Jacky Woodward

also
Best wishes Mick Greene
& 1 Sgr. K.B. Akuantan,
& Kofa Qede.

THREE TIMES LUCKY

By

Jack K. Woodward

First published in 1991 by Boolarong Publications
with J. Woodward, 121 Jensen St, Whitfield, Cairns.

Copyright © Jack Woodward

National Library of Australia
Cataloguing-in-Publication data.

  Woodward, Jack K. (Jack Keith), 1916-
    Three times lucky.

    Includes Index.
    ISBN 0 646 02970 3.

    1. Woodward, Jack K. (Jack Keith), 1916-   . 2.
    Australia. Royal Australian Air Force — Airmen —
    Biography. 3. World War, 1939-1945 — Personal
    narratives, Australia. I. Title.

940.544994

BOOLARONG PUBLICATIONS
12 Brookes St., Bowen Hills, Brisbane. Qld. 4006
Design and phototypesetting by
Ocean Graphics Pty Ltd, Gold Coast, Qld.
Printed by Fergies Colour Printers, Brisbane.
Bound by Podlich Enterprises, Brisbane.
Film Production: Graphic Investments, Brisbane.

PROUDLY PRINTED IN QUEENSLAND

THREE TIMES LUCKY

By

Jack K. Woodward

IN THREE PARTS

PART 1 — WITH THE BLENHEIMS IN MALAYA

From the Wartime Diaries of the Author

From Enlistment in the Royal Australian Air Force (R.A.A.F.) on the 3rd January, 1941, with the Classification of Observer (Navigator).

Training Days in Australia.

Travelling to Singapore, and Posting to 27 Squadron, R.A.F., at Sungei Patani in Northern Malaya.

Invasion of Malaya by the Japanese on the 8th December, 1941, and Declaration of War on Japan by the Allies.

Evacuation to Singapore, Operations in Palembang on P2.

Crash Landing at Night in Java (Indonesia) and Experiences in Java.

Evacuation by Sea from Tjilijap in Java (Indonesia) to Ceylon (Sri Lanka) and Ultimate Return to Australia.

PART 2 — FROM THE BOSTONS TO THE LIBERATORS

22 Squadron — Boston Aircraft (A 20).

11 Squadron — Catalinas (PBY).

Bairnsdale — General Reconnaissance School — Instructional Duties and Crash Landing in Bass Strait (Victoria).

12 Squadron — Liberators (B24).

PART 3 — POSTSCRIPT

Short Account of the Fates of the Other Fourteen Members of the Group who Travelled to Singapore on the ''Marella'' with the Author in 1941.

Foreword

The Author, through the book, has found the ability to relate in simple, sincere terms an overlay of the RAAF during the years of hostility from 1939 to 1945.

"Three Times Lucky", as seen through the eyes and experiences of Jack Woodward, can be reflected in many similar but different incidents, and of course, is applicable to many other spheres of Air Force operations.

Jack, like many of us, was a product of the Empire Air Training Scheme, and its value and assistance to the war effort was immeasurable. All countries, as part of the British Empire, participated resulting in a huge abundance of well-trained aircrew. No like-training system existed before or has been attempted since, and great credit lies with the initiators who devised and instituted the training program within weeks of the declaration of war.

Fortunately, a few aircrew like Jack Woodward were mindful of retaining personal records of the highlights of these very eventful years, so that one day they would be able to put to print their exploits for all to read. Many ageing memories will be refreshed by reading "Three Times Lucky", and I'm sure many will feel part of the scene in the simple way the book unfolds for its readers.

I well remember the flight that Jack relates from Richmond to Charters Towers under the leadership of Ken MacDonald. Ken, pre-war, was a racing car fanatic and was inclined to fly the same way. He and his crew were lost in action soon after arriving in New Guinea with his own bombs blowing up soon after release. Luck played a major role in survival in those days, and "Three Times Lucky" is a typical example.

Jack McMaster, AM, DFC
(Flight Lieutenant Ex-RAAF)

THREE TIMES LUCKY

By

Jack K Woodward

From the Wartime Diaries of the Author

PART 1 — WITH THE BLENHEIMS IN MALAYA

Contents

PART 2 — FROM THE BOSTONS TO THE LIBERATORS

PART 3 — POSTSCRIPT

Part 1

With the Blenheims in Malaya

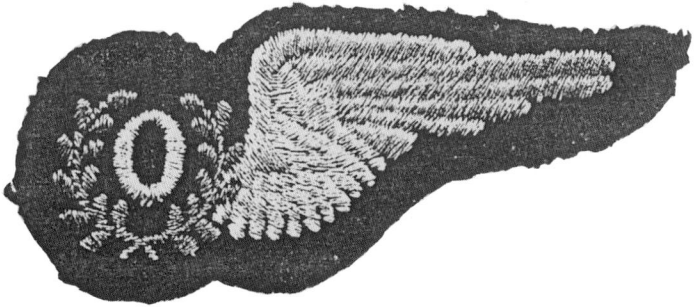

OBSERVER'S BADGE

The author and his wife on his return from Singapore.

Author's Foreword

I was born in Cairns in North Queensland during the First World War. Like most children of that era, I was often reminded by our school teachers and public figures of the futility of war, and the wanton destruction and misery that it created.

During my school days, remembrance of the landing of the Anzacs at Gallipoli on the 25th April was observed throughout the country, and the day was a very solemn affair. Armistice Day was also observed on the 11th November, but not to the same extent as Anzac Day. Apart from those sombre occasions, the early childhood school days of my life were very happy, and I made many good lifelong friends.

During the early part of 1929, I contracted a very severe bout of typhoid fever whilst on a youth tour of the southern states. The source of the fever was traced to drinking water from a fountain drawn from a city lake. This resulted in a crucial loss of nearly four months of schooling in Scholarship year (the entrance to secondary education). However, I managed to obtain a reasonable pass and spent the next two years at Brisbane Grammar School, passing my Junior (Intermediate) high school examinations.

This was a very happy part of my youth, and I would have liked to carry on to the Senior exams. However the world-wide depression had descended upon the country, and my parents could not afford to give me the opportunity of further education.

The depression had an enormous effect on the country, and the financial ruin of so many people and resulting unemployment led to desperate times. Jobless people moved from city to city and into the country by whatever means they could. Climbing on to moving trains was called "jumping the rattler"; drivers always slowed the trains down at convenient spots to help these travellers climb aboard and prevent accidents.

There was no dole or unemployment benefit to assist the unfortunate, and it might seem surprising, with today's standards, that the country remained reasonably calm, and did not break out in rioting or civil disorder. "Soup kitchens" were provided for the itinerant unemployed by men and women in more fortunate circumstances. They were very difficult and trying times.

Upon returning home, I attended Cairns High School learning typing and other commercial subjects, and took casual employment for six months. I commenced work in an accountant's office, which lasted two and a half years. I resigned when I felt that I was being exploited because of the difficult times, but was able to obtain a very good position with the Babinda sugar mill as a weighbridge clerk for the sugar season. Unfortunately it was only for the season, and the following year the regular clerk returned to the mill.

For the next twelve months I took whatever jobs were offered — some good and some not so good. In 1937, I applied for a temporary position in Atherton, and when this expired obtained further work in Cairns. Then followed a permanent position with an insurance company, which led to a transfer to Townsville.

During my stay in Townsville, I was able to concentrate on my favourite sport, rugby league football. I played on the wing three-quarter and was chosen to represent Townsville. In my second year there, our team won the club competition and Townsville won the intercity competition, the Carlton Shield.

Whilst working in the accountant's office, I had undertaken a correspondence course in accountancy. Although hampered in my studies by the difficult times, I persevered and was successful in passing my final examinations just prior to being called up by the R.A.A.F. in January, 1941.

During this period of the 1930's, the world was in turmoil, with Germany and Italy being taken over by the dictators Hitler and Mussolini. Brute force reigned over commonsense, and those who attempted to resist were quickly overcome. With the invasion of the neighbouring countries in Europe, it became evident that Hitler was determined to conquer the world, and thereby reign supreme.

Appeasement by diplomats and leaders of others countries was to no avail, and so war faced all the free countries of the world. It was a most serious situation, and the whole population of our country was very concerned about what might occur.

During the period leading up to the Second World War, queries were raised as to whether the youth of Australia would respond to the call to volunteer in the same way as the men did in the First World War. In some quarters it was implied that the fighting spirit which was displayed in the previous war would not be as evident in this coming conflict.

The young people of my age thought of the coming conflict in very sober terms, and certainly did not rush in to enlist as occurred in the 1914-18 war. When groups of us assembled, we discussed the war which had just started, realising that we were not trained, and would be thrown against an enemy who was well equipped and organised. It was a frightening thought, but nevertheless the enlistments followed, with young women also joining the Voluntary Aid Detachment and other services.

Like so many others who were eligible I tarried, just in case the war might be a fizzer — perhaps Hitler and his cronies might suddenly listen to reason. I was very confused as to what I should do. Many of my friends in Townsville enlisted with the A.I.F., particularly those who were volunteer reserves in the 31st Army Battalion. Those who were in the Naval Reserve enlisted with the R.A.N.

The service that appealed to me was the Air Force. It was very difficult to get information about the R.A.A.F. and how to enlist. Stories circulated that some young men with a pilot's licence had tried to join the Air Force on the outbreak of hostilities, but were not accepted. They had then paid their own fare to travel by ship to England, and were immediately accepted into the Royal Air Force.

This was most confusing to young people like myself, who were seriously contemplating enlisting with the R.A.A.F. As a result, I was just about ready to toss a coin to see whether I would join the A.I.F. or the Navy. Suddenly an advertisement appeared in the "Townsville Bulletin", notifying young men in the area that a recruiting office would shortly be opening for a period to interview potential recruits for the R.A.A.F.

So in April, 1940, I made my way to the recruiting office to offer my services for air crew in the R.A.A.F. I passed my medical examination, with the proviso that my nose had to be fixed. The medical officer maintained that there was a distinct blockage due to my nose having been broken at some time in my life. Thinking back, I had suffered a decent smack in my younger days playing football.

I was under the impression that the Air Force might be able to fix my nose, which had not worried me at all. However, in the very early days of recruiting the Air Force was very particular, demanding only very fit recruits. Evidently it was considered I could have difficulty in breathing, particularly at high altitudes. Being keen to enlist I had a minor operation, and on reporting back I was accepted into the R.A.A.F. for aircrew training.

Time marched on, and I began to wonder what had happened to my enlistment. I had volunteered in early April, 1940, had the operation in the middle of that month, and was re-examined in May and accepted. However, I heard nothing further until the middle of November.

All of a sudden I received notice to report to the Eagle Street Depot of the R.A.A.F. in Brisbane on the 3rd January, 1941. In the meantime, my fiancee Vera Mazlin and I had decided to marry in Cairns on the 25th November, 1940.

Vera worked in a chartered accountant's office as senior clerk and secretary. Our wedding date hinged on the return to that office of young men doing their term of National Service training. Vera was a member of the Voluntary Aid Detachment (V.A.D.) Q. 142, having done considerable hospital training with the Cairns Base Hospital after office work hours.

After our marriage on the 25th November, 1940, we had our honeymoon at Trinity Beach. A few days later, I reported back for work in Townsville, where we rented a house on Stanton Hill for three weeks. I finished work with the insurance company coming on to the Christmas period. We had a few days together before leaving by train for Brisbane. I reported to the depot on Wednesday, the third of January, 1941, and was sworn in for the duration of the war and up to twelve months later if required.

Training Days Sandgate — No. 4 I.T.S.

And so on to the Training Days of my Air Force career. I just did not know what to expect. In fact, I was overawed at the thought of being called up — a thought that must have gone through the minds of everybody in a similar predicament. Was it going to be a wonderful adventure, seeing and doing many new things, and with the likelihood of going overseas? When I eventually arrived home after much action, would I be called a hero and be given a rousing reception by all and sundry?

And then crossing my mind was the sobering thought — Would I survive the war, or possibly be a casualty and become permanently incapacitated and a burden not only to myself but to the community? I had seen the effect of injury on many who had returned from the previous war.

The thought of adventure and the possibility of going overseas was ever in the back of my mind, but no doubt the main purpose of my enlisting was to defend our way of life from the dictatorship and oppression which was occurring on the other side of the world. All these thoughts were often discussed with other young people in those turbulent times.

My first entry in my diary was Thursday the 27th day of March, 1941. It was rather late to start a diary seeing that I was called up on Wednesday, the 3rd January, 1941, so I gave a resume of my doings up to this time.

I entered the Initial Training School (I.T.S.) of Sandgate after passing a thorough medical examination. The eye test was particularly severe, checking all sorts of things I did not understand but especially looking for signs of colour blindness. Quite a few who had initially been passed at their preliminary volunteer site were failed, and whilst some decided upon a ground staff position, others were given the opportunity of enlisting in either the Army or the Navy.

After being passed medically, the recruits loitered around the Creek Street Brisbane enlistment centre until the examination of the balance of those in the call up was completed. We were then gathered together with some semblance of order, and sworn in for the duration of hostilities and twelve months thereafter. My rank on entering was Aircraftman, Second Class, or in its abbreviated form — A.C.2. My pay was five shillings a day, or in today's money, fifty cents a day.

We could be called upon for duty seven days a week, so therefore we received a weekly pay of 35 shillings a week, or $3.50.

Being married, my wife was entitled to receive three shillings a day, which amounted to $2.10 per week. For her to be entitled to receive this sum, I had to allot to her an equivalent amount out of my pay. Needless to say, airmen in their initial training days did not have much spare money.

Sandgate Initial Training School was located about 20 km. on the coast north of Brisbane and was still under construction, so we were sent off to Amberley Air Force Station, located just west of Ipswich. Our training school then became known as "Sandgate attached to Amberley". Altogether there were about 120 trainees, and much to the dismay of some but to the delight of others, even before we arrived at the Enlisting Depot it had been determined whether we would be pilots or observers.

Everybody hoped to be trained as a pilot — whether for fighters or bombers, it did not matter much, so long as one was mustered as a pilot. And I do not think that I was any different to the other trainees in this hope. It did intrigue us, though, how this was decided in advance of our mustering. We never did find out, and perhaps it was just as well.

We were then allotted our Air Force Number. Those in our group selected as pilots had numbers commencing from 404900, whilst those selected as navigators had numbers commencing from 405001. The numbers were allotted in alphabetical order and mine was 405030. As there were two enlistments with the name of Roberts, it was decided to separate the numbers, and Graham Roberts was allotted the number following mine, 405031.

I had known the Roberts family in Townsville, and in particular was good friends with Ian (Graham's older brother). They had been, and still are, a very well known and respected family in the legal profession. In addition to Graham, another Townsville enlistment was Ernie Ginn.

The system of training was named the Empire Air Training Scheme, and was designed to train air crews from all the Dominion countries — Canada, Australia, New Zealand, South Africa, and India, though India did not have the same training facilities as the other countries. Every four weeks, another group of volunteers was to be called up creating another new Course, with a gradual increase in the numbers involved. The Course I was trained under was numbered Ten. This continued until nearly the end of the war, and by that time over forty Courses had received training.

The pilots would leave after their I.T.S. (Initial Training School) for E.F.T.S. (Elementary Flying Training School) and from there would be selected for either fighters or bombers. Their training lasted eight months, and on conclusion they were presented with a cloth badge bearing two spread wings, signifying that they were pilots.

The observers, as we were dubbed, were navigators and bomb aimers. After our Initial Training School, we were to proceed to Cootamundra in New South Wales for twelve weeks training at the A.O.S. (Air Observers School). From there we would go to Evans Head to the B.A.G.S. (Bombing & Air Gunnery School), and then complete our training at Parkes at the A.N.S. (Astro Navigation School).

The navigators in our call-up appeared to include a large percentage of school teachers and bank clerks. Perhaps it was considered that their training with figures would assist learning navigation. If this was the case, having just passed my accountancy examinations would have had some bearing on my mustering.

On finishing our training we were presented with a cloth badge bearing a single wing with a large O. Later on the Observers Course was split, with the term "Observers" being discarded and separate training instituted for navigators and bombardiers. The navigators were issued with a half wing with the letter N, and the bombardiers with the letter B.

The early observers held on to their old badges with the O (known throughout the Air Force as the "Flying Arse-hole"), even though the badge was redundant and disciplinary action was threatened against those continuing to wear it. We defied this order and our action was eventually accepted. No more were made or issued, and some of the Flying O's worn on observers' tunics were rather battered by the end of the war. I managed to obtain extra badges from the Equipment Store before they were withdrawn from issue.

The Wireless Air Gunners (W.A.G's) received their call up and enlisted the day after us, the 4th January. They spent only four weeks at the Initial Training School, then moved on to the Wireless Training School at Parkes before their final four weeks at Evans Head for Air Gunnery. The badge for the W.A.G's was a half wing with the letters W.A.G., whilst those who had been unable to absorb the radio training and elected to fly as a straight air gunner, had the half wing with the letters A.G. Their Course was much shorter than the W.A.G's.

Prior to 10 Course, all recruits from Queensland commenced their training at Bradfield Park, in Sydney. The Empire Air Training Scheme had schools in Sydney, Melbourne, Adelaide and Perth, and various training centres spread over the whole of Australia. There was a shortage of aircraft, and many pilots and navigators were sent overseas immediately after their Initial Training School, proceeding mainly to Canada to complete their training. This also applied to quite a number of trainees from New Zealand.

Such is a short summary of the training that existed for air crew. In addition, the personnel of Ground Staff, Office Staff, and the

W.A.A.F. all played a major part in the overall training of air crews, from mundane jobs to most important management positions.

Prior to being called up, quite a number of centres provided facilities for training personnel in such subjects as Advanced Maths in preparation for their coming studies. This refresher course proved of great assistance to those to whom it was offered.

The course at the Initial Training School was rather intense, with five classes and thirty in each class. Absorbing advanced maths, trigonometry, and various other subjects proved quite difficult. Only the very young trainees not long out of school with these subjects fresh in their memories, and those afforded the refresher classes, were able to immediately grasp all that was being taught.

To the credit of the trainees of the Course, however, there were very few failures at the end of the two months. Those who had some difficulty in absorbing all the instruction were held back for a further month only, and then joined the following Course, No. 11.

The I.T.S. was of four weeks duration for the wireless air gunners, and eight weeks for the navigators and pilots. Our Course commenced on the 4th January, 1941, and concluded at the end of February, when we were transferred to the Air Observers School at Cootamundra, in New South Wales.

At the end of this initial training, those who were moving on decided to let their hair down, and had a passing out night to celebrate at the Grand Central Hotel in Ipswich. We were a little late in finishing, about 11 p.m., and so missed the last bus to take us back to Amberley.

Quite a number had difficulty in getting past the guards on the gate. Our group hired a taxi, taking one of the instructors as insurance, and safely got through the gate. However, after bidding good night to our instructor, we were accosted by the Orderly Officer and the Orderly Sergeant for singing on our way back (a problem being that the song had the name of an Officer embodied in it). Our names were taken, and as a result we were arraigned before the C.O. the following morning.

Unfortunately for us, two of the chaps (trainee pilots) arrived back at camp a little the worse for wear, and as they could not contain themselves decided to relieve themselves beside one of the huts. Unfortunately for them (and for us too, as it turned out), the Orderly Officer and Sergeant came across them and raucously enquired what they were up to. In typical Aussie fashion, the two informed the officer and sergeant what they could do, at which point the Orderly Officer informed them of his rank. Trying to do the right thing, and not being able to contain themselves, they turned around and saluted the officer, at the same time urinating on the officer's leg.

They were both charged under Section 40 with conduct to the prejudice of good order and Air Force discipline, that they at such and such a time and at such and such a place, urinated on the Orderly

Officer's leg. As a result, they and the rest of us who were caught on any trivial thing that night, were charged and given four days C.B. (confined to barracks). All our inter-school leave was cancelled, and this was dished out to 38 of us altogether, on 61 charges.

Evidently this episode became well known throughout the R.A.A.F., and in years to come, when I mentioned to others in conversation that I was on 10 Course and had gone through Sandgate attached to Amberley, I was invariably queried whether I was the culprit who urinated on the Orderly Officer's leg. Needless to say, I always denied the allegation.

I was not very popular with Vera, as she then had to come out to visit me at Ipswich. Ben Westerman (a trainee pilot) was in a similar predicament. and we arranged for the two girls to meet at Central Station and come out to Amberley together, and for the two wives to talk to us the following day through the fence. On the Sunday, however, I asked for an interview with the C.O., and he gave permission for both wives to come on to the Station, which was quite considerate. We were finally allowed off the Station early on the Monday morning, but I had to catch the mail train for Sydney at 11 a.m., so the leave between courses was virtually lost.

Whilst awaiting the train to leave from South Brisbane that morning, I was very pleased to find that Tom Williams had come down to the train to see me. Tom worked with me for Commercial Union in Townsville, and we had boarded together for two and a half years whilst there. In fact, Tom was the best man at my wedding in Cairns the previous November.

Tom had initially been a volunteer with the 121st Heavy Battery, but had applied to join the R.A.A.F. The application was withheld for a time, but then allowed to proceed. He was immediately called up with the R.A.A.F. and was reporting to Sandgate that morning. He went through 12 Course as a trainee pilot, and became a captain on Catalinas.

Cootamundra — No. 1 A.O.S.
— Air Observers School

We arrived in Sydney in the early hours of the following morning, and had the day there prior to catching a train to Cootamundra late at night. There were twenty-three of us from Sandgate I.T.S., and we arrived at Coota at 7 a.m. On arrival, we were informed that we were not expected until the following night. This did not make us very happy, as we could have had an extra day in Sydney.

Those from Queensland were joined by twenty-five other trainees from Somers I.T.S. in Victoria, and also five wireless operators, making a total of fifty-three doing the Course. Of our original thirty-one commencing in Queensland, two had been re-classified as pilots, whilst the other six were held back to 11 Course.

There were too many to have in one class, and the numbers were divided into two, described as 10A & 10B. Within a couple of days, we were called upon to elect a Course Captain, and Tom Wilson was elected as the Course Captain for 10A. Probably because nobody was keen to take on the position in 10B, I was appointed.

We commenced on the 5th March, 1941, and being summer, we enjoyed the warm days and the coolness of the nights. However, it proved to be a cold winter, and before the Course finished on the 29th May, we were to experience many cold days with frost lying over the ground and water pipes frozen. However, in other ways it was a very pleasant time, and we found the instructors were keen to help us.

On arrival at Cootamundra, all of the trainees were promoted to the rank of Leading Aircraftman, (L.A.C.). That may have not meant so much, except that we all had a raise in pay of an extra 4 shillings per day, bringing us to 9 shillings a day (90 cents in present money).

The personnel for the two sections were as follows:-

10 A		10 B	
LAC	Atherton P.F. (Peter)	LAC	Ahern J.A. (Jack)
''	Beacham N.T.G. (Nev)	''	Camm M.B. (Max)
''	Brennan W.F. (Judge)	''	Duce E.B. (Eric)
''	Buckland J.C. (Jack)	''	Dyson F.V. (Frank)
''	Carmichael C. (Col)	''	Forrester N.S. (Nev)
''	Cooper A.R. (Bert)	''	Gluck N.W. (Nate)
''	Champaign K.D.	''	Gray J. (Jim)
''	Foster G.A. (George)	''	Green L.R. (Les)

12

''	Hall N. (Nev)	''	Hargrave N.C. (Neil)
Cpl	Hawthorne R.K. (Reg)	''	Hawkins S.H. (Stan)
LAC	Holmes K.G. (Ken)	''	Hull W.T. (Bill)
''	Jones Ack	''	Leitch T.G. (Tom)
''	Lynch W.D. (Bill)	''	Millgate K. (Toss)
''	Logan W.A.B. (Lex)	''	Murray-Prior T.L. (Tom)
''	Martin L.J. (Lionel)	''	McConville D.W. (Doug)
''	Moon L.W. (Bill)	''	Norris M.A. (Murray)
''	McDowall R.G. (Rob)	''	Oliphant D.C. (Clyde)
''	O'Sullivan C.F. (Sully)	''	O'Brien B.P. (Brian)
''	Perry T.F. (Trevor)	''	Peters V. (Vin)
''	Purdon N.D. (Don)	''	Robinson T.F. (Fred)
''	Sheppard D.R.	''	Romans K.A. (Tony)
''	Smith J.L. (Jack)	''	Rowe B.C. (Barnie)
''	Ward K.W.	''	Taylor S.W. (Stan)
''	Williams J.M. (Maurie)	''	Weston I.D. (Ian)
''	Wilson T.S. (Tom)	''	Whitehead N.G. (Noel)
''	Winzar F.R. (Ron)	''	Woodward J.K. (Jack)
''	Wright J.C. (Joe)		

We were told that we would be flying in pairs, and so we were given the choice of selecting our own partner. Tom Murray-Prior and I decided to pair together, and from that sprang a friendship between us and our respective wives that still exists today.

Tom's wife, Lilian, and my wife, Vera, arrived soon after, and at first stayed at the Central Hotel. This was very pleasant, but it was quite beyond the means of an aircraftman on 9 shillings a day. The girls then had a good look around the town, and eventually found a boarding house where they stayed for the rest of the time we were there. We were also able to visit them when we had leave at night, which was appreciated.

At Cootamundra A.O.S. there were three courses in training at any one time, totalling approximately 150 trainees. The number of personnel involved would no doubt have exceeded two thousand, and when considered with other training stations in the Empire Air Training Scheme, the total manpower involved in training was enormous.

With similar effort taking place in Canada, New Zealand, South Africa, and other countries of the Empire, the combined result was a tremendous contribution to the defence of Britain and other parts of the Empire under attack. Later the airmen trained under the scheme served to carry the offensive to the enemy, and the success of the whole operation was a just reward for the careful planning.

Whilst training was the major concern, it was nevertheless considered that physical fitness was most important. Each afternoon, after the completion of classes, we would be put through physical training exercises, and that would often be followed by a long distance race round the aerodrome, the distance being approximately three miles.

All training flights involved three course members. There was a trainee navigator and his partner, who would also do a secondary log and duplicate the navigation. A third trainee would be expected to carry out map reading. Even on night time flights this was carried out, and it was important for the third navigator to be able to recognise towns which showed up through their lights.

The main part of our training was undoubtedly flying. Although some of us were affected by air sickness (it could get very rough in the air over the inland part of New South Wales), still we persevered. There were some casualties in this training period; a small minority of the chaps just could not cope with continually getting sick.

The Dehavilland Rapides were very light planes, and the least bit of turbulence made them lurch and buck in all directions. I was airsick on a couple of occasions, but kept at it and seemed to grow out of the problem by the end of the course.

Clyde Oliphant had an interesting experience. On our arrival at Coota, we were issued with overalls and a beret to wear when on flying duties. One day Clyde was quite airsick and used his beret as a receptacle as nothing else was available. Rather than take it back to base, he threw the beret with the contents out of the door window. To his astonishment and embarrassment, a week later he received a small parcel in the post with the beret nicely laundered and a letter from a woman who had found it near her house, wishing him well. Clyde's name was marked inside the beret, and she checked and found that Clyde was a trainee at Cootamundra. Needless to say, the course never let him forget the incident.

We were given leave over the Easter period, and Vera and I went to Sydney to stay with a friend at Bondi. We found June quite upset and concerned, as her husband Ted was with the A.I.F. and had boarded the "Queen Elizabeth" the previous day. During the morning we saw the "Q.E." with other ships draw out of the Harbour and join up with warships outside to form a convoy, destined for overseas. That date was the 11th April, 1941.

At Cootamundra it was agreed that the meals were quite good, but there was always a preponderance of carrots in the diet. With practically every meal and in particular the main meal in the evening, vegetables were served with large quantities of carrots. Many months later we found out the reason for this dishing up of carrots, carrots, and more carrots.

In the previous year, 1940, the German Luftwaffe made their massive air attacks on Britain in daylight raids, and were repelled in the Battle of Britain, with tremendous losses and casualties on both sides. The Spitfires and the Hurricanes were the main defensive fighters of the R.A.F. The Germans then took to night raids on Britain, using their full force of bombers. To combat this offensive, the British used their night fighters which were equipped with radar, a new and secret device which could pick up aircraft at any time.

This was most disconcerting to the enemy, and they were nonplussed at the number of their aircraft being destroyed or damaged. Enemy agents were called upon to investigate this secret weapon, and the reply came loud and strong that carrots were very good for the eyesight, and assisted particularly in being able to discern objects at night time.

They also found out that aircrew being trained throughout Allied countries were being served with massive quantities of carrots, and so when going into battle, particularly at night time, possessed unique eye sight. This deception must have been successful, and it was some time before the Germans did find out that it was just hogwash. However, the feeding of carrots to us persisted, no doubt much to the satisfaction of the growers of carrots throughout the Allied countries.

The subjects covered in the Air Observers Course were D.R. Navigation (Dead Reckoning Nav), Map Reading, Meteorology, Maps & Charts, Compasses & Instruments, Reconnaissance, Photography, D.F. and practical work. I passed all subjects, though I found some rather difficult. We flew in Avro Anson, Dehavilland 86, and Dehavilland Rapide aircraft. The D.H. machines were civilian aircraft which were absorbed into the R.A.A.F. The total hours flying time for each trainee was between 40 and 50 hours, with six of these being night flying.

Air Observers School at Cootamundra was quite refreshing, and really enjoyed by all. We had sports midway through the twelve week course, and I did reasonably well, running second in the 100 yards and 220 yards. With Maurie Williams I was chosen to compete with the R.A.A.F. against the Army and Navy at the Sydney Cricket Grounds. I ran in the 100 yards, the long jump and also the sixteen man relay over a mile distance, whilst Maurie took on the 220 yards and the hop step and jump, and also the relay. I won my first heat of the 100 yards in 10.4 seconds on a waterlogged track, and then came fourth in a blanket finish in the semi final. This was the first time that I had run in running shoes, and the pair that I borrowed were two sizes too big, and had to be stuffed with paper to fit.

I also had a very successful season playing rugby league for Cootamundra against neighbouring towns, including Young. I played on the right wing, and in the team from the town of Young and playing on the left wing against me was Merv Denton, who was the New South Wales representative. In five matches I scored eight tries, which gave me a very good feeling.

Before playing my final game against Young, I was presented with a pen and pencil set from the officials and players of Cootamundra.

R.A.A.F. — No. 1 AIR OBSERVERS SCHOOL
COOTAMUNDRA — No. 10 COURSE — March/May, 1941.
Rear Row: Tony Romans, Max Camm, Vin Peters, Ken Holmes, Doug McConville, Norm Forrester, Jack Buckland, Ian Weston, Tom Leitch, Bill Hull, Lionel Martin.
2nd Rear Row: Don Sheppard, Reg Hawthorne, Bill Lynch, Joe Wright, Don Purdon, Stan Taylor, George Foster, Nate Gluck, Ron Winzar, Judge Brennan, Noel Whitehead, Eric Duce, Tossil Milgate, Jack Smith, Bert Cooper.
2nd Front Row: Nev Beacham, Bob McDowall, Murray Norris, Ken Ward, Tom Wilson, Brian O'Brien, Tom Murray-Prior, Clyde Oliphant, Jack Ahern, Morrie Williams, Bill Moon, Jim Gray, Barney Rowe, Neil Hargrave, Neville Hall.
Front Row: Trevor Perry, Arthur Jones, Jack Woodward, C.F. Sully O'Sullivan, F/O Bain, P/O Clarke, Fl/Lt Marsh, Fl/Lt Smibert, F/O Hunt, P/O Jones, Lex Logan, Peter Atherton, Les Green, Frank Dyson, Colin Carmichael.
Absent: Ken Champain, Stan Hawkins, Tom Robinson.

They thanked me for my efforts, and wished me a safe return from the hostilities of war. During this last game and unknown to us there were two N.S.W. selectors watching us play. After the game they approached me to see whether I would be available to go to Sydney and play for the Country Team against the Sydney City team, and be available for selection of the New South Wales team against Queensland. I suggested that they should see the C.O., and obtain his permission. They did this, I was told, but were given the answer — "Don't you know that there is a war on?"

One of the highlights of our training at Cootamundra was a visit to the Station by Wing Commander Garing, C.B.E., D.F.C., later to be promoted to Air Commodore. He addressed the three Courses (9, 10 & 11) on navigation, and also on his experiences as Commanding Officer of 10 Squadron, a reconnaissance squadron patrolling out from Britain on Sunderlands over the Atlantic. Needless to say, he kept

" Per Adua ad Albion.'

No. 1 Air Observers' School
COOTAMUNDRA

No. 10 Course
Passing—Out Dinner

Albion Hotel . May 28th, 1941

Course Captains : 10A : LAC T. S. WILSON
10B : LAC J. K. WOODWARD
Committee : LAC F. V. Dyson
LAC L. J. Martin,
Chairman : LAC T. S. Wilson

— Log of Proceedings —

Time g.s.t.	Observations
2000	Reeling in.
2010	Glasses Synchronised—Juice On Bar Pressure—High. Temp.—Hot (red on red)
2015	Liquorborne Coota.
2020	W.C Go.—No. 1 Running Fault.
2021	Tomato S/C Puree.
2025	T.D.S. (True Drinking Speed) 2 9's per hour E.T.A. Insobriety 2100.
2030	Position Vague.
2035	Waitress Bearing 200 Asparagus. A/c to Intercept.
2040	Ordered carry out R. of A. from Turkey · Avoiding Greece
2042	M.T.B. (1) (Mission to Bathroom)
2056	Visibility Hazy.
2057	Rhubarb Merv Tarts, with 60% Overlap Cream Bears 30 Red.
2058	I'se Right (Hic)
2100	Insobriety S/C. Blackout E.T.A. 2140
2105	Saturation Point—No. 1 Running Fault Again.
2107	T.T.T. (Tonic To Teetotallers) White Coffee T.O.I. (Trouble of Inebriates) Black Coffee.
2110	Critical Point—Maintaining Track Drift 10 to Port (Royal Reserve)
2120	Blind Flying Conditions—4 T.Ts. Baled Out.
2132	Olives and Castellated Nuts.
2135	Reeling Out. E.T.A. Base ? ? ?

everyone's attention, and at the end of his talk was bombarded with questions. We really enjoyed his address, which was very instructional and down to earth.

And so on the 29th May, 1941, the whole of 10 Course, our numbers just over fifty, entrained from Cootamundra and proceeded to Evans Head, where we would do our training in Bombing & Gunnery.

Evans Head

No. 1 Bombing & Air Gunners School
(No.1. B. &. G. S.)

We arrived at Evans Head in early June, travelling from Cootamundra to Sydney and then by train on the "Brisbane Mail" to disembark at Lismore for our destination — Evans Head. A lovely place, right on the sea, and certainly a lot warmer than Cootamundra. This was appreciated, as Coota was getting very cold, especially for the northerners from Queensland.

Jim Gray and his wife Enid had obtained a flat in the township, and offered to share it with us, which was most pleasant. Vera & Enid had met each other quite often in Cootamundra, and got on well together. This was really great, especially as Jim and I had to report each day to the station, firstly for our studies in bombing, and then later for air gunnery.

Lil & Tom Murray-Prior had a flat on the other side of the inlet. This sounded good, being on the sea front, but proved awkward and inconvenient. They had to row across in a boat if they wanted to go to town, and Tom had to report to the Station very early each day for training. Within a week they had had enough, and searched Evans Head for other accommodation. This was not at all easy, with the influx of personnel and trainees to the township. However, they managed to get a flat after a few days, sharing one like we did.

The total course lasted eight weeks, with four weeks allotted to bombing, and the last four to gunnery. Let me recount from my diary the procedure:-

Fairey Battles were the aircraft that were used, being a single engine low-winged monoplane, with economical cruising speed of 150 m.p.h. That was, therefore, the speed which we used for our bombing and gunnery exercises. Quite a number of the planes at Evans Head had already seen active service, serving at the evacuation of Dunkirk and again in the Norwegian campaign.

Although considered a fighter bomber, with an open cockpit behind the pilot and a mounting for single or twin machine guns, they were no match against the German M.E. 109 and 110. In one raid over Norway they mixed it with the German fighters, and only one returned from a flight of twenty-four. As a result, they were

19

considered to be obsolete, and were taken off combat duties and assigned to training. They were certainly very suitable for our type of training.

For our bombing exercises, we used practice bombs weighing eight and a half pounds. These were filled with stannic chloride, and upon striking the ground they exploded and gave off bluish smoke which could be seen for about five minutes. Occasionally the bombs did not explode on impact, but this was quite rare.

When detailed for a flight, it was necessary to be on the tarmac fifty minutes before the detailed time, and to check with the noticeboard that the flight had not been cancelled. Often the aircraft were U/S (unserviceable). If the flight was proceeding, we then had to note the aircraft's number and the pilot's name. The latter was eagerly checked, as it quickly was made known from previous courses which pilots were good, and which were not so good. This could make a big difference to the result of an exercise.

The next duty was a final check on the plane with the mechanics, making sure it was serviceable. Then a visit was made to the armoury to collect eight practice bombs, and also a dummy bomb used to check the release switch on the aircraft. With the assistance of the armourer, the bombs were loaded on to the carrier. After collecting a parachute and other equipment, we would test the bomb carrier and then await the arrival of the pilot.

After starting up the engine, chocks would be pulled out from in front of the wheels and the safety pins extracted from the practice bombs. The plane would then taxi out to the strip with the trainee taking hold of the tip of the starboard wing — the starboard side being most convenient, as we had to enter the rear cockpit on that side.

On reaching a reasonable height, the bomb sight and other gear had to be assembled, and made ready for the bombing exercise. We bombed from 6,000 ft and also 10,000 ft, and had to find the prevailing wind direction and its velocity at each height. This was necessary for accurate bomb aiming. Upon releasing each bomb, it was necessary for us to record where it landed. At the same time, the blue smoke marking the landing position was plotted at the target area by personnel observing from three quadrants. It was very well thought out, and there were no errors (or rather, there were not supposed to be). Altogether each trainee carried out about ten bombing flights, lasting approximately ninety minutes.

The gunnery training flights were also carried out in the Fairey Battles, with approximately eight to ten flights. The method varied, with some exercises firing on ground targets and others on drogues towed by other aircraft. These flights lasted about forty-five minutes. We used Lewis and Vickers machine guns, but not Brownings, as there were none available other than the one used for instruction purposes.

EVANS HEAD — No. 1 Bombing & Air Gunnery School
A Ten Course Training Flight at No. 1 B.A.C.S. — Evans Head

Back Row: J.C.Wright, F. Robinson, M. Williams, J. Smith, D. Sheppard, B. Rowe, D. Purdon, K. Romans.
Front Row: T. Perry, I. Weston, R. Winzar, S. Taylor, N. Whitehead, J. Woodward.

The Station was very well run, with a good Commanding Officer, Group Captain Hancock. After the war he was promoted to Air Vice Marshal with the Air Board, in charge of Personnel. A story about Group Captain Hancock — in November, 1944, when I was an instructor of navigation at Bairnsdale, he arrived in Bairnsdale to do a crash course on various important navigation subjects. The length of the course was two weeks, and he was detailed special instructors to qualify him for general reconnaissance duties.

His special instructor for Dead Reckoning Navigation 1 & 2 was a chap called Jack Lewers, who was a Warrant Officer, and who would not take a commission for various reasons. On the last day of the course, Group Captain Hancock did a flight exercise, and at its conclusion wanted W/O Jack Lewers to go through the exercise and correct it. Jack put him off with the excuse that he felt that he had had a very heavy week and needed a rest, but he would go through the log the following day. Jack couldn't tell G/C Hancock the real reason, which was that he was the unofficial S.P bookmaker for the Station and as such was otherwise engaged for the day.

The Station at Evans Head was conveniently located close to the seashore. After instruction periods, we often would have the opportunity of racing down to the beach and slipping off our clothes

No. 1 — B.A.G.S. Evans Head Football Team 1942.
Taken in front of a Fairey Battle.

for a swim in the sea. Occasionally there was some really good surf, which was most enjoyable.

Those of us who were living out were given plenty of opportunities to invite our ladies to the station, particularly on passing-out days and parades. Every second Sunday night there would be a church service on the station, and the ladies were invited to join us and stay for tea and biscuits afterwards. This fellowship meant quite a lot to us as trainees, and meeting with the N.C.O's and officers on occasions like this gave us all a great feeling towards Evans Head.

During the Course we played six games of rugby league in the Lismore local competition, losing the first five though not by much. We were weak in the forwards, which made the backs work so much harder. I had to leave my regular position on the wing and go in as five-eighth to help bolster up the defence. The Saturday before the end of our training, we played against a team of aboriginals from Cabbage Tree Island. They had a good coach, and whilst there was no outstanding player in the team, they were all good and in top condition. They had a philosophy when being tackled with the ball, of pushing it back to someone backing up. This made them a very tough team to play against.

The Lismore Star, in its notes prior to the game, forecast that we would be well beaten, but did not venture to say by how much. We were determined to get into it, and the captain, Flying Officer Brown, called on the players to exert themselves to the fullest. I played at five-eighth, and with five minutes to go scored my third try, bringing the score to 22 to 20. They scored again with a conversion, bringing them to a lead of 25 to 22, and our position seemed hopeless.

With only a short time to go, we were on our line with a five yard scrum, when the final siren sounded. We somehow won the ball and the half back kicked it over the scrum. I raced through, won the ball from a lucky bounce, and raced down the field with the whole team of Cabbage Tree Island chasing me, and placed it under the posts. What our team threatened F/O Brown with if he didn't convert the try was nobody's business, but he did manage it. The Island team was really a great team, and we spoke to them afterwards, and congratulated them on their outstanding performance — they were indeed unlucky not to win that match.

The following Friday, we had our passing out ceremony, and being winter, we paraded in our blues. The full station with all the trainees turned out, and it was a very impressive day. That was Friday, 25th July, 1941. We left the following day for Parkes to do our Astro Navigation course, which we were all looking forward to. That would last a month, and then our course would be finished, and we would be due for overseas posting.

Parkes — N.S.W.

Astro Navigation — No. 1 Air Navigation School

My first entry in the diary for this period was on Sunday, 27th July, 1941. We were in Sydney, having just arrived from Evans Head on our way to Parkes in western New South Wales. We would be in Parkes for four weeks, with quite a lot of evening study recognising the stars. Vera decided that she would return to Brisbane, and I would meet her there after the course finished. Bert Cooper's wife, Mary, made the same decision, and consequently Bert and I travelled with the girls by bus to Casino, and saw them off on the Brisbane Mail train.

We spent just under four weeks at Parkes, learning the theory and the practical side of astro navigation. It was a very absorbing and interesting time. Although we felt that we had been treated well at Evans Head, the time at Parkes was very different. We were there to learn and be taught if we wanted to, and it was up to us. The instructors were excellent, and in particular F/O Brandis. He was a marine officer, and his previous occupation was marine navigation. He left us to our own resources, but was at our beck and call for any information on astro navigation that we required. Consequently, everyone worked enthusiastically at their studies, and all were keen to gain more knowledge on this absorbing subject.

I enjoyed this stay, and it was the ultimate in my studies as an observer with the R.A.A.F. Having passed through the various training centres of the course, struggling at times, I really enjoyed the challenge of it all. Parkes was an ideal location for astro, a small town without many bright city lights giving a clear dark sky at night to observe the stars and the moon.

Within a few days of our arrival, flying exercises were in full swing. With three trainees being grouped, the crew of each flight comprised the pilot, wireless operator and the trainee group. One of us would be detailed to navigate by dead reckoning, whilst the other two would be busy during the flight continually taking readings using the sextant, and then calculating their position.

We flew in Anson aircraft, a twin engined plane with an airspeed of approx 120 miles per hour, very stable and ideally suited for our training purposes. Over eight flights, five of which were in daylight and the others at night, we logged up over 33 hours.

Most of our flying time was in ideal weather conditions, but we did strike one night when a cold front with volumes of cloud was passing through the area. It was necessary to climb above the cloud so that astro shots could be taken, and we reached 11,000 feet. It was freezing cold, with the temperature at minus 11 degrees (C). We persevered for some time, but it was too cold without the proper equipment and we returned to base. In this part of New South Wales with rather a dry climate, there was usually very little obstruction from cloud.

On another occasion at night time, we had a close call. Coming in to land we suddenly saw another aircraft immediately on our port side also heading in. I was sitting alongside the sergeant pilot and noticed the plane, and immediately drew his attention to it. He quickly took action to avoid any collision and climbed away, circled to make another approach and landed without any further alarm. It was very close.

On another flight, a daylight exercise, Ron Winzar, Joe Wright and I were together, and we had been out about two hours (on a four hour flight) when the pilot felt the call of nature and wanted to go to the rear of the aircraft for relief. I was sitting beside him at the time, and he asked if I had flown a plane before. I hadn't. He assured me that I would be all right — just keep it on an even keel, and on a straight course.

He had just reached the tube which was used for that purpose, located at the rear of the plane, when I noticed that the plane was off course. I tried to straighten it, but suddenly it dipped its nose, and got further off course. Ron Winzar by this time was sitting next to me, and as he had been a scrubbed pilot, I made him take my place. Ron also had great difficulty with the aircraft, trying to get it on an even keel, but I felt he knew more about flying than I did.

The pilot struggled to make his way back to the front of the aircraft, resumed his seat, and ridiculed us for not noticing that the port engine had stopped, being out of fuel. We should have known to switch it over to the extra fuel tank. He switched on the tap, and immediately the port engine came alive, but in the meantime we had dropped about 2,000 feet, and were practically on a reciprocal course.

Joe Wright was the navigator at the time; he had difficulty in making the necessary corrections to his exercise in his log, and let us know about it. Ron told him he could be thankful that this was all he had to worry about, as it could have been far worse.

During the 24 days we were at Parkes, we completed all the theory on astro navigation. We took over 200 sightings through the sextant of the "heavenly bodies", as our instructors liked to call them, and completed plotting them on to maps. We were taught that at any time of the night sightings could be made, and from these, accurate positions calculated anywhere on the earth's surface. Also, in daylight, sightings could be taken on the sun, though these would be single bearings. It took quite a few days for this to be fully appreciated, and to realise just how it could assist our future navigation, particularly in war operations, when out of range of radio contact.

We were taught all the workings of the bubble sextant, which was the instrument used in aircraft — as distinct from the marine sextant, the latter using the real horizon to measure altitude. The bubble sextant relied upon a bubble which transformed showed an artificial horizon, from which the altitude of the star or sun could be determined. It was all very confusing when first explained, but eventually understood.

Under these circumstances, night time was a most valuable commodity in our calendar. Not only did we have to learn the exact location of the planets and constellations, but at any given time to recognise them, making an instant reading. Three sightings and readings would be made and then plotted, and from these the exact position of the aircraft could be calculated.

At the conclusion of this course, we were considered to have fulfilled all the training requirements for an observer, and could then be posted to an Operational Training Unit (O.T.U.), whether in Australia or some place overseas. With other air crew we could then be grouped into a crew, the personnel and number depending upon the type of aircraft and its operational function. Training in a practical manner would then ensure that the crew would have operational guidance before going into serious operations.

Before coming to Parkes I had some difficulty with the theory part of the course, which could have been brought about by spending too much time playing football, and also fishing. I therefore decided that whilst at Parkes, I would not play any football, knowing also that there would not be any opportunities for fishing. This would allow me to concentrate on my studies on astro nav. I was dismayed, however, on the first Friday after arrival to be called to the Orderly Room. Fronting the Adjutant, I was informed that I had been selected to play football for the Parkes representative team the following Sunday afternoon against Dubbo.

I told the Adjutant of my desire to do well with my studies at Parkes, but was informed that the C.O. expected me to play, as the Air Force station had to maintain good public relations with the townspeople. On turning up for the game, I asked the authorities how they knew of me, and was told they had heard from Cootamundra that I would be in Parkes on this Course, and been given my expected arrival date.

It was a disappointing game, as I was starved of the ball on the wing, and Dubbo defeated Parkes by 18 to 14. The following fortnight, I was called on again to play in a combined team of Parkes and Canowindra against Newtown, one of the top Sydney clubs. Several notable players were in their team, and it was rather a good match.

We were defeated only narrowly by 16 to 12. I felt that I had a much better match on this occasion.

When the Course ended on the 2nd August, 1941, six members were selected for commissions as officers, namely Nev Beacham, Lex Logan, Murray Norris, Col Carmichael, Jim Gray and Tom Leitch. The rest of us who passed out successfully were promoted to the rank of sergeant. I did quite well with my exams here, being in the first ten, which was an improvement on my efforts at Evans Head. The final marks were not noted on our certificate — simply passed or failed.

Before commencing our pre-embarkation leave, we had to have a complete medical examination, checking teeth, eyes and ears, and various other tests. Three did not pass, and had to go to Sydney for further testing. It was found that Trevor Perry was colour blind — how he was allowed to commence training was hard to fathom. Vin Peters was also suspect, having a defect in one eye evidently due to an accident in his younger days, whilst Nev Hall had ear and hearing problems. Nev was kept in Australia, and eventually was discharged. The last we heard of Trevor and Vin on leaving Parkes was that they were being considered as instructors, which would have made good use of their talents.

On leaving Parkes, we were given six days pre-embarkation leave plus travelling time to our home and return to Embarkation Depot (known as E.D.) The E.D. for the Queenslanders was Sandgate, outside of Brisbane. As I reported living in Cairns, they also allotted me an extra six days travelling time, from Parkes to Cairns and return to Brisbane. I did not inform them that my parents and wife were in Brisbane, which gave me that little extra time with them.

Sandgate

No. 3 E.D. (Embarkation Depot)

My father and mother came to Brisbane and rented a house at Sandgate, and Vera and I joined them there for a while. We spent four weeks at Sandgate Embarkation Depot, and were given lectures and advice on what to expect when we went overseas. Most of it was hopeless, as the lecturers did not have a clue on their subject.

One day we were told that the lecture that afternoon would be a talk from the padre. This would just have to be the last straw, and all thought what a boring afternoon it was going to be. Most of the lads settled down with their heads on the desk after the padre was introduced, determined to have a good sleep. However Padre Debenham had been a Digger in the First World War, and had seen quite a lot of service in France. He commenced by saying that he could well imagine what we thought we could expect from his talk, after having listened to so many boring lectures, but his talk would be different from those previously heard.

His subject would be, "How to do it, and get away with it". All heads came off the table, and eyes and ears opened to listen to him. His talk went on for over an hour, and question time lasted at least another hour. His main talk was sex, and the associated diseases which could be experienced in the distant lands. He was most frank, and his final advice to all and his concluding sentence was — "Don't do it". He was given a terrific ovation at its conclusion, and all vowed that this was the best advice which we had received whilst at Embarkation Depot.

On Wednesday, 1st October, a group of thirty-five or so comprising pilots and W.A.G.'s were handed a green band to put round their kit bags, and they left that morning for Sydney. We found out later that they boarded the "Queen Elizabeth" which left a few days later. As soon as they had gone, my group of fifteen (eight observers and seven W.A.G.s) were told that we could go on leave from 12.15 until 15.15 the next day, and that the following night would be a closed camp. We were not sure where we were heading, but were certain it was to a tropical area, being issued with tropical kit. My parents had shifted to Brisbane, and so had Vera, so I telephoned to meet her in the city.

The following day, Thursday, I returned to Sandgate, Vera coming down with me to be together to the last, and I bade farewell to my parents at Central Railway Station. Although it was closed camp, Vera came to the Air Force Station and I sneaked out to be with her as long as possible. She then returned to Brisbane in a late train.

Friday, 3rd October, 1941.

And so this day — *recording from my diary* — we thought we knew where we were heading. After leaving Vera the previous night, we all assembled in the Sergeants Mess, and with the others who had not been posted, had a farewell party. We left the Station just after 1 p.m. being handed presents and parcels from the Comforts Fund and also the R.S.S.I.L.A., and were addressed by the C.O. and the padre, wishing us all the best.

There were fifteen of us in all, two pilot officers and thirteen sergeants.

Pilot Officer	Lex Logan	(O)	Sergeant	Jim Axon	(W.A.G.)
,, ,,	Ted Eckersley	(O)	,,	John Blunt	(,,)
Sergeant	Peter Atherton	(O)	,,	Arch Buchanan	(,,)
,,	Bert Cooper	(O)	,,	Jim Barnes	(,,)
,,	Ken Holmes	(O)	,,	Gordon Clarke	(,,)
,,	Don Purdon	(O)	,,	Cyril Donovan	(,,)
,,	Ron Winzar	(O)	,,	Flash Gordon	(,,)
,,	Jack Woodward	(O)			

We were taken to the Newstead Wharf, and boarded the S.S. "Marella". We were allotted first class cabins, some three berth and some two berth. Ken Holmes and I had spent quite a lot of time together in training from enlistment days, and so we quickly decided that we would share the same cabin. As we had a three berth cabin, we asked John Blunt would he like to share, and in his inimitable style he answered that he would be delighted. For the next three weeks that we were on board, we all got to know each other really well, and, in fact, a bond of friendship sprang up between the whole fifteen of us.

We found out that we were travelling as passengers to Singapore, and not in convoy. We then asked the purser whom should we report to, and he was nonplussed. On enquiring when we would be leaving, he was not certain, but was sure that it would not be before 10 p.m. When asked could we go ashore, he just replied, "Please yourself". And so there was an immediate rush to go ashore — I caught the New Farm ferry across the river, and then on to East Brisbane, where Vera was staying. Of course, she was surprised to see me, and we had a few more hours together. She came back with me to the wharf, although I was very concerned with her going unaccompanied through New Farm Park to catch the ferry and then a tram home. A couple of days later when the ship called in at Townsville, I rang her, and was relieved to know she had had no worries.

It was not easy to say farewell, particularly as Vera was pregnant, being due sometime in January. It was war time, and at that stage things were not going at all well, with France, Holland and Belgium having fallen, and the air battle over England still being waged most fiercely. So it was we parted — not with feelings of despair, but rather of hope that we would be united again sometime, someday. And this applied not only to us, but also to many thousands of troops — Army, Navy and Air Force — who had enlisted like myself. I did not sleep at all well that night, and I am sure that Vera didn't either.

Singapore Bound

On board S.S. "Marella"

Saturday, 4th October, 1941.

The "Marella" cast away from the Newstead Wharf at 6 a.m., and when I woke and looked through the port hole, we were just clearing the mouth of the Brisbane River and entering Moreton Bay. On going down to breakfast, we were waited on by the stewards in grand style. This was not hard to take. It was certainly not like the troop ships that most of our fellows going overseas experienced, and was indeed very comfortable.

Sitting down to breakfast, we were all allotted the same table. It was with relief we checked that all fifteen were present, nobody being carried away in some form or another and missing the boat. We were not sure just how long the journey would last, but it was estimated that it could possibly be three weeks.

Besides ourselves, other passengers on board the ship were about thirty or so navy men, also bound for Singapore to man the destroyer H.M.A.S. "Vampire" being refitted there. One of these naval officers I happened to know from my days at the Brisbane Grammar School in 1930-31 — "Tubby" Russell, the medical officer. Also on board were two R.A.A.F. nursing sisters, bound for the R.A.A.F. Hospital at Darwin. I did not record their names, but they were keen on bridge, and Lex Logan and I made a four with them on many occasions between Thursday Island and Darwin, where we bade farewell.

Also on board as passengers were civilians returning to Singapore after holidaying in Sydney. They comprised more than half the complement of passengers on board ship. One of them was Tiger King, from Sydney but returning to Malaya — he had vast interests in mining and rubber. Also on board were Reg Young and his wife, a very friendly couple. I got to know them quite well, and they invited me to visit them in Singapore, if ever I had the opportunity. All the passengers were most hospitable and provided a wonderful party for us just before we reached Singapore.

On pulling out from Moreton Bay we kept inside Moreton Island, and soon dropped the pilot, the launch "Matthew Flinders" taking him on board. We then followed the coast for the rest of the day, coming in sight of Fraser Island. In the passage were quite a number of large fish, either marlin or dolphins. They would come out of the

31

water and stand on their tails and fall back into the water with a resounding splash. They seemed to enjoy themselves, and we also enjoyed their performance.

The day we left was the running of the Epsom Handicap in Sydney, and the passengers decided to run two sweeps. This put us in mind to run a sweep amongst ourselves to be called the "Chunder Derby", each one of us putting up a pound and drawing someone else from our group as their horse. The first person to become seasick had to acknowledge the fact, and the person drawing him would take out the whole of the prize, which would be worth fifteen pounds ($30). We had a very smooth voyage all the way, and nobody took ill. The whole of the proceeds were added to our bank for the party we provided for the navy and civilians, on the night prior to arriving in Singapore.

We had a black-out on board, and no lights were visible. All our port holes were blacked out, and if we wanted to look out at night or get some fresh air we had to make sure that the lights were out in our cabin. The main lounge on the top deck was also blacked out (lights being on inside), but to enter, one had to go through a door which closed on entering, through a short passage which had a very subdued light, and then through another door into the lounge and bar.

The "Marella" was a very interesting ship in many ways. She was built before the First World War, and was, we were told, the German Kaiser's yacht before the outbreak of hostilities in 1914. After the First World War, she was taken over by the Allies, and in some way or other, came into the hands of Burns Philp & Co. Ltd. (a large firm which originated in Townsville, later having its head office in Sydney). At the end of the passageway in the cabin area was a plaque, signifying that it had been the Kaiser's yacht, but apart from that, there were no other signs of the ship's earlier days.

The "Marella" was a ship of about 6,000 tons, with a cruising speed of approximately fifteen knots. Late on Sunday night, we passed and observed the light on Flat Top Island. This island was the anchorage for the town of Mackay, with all goods and passengers being transhipped by lighter from this point into Mackay via the Pioneer River. The following day we journeyed through Whitsunday Passage, passing close to Daydream Island. People holidaying on the island came down to the beach and waved to the ship, the "Marella" replying with a long blast on its siren. We arrived outside Townsville during the night and anchored, entering the port early in the morning.

We had leave all day in Townsville, and I was able to visit my previous office of employment and friends, and eventually made my way back on board just after midnight. By 10. 30 a.m. the following day we left Townsville to continue our journey. The scenery passing the islands northward was really picturesque, and by midnight we passed outside Cairns.

Travelling inside the reef northward to Thursday Island provided a different type of scenery, abounding with coral reefs and islands. We passed several ships; one was a Dutch ship which was quite large, but we could not recognise its name.

Another very large ship was the "Stirling Castle". I recorded that she was a ship of about 15,000 tons, but found out later that her size was closer to 25,000 tons. The chaps on board remarked they would like to travel on her, with which I agreed, little realising that six months later I would be wending my way back home to Australia on that same ship. It was only on reading through my diaries much later that I remembered the day we passed the "Stirling Castle" in North Queensland waters. Two days after leaving Townsville, we passed Cape York in the distance, and then pulled into Thursday Island, discharging cargo (mainly cartons of Fosters Lager) and also some passengers.

We arrived in Darwin on Monday the 13th October, and spent two days there, leaving on Wednesday afternoon for Sourabaya in Java. Whilst in Darwin, we had the opportunity of looking through the town, and also visited the R.A.A.F. Station. We met two of the observers from 9 Course, Jack North and Bob Kelleher, who had been posted to one of the Hudson Squadrons in Darwin.

On leaving the R.A.A.F. Station, Peter Atherton and I decided to get a taxi to take us back to the ship, and on the way asked the driver to call at the Post Office so that I could post a letter home. As he was turning he noticed another taxi coming towards him, and swerving almost went down a steep incline, only a fence of steel railing saving the taxi and us. We were told that there were no effective brakes on the taxi, but this was not unusual in Darwin at those times. We all went to the pictures that night, half of the "theatre" being open air. The other half had a roof and was classed as the dress circle, and was also more expensive.

Wednesday, 15th October, 1941.

The "Marella" was able to finalise the discharge of her cargo, and left at 2.30 p.m. for Sourabaya in Java. On the day of our arrival in Darwin the wharfies were on strike, and so the discharge of our cargo took twenty-four hours longer than the captain would have liked. Soon after, we had our last glimpse of Australia, some of us for six months, but for quite a number who became P.O.W.'s the last for four years. All wondered just what the future would hold.

We arrived in Sourabaya the following Sunday, the 19th October, passing close to many of the islands, including Bali. The harbour was heavily mined, and it was necessary to have a pilot to guide the ship through the minefield into the harbour. We berthed at 2.30 p.m. Some of the passengers threw coins into the water and were given a great exhibition of diving by the natives, who were able to retrieve coins before they got out of sight. The captain prevailed on us all to stop, as the natives would not work whilst they were diving for coins. We had the day and night ashore, which was a real education to us, visiting night clubs, and seeing the canals of the Far East.

The following day we left for Semarang. The "Marella" anchored off-shore, and we went ashore on the tender "Wilhelmena". On arrival at the jetty, all air force and navy personnel were met by six army buses and two cars, and taken for a tour of the area, visiting the hills behind the town. We passed through quite a number of sugar cane farms.

We had thought that Sourabaya was beautiful, but this place was a complete gem — lovely homes and magnificent gardens. We were taken to a hotel, where we were able to have a swim, and from there to a club and treated to a sumptuous lunch, and with plenty to drink. We were told that the British Consul at Semarang was responsible for organising the entertainment and the dinner, which was so lavish and enjoyable.

Our time ashore was three hours, and at 1 p.m. the ship got under way and on to Batavia, now known as Djakarta. As on the day before, we were met and taken out to a hotel with beautiful gardens and grounds, and were well entertained. Mid afternoon, we boarded buses to take us back to the ship, and they deviated to show us the rich Chinese and Japanese quarters. They had really magnificent homes, and it was easy to tell the difference in the architecture. The two areas were, of course, separated. The Japanese buildings were all unoccupied, their owners having returned to Japan. Erna, our special guide, explained that there was intense rivalry between the two areas, each one trying to outdo the other.

We invited our guide Erna to come aboard, and showed her over the ship and also took her for a drink. Her father was in Sourabaya, and her mother and two brothers in German occupied territory in Holland. She had not heard from them for over six months, and was very worried about their welfare. Erna worked with General Motors in Batavia, and spoke English fluently.

Peter Atherton and Don Purdon had quite an experience when returning from the entertainment that had been provided. They were in a car with some Dutch journalists when it was involved in a collision with a native Javanese, who walked into the mudguard of the car. He appeared to be badly injured, bleeding from the nose, mouth and ears, and was unconscious. It happened near a police post, and Peter and Don were amazed at the apparent indifference of the police and the Dutch people present towards the injured Javanese. Peter and Don were driven back to the "Marella", but it was a very sobering experience to both of them.

And so we left Batavia, on our last leg to Singapore. We followed the coastline of Sumatra on our port side, and passing tropical islands on the other side made a very picturesque end to our voyage. Singapore Harbour was an eye opener — being so vast and with much shipping about. We were really impressed. We disembarked at the wharf at 4 p.m. on Friday the 24th October, 1941, after bidding farewell to the navy and civilian friends with whom we had had such a pleasant journey.

We were all apprehensive as to what to expect in the very near future, and did not have to wait very long to find out.

Malaya

Sungei Patani

Disembarking from the "Marella" at the Singapore wharf, we all wondered what would happen — whether we would remain together, with the possibility of being posted to an Operational Training Unit.

We were met on the wharf by several air force men, and informed of our postings. Nine were to remain in Singapore in various squadrons, whilst the other six were posted to squadrons located away from Singapore. The six were Lex Logan, Don Purdon, Ron Winzar and myself, all observers, and Gordon ("Clicker") Clarke and Cyril Donovan, both wireless air gunners. We gathered our kits, and were taken by motor transport to the transit camp, located in a belt of rubber trees near Seletar aerodrome.

We were informed that we would probably be advised of our posting the following day, and would be on the move within the next twenty-four hours. As it seemed we would only be in Singapore for a short time, we decided that we had better make the most of it and travel into the main part of town.

There was one problem, however — we only had Australian money, and there was no chance of changing this after 5 p.m. Lex Logan was not with us, having been taken to the officers quarters. This left the five of us together, all sergeants.

We had been told that on arrival in Singapore, we would be advanced the sum of $20 (Malayan). I made an approach on behalf of us all to the Finance Officer, who happened to be an Australian — Pilot Officer Isaacs, from Sydney. He contacted the Finance Officer from Seletar, who was supposed to be arranging the advance. He said that it was too late to give it to us, as it was after 5 p.m. (typical of the R.A.F., as we lived to find out).

When P/O Isaacs asked could he give us a loan till the following day, he was told that various forms would have to be filled out and signed and countersigned. Exasperated, Pilot Officer Isaacs said, "Buggar him, I will lend you the money personally, and you can give me an I.O.U.". This was done, and was much appreciated.

We had the evening meal shortly afterwards — stewed rabbit — cooked R.A.F. style and not at all appetising. If this was a sample of the eating style of the R.A.F., we agreed that we would not be looking forward to future meals. Perhaps we may have been spoilt somewhat by the excellent quality of the food on the "Marella".

*Sgts Ginge Hooper, Slim Richardson and Barney Barnum from 27 Sqdn.
with girls on Penang Island.*

Iggy, Clicker and I left by taxi, with Ron and Don deciding to stay behind. We passed Raffles Hotel on our way to the General Post Office, where the taxi let us out. Raffles Hotel was very spacious and very superior, but we were informed that it was out of bounds to all ranks except commissioned officers. It remained this way even after the Japanese entered the war, and all I ever saw of Raffles Hotel was the outside.

We walked around for a while and then through some Chinese quarters. It was much different to Java in that the streets seemed better, and cleaner too. We appreciated the absence of the native cigarette vendors, who proved such a nuisance throughout Java.

It wasn't long before we felt thirsty, and so looked for a hotel to try out the local product. We duly came across one and were directed to a lift which took us up to the roof garden, which was actually the fourth floor. It turned out to be a Chinese hotel, and the tea garden was full of Chinese sipping tea. A menu was brought to us, and by signs we made them understand that we wanted "dua bottles beer", and nothing to eat. The girl waitress brought us the beer — Tiger Beer — and then brought along some cigars.

During this time we noticed two girls on a raised platform, and one was singing — a love song, we found out later — to the accompaniment of the orchestra. It was a wailing song, and to us it sounded more like a funeral dirge than a love song. The Chinese patrons sitting round did not seem very much impressed by the singing, for they were talking away their hardest. After finishing the beer, we decided to try some China tea, but all agreed it was most vile.

Sungei Patani today. It is now an army camp.

After leaving I suggested going to a Chinese play. Clicker and Iggy were not amused at the prospect, and we went to the New World Cabaret. Inside we found Lex Logan with two R.A.F. officers, the adjutant and the transport officer of the transit camp, and joined them.

The cabaret commenced, and the taxi dancers took their place around the tables allotted to them. They were very pretty girls — Chinese — and beautifully dressed. They were also excellent dancers, and their charge for a dance was 25 cents. Lex and the two R.A.F. officers were enjoying their dancing, when suddenly two military police threatened to take action against the officers if they didn't cease dancing with the girls, as it was just not allowed.

We then moved to another cabaret, but only stayed for two dances, as a brawl seemed imminent and there was a likelihood that we could be dragged into it. We visited another place, but soon cleared off, leaving the two R.A.F. officers from the Transit Camp to their own devices; they appeared to want to make a night of it. The four of us cried enough, and went back to the camp and to bed.

Saturday, 25th October, 1941.

The first thing we did was to visit Seletar Station, where we were given our $20 dollars (Malayan) advance. We ran into several of the chaps who had been posted to squadrons at Seletar, and they seemed quite satisfied and pleased. We had not received our definite postings at that stage. We decided to go into the city and changed our Australian money into Malayan dollars, receiving $6.72 for each Australian pound.

I left the others and found the Post Office, and sent a cable home to Vera. Nearby, I noticed the office of the Commercial Union, the insurance firm I had worked for in Townsville. I called in and met the manager, Mr. Potts, and told him that I thought I had been posted to the north of Malaya. He gave me the name of their manager at Penang, in case I visited that centre.

Two young men from the insurance office drove me to the Cricket Club, and we had some drinks and were shown around. It was rather imposing, very spacious, with a very good cricket field. Evidently, the cricket season was clearly defined, even though Singapore is close to the equator and it would not matter very much when cricket was played. In what they termed the off season, the field was used for rugby union and hockey. They then drove me to the Anzac Club where I expected to find my companions, but not finding them, I hired a taxi and returned to the transit camp.

We were informed that an air force tender would be leaving camp at 6.45 p.m. in time to catch the train north at 8 p.m. Ron Winzar and I were posted to 27 Squadron at Sungei Patani, just north of Penang, and Clicker and Iggy to Alor Star with 62 Squadron. They were both British R.A.F. Squadrons. We were not given any movement orders, but just train tickets for our destination. Lex Logan and Don Purdon were posted to No. 60 Squadron, R.A.F., stationed at Rangoon in Burma, and they were to leave by boat the following Wednesday. The four of us travelling north caught the train, which pulled out right on time at 8 p.m.

Alor Star, where 62 Squadron was stationed, is approximately 30 miles (50 km.) south of the Thai border, whilst Sungei Patani is about another 30 miles further south. S.P., as we called Sungei Patani, is about 25 miles (40 km) north of Butterworth, the town on the mainland alongside the island of Penang.

The following day, Sunday, was very dreary. Arriving at Kuala Lumpur at 7 a.m., we wandered up town to the Anzac Club, and had a shower and breakfast. We changed trains here, and caught the train leaving north at 8.30 a.m, passing many rubber plantations, tin dredges, and lots of jungle. We had to change trains again, and finally arrived at Sungei Patani at 7 p.m., only to find that there was no one there to meet us.

Ron and I were given a lift out to the guard house of the R.A.F. station in an army tender. The Orderly Sergeant was then notified, and took us to the Sergeants' Quarters, where the accommodation proved quite to our liking. Apparently they were not expecting us, and had not received any signals from the Transit Camp about our arrival.

Far East Command Map

Johore Bahru
SEMBAWANG, 8, 453 Sqns.
SELETAR 100, 205 Sqns R.A.F.
Dutch Nav. Air Service
TENGAH
34 Sqn R.A.F.
SINGAPORE I.
Straits
Changi
Tanglin Bks
KALLANG, 243 Sqn R.A.F.
488 Sqn R.N.Z.A.F.
Singapore
Alexandra Bks
Keppel Hbr.
Johore
0   5   MILES 10   15

THAILAND

Singora
Had Yai
Khlaung Ngae
Patani
Ban Sadao
Jitra
62 Sqns R.A.F.
Alor Star
Kota Bharu
1 Sqn R.A.A.F.   36 Sqn R.A.F. (Det)
243 Sqn R.A.F. (Det)   1 Photo-recce Beaufort
21 Sqn R.A.A.F.
27 Sqn R.A.F.
Sungei Patani
Kroh
Gong Kedah
100 Sqn R.A.F.
Machang
Georgetown
Penang
Butterworth
Kuala Krai
Lubok Kiap
K. Trengganu
Taiping
Kuala Kangsar
MALAYA
Perak
Ipoh
Sitiawan
Kampar
Kuala Lipis
Telok Anson
Jerantut
Slim River
Kuantan
8 Sqn R.A.A.F.
36 Sqn R.A.F.
60 Sqn R.A.F.
Fraser's Hill
K. Kubu
Selangor
Kuala Lumpur
Port Swettenham
Gemas
Endau
Port Dickson
Segamat
Labis
Mersing
Malacca
Kahang
Jemaluang
Muar
Yong Peng
Kluang
Rengit
Tebrau
Johore Bahru
Singapore

Occupied Airfield
Unoccupied "
Landing Ground

MILES 20 10 0   20   40   60   80   100 MILES

HUGH W GROSER

We were welcomed into the Sergeants' Mess, and had dinner there, being agreeably surprised with the quality of the food. The sergeants present insisted on our having a few beers, and we were struck with their generosity and friendliness, and looked forward to some happy days ahead. We did not stay late, but retired to our rooms to unpack our kit and get to bed.

We each had our own room, quite a good size and well ventilated, and no doubt originally designed to hold two people. The Sergeants' Mess was also spacious, the dining hall having a kitchen on one side and mess bar on the other. No doubt it was designed to accommodate a much larger number than there were in the squadron.

The squadron was not large, with approximately 600 to 750 men. The administration section was quite efficient, comprising Royal Air Force personnel. We were equipped with Mark 1 Blenheim aircraft — (known as short nosed Blenheims) — twelve in all, with six of them being deemed fighter aircraft and the other six bomber aircraft. The Blenheim was quite a manoeuvrable aircraft, and was considered probably the most efficient aircraft of the R.A.F. in the mid 1930's.

The top speed was over 250 miles per hour at 15,000 feet, but this was considerably reduced when armour plating was installed for the protection of the pilot, and also by the installation of the mid upper gun turret. We considered the top speed of the aircraft to be about 170 m.p.h., with a cruising speed of 135 to 140 m.p.h., with a range of three and a half hours safety. The navigator took up his position alongside the pilot.

All the buildings in the station, which included those for the officers, N.C.O.'s and airmen, were located in an area which was previously a rubber plantation, and were well camouflaged with many of the trees left standing. They were huge trees, and from the air it was difficult to see the buildings. The administration buildings were in the open, and in close proximity to the aerodrome. The drome itself was quite large with two cross strips, sufficiently long to land or take-off any plane in operation in Malaya.

The landing strips themselves were of natural turf, topped with gravel or some similar material to assist in the taking off and landing of aircraft in wet weather. However, although reasonably well drained, the strips could not cope with the heavy tropical rains which always affected flying conditions. This usually happened in the afternoons, and as a result, most of the flying was carried out in the mornings.

The station itself was very new. In fact, there were hundreds of Malay natives, male and female, employed on drainage still under construction. Our 27 Squadron occupied the area on the western side of the drome, where the Administration Section was located. The duty pilot's tower building was on the edge of the strip, but there was

Sgt. Michael (TIT) Willows holding monkey mascot.

Sgts. John Hodgson, Ginge Hooper and Jock Kennedy.

A pet monkey given to the sergeants by a rubber planter was being tamed as a mascot.

Self with W/O Jock Kennedy. Jock liked our Australian Hats.

no tower on this building. It was only a timber building on high blocks, and comprised one room with steps on the outside.

In the short time I was at Sungei Patani, I did not have the opportunity of inspecting all the buildings. I believe those of the officers and other ranks were somewhat similar to those of the N.C.O.'s. Our mess had a well provisioned kitchen with plenty of facilities.

Malayan and Chinese staff were employed to man the kitchen and serve food, and also to serve in the bar. They were supervised by N.C.O.'s, and were, I thought, very efficient. We also had native staff to help with our rooms, for which we paid $1 Malayan per week. They kept the rooms clean and tidy, carried out some laundry, and also cleaned the precincts of the quarters.

On the northern side of the drome we could see a new complex under construction, though I never had the opportunity in the short space of time to make an inspection. We were informed that it was to accommodate another squadron. On the 24th November, 1941, the new squadron arrived, with twelve Buffaloes of 21 R.A.A.F. Squadron being escorted into Sungei Patani by a Lockheed Hudson. It was reassuring to see them arrive, even though they had not had too much experience in flying the new fighters — the Buffaloes.

On my first day of arrival in S.P., I reported to the Orderly Room and met the O.C. of "B" flight (Fl/Lt. Smith) to which I had been assigned, with Ron Winzar allocated to "A" Flight. The Commanding Officer, Squadron Leader Fowles, was away in Singapore, but we soon met him on his return a few days later. However, I had a joy flight or familiarisation flight with Fl/Lt. Carmichael, flying round Penang and looking at the countryside.

Ron and I at first found the personnel of the squadron a little standoffish, and for quite a few days were at a loss for something to do. Perhaps this was to be expected, as the R.A.F. was so different to the R.A.A.F., being very conservative. On making enquiries as to our role we so often were given the phrase — "Ti Dapa", a Malayan term meaning — "It doesn't matter".

We were, however, given the go ahead as navigators (even though we only held the rank of sergeants) to have access to the Intelligence Section. There was a great deal of interesting and informative "gen" (information) available. We also spent quite a lot of time in Operations Room, watching and having explained simulated operations of enemy actions.

We were under the impression that we were the only two Australians in the squadron, but were pleasantly surprised to meet another Australian who was in charge of an operations exercise at the time. His name was Pilot Officer Huck Findlay, previously the Queensland manager of the A.B.C.

Singora

Haad Yai •

Patani

**RAF Unit Location in the
Malay Peninsula, 8 December 1941**

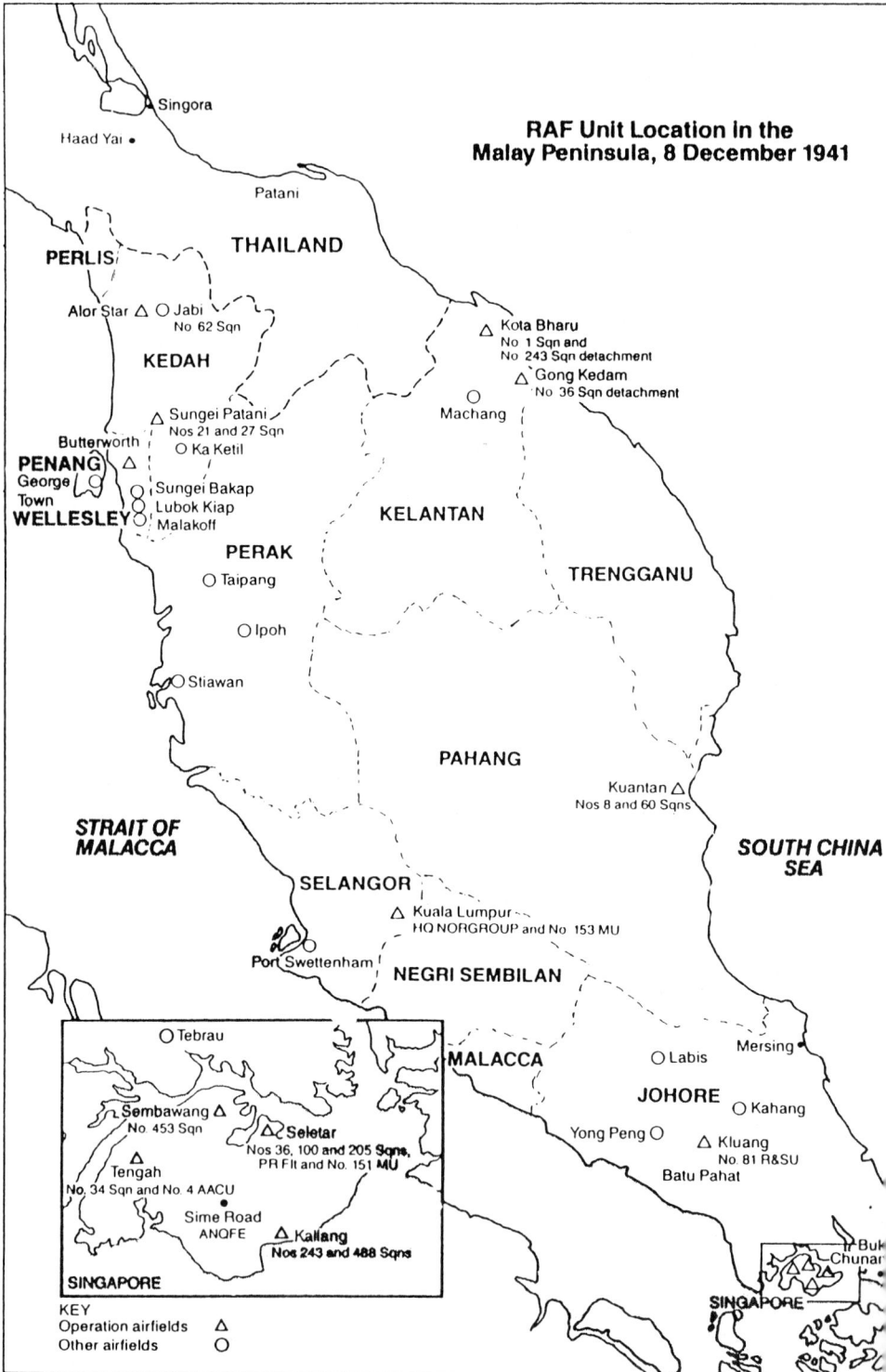

THAILAND

PERLIS

Alor Star △ ○ Jabi
No. 62 Sqn

KEDAH

Kota Bharu
No. 1 Sqn and
No. 243 Sqn detachment

△ Gong Kedam
No. 36 Sqn detachment

△ Sungei Patani
Nos 21 and 27 Sqn
○ Ka Ketil

Machang

Butterworth
PENANG △
George
Town
WELLESLEY

○ Sungei Bakap
○ Lubok Kiap
○ Malakoff

KELANTAN

PERAK

○ Taipang

TRENGGANU

○ Ipoh

○ Stiawan

PAHANG

Kuantan △
Nos 8 and 60 Sqns

STRAIT OF
MALACCA

SOUTH CHINA
SEA

SELANGOR

△ Kuala Lumpur
HQ NORGROUP and No. 153 MU

Port Swettenham

NEGRI SEMBILAN

○ Tebrau

MALACCA

○ Labis

Mersing •

△ Sembawang △
No. 453 Sqn

△ Seletar
Nos 36, 100 and 205 Sqns,
PR Flt and No. 151 MU

△
Tengah
No. 34 Sqn and No. 4 AACU

Sime Road
ANQFE

△ Kallang
Nos 243 and 488 Sqns

JOHORE
○ Kahang

Yong Peng ○
△ Kluang
No. 81 R&SU
Batu Pahat

SINGAPORE

Buk
Chunar

SINGAPORE

KEY
Operation airfields   △
Other airfields   ○

The working hours of the squadron were:- Rise about 0615, get cleaned up for the first parade at 0650, work till 0830, then have breakfast. Second parade 0915, work till 1300, when all flying personnel stood down for the rest of the day. Ground staff worked till 1600 hours. Tiffin (mid-day meal) was held at 1300, and dinner at 1930. Lights out any time you like.

We found out that there was another "colonial" in the Squadron, Sgt. Ginge Hooper who hailed from South Africa and had been trained there. Another pilot with whom we became quite friendly was Sgt. Michael Willows — he quickly was given the nickname of "Tit". He came from England, but had worked in Assam in India in connection with tea agriculture. On the outbreak of war he enlisted in India, trained as a pilot, and received his wings and his posting to 27 Squadron just prior to our joining the Squadron.

There was one person with whom I became very friendly, John (Jock) Kennedy. Jock was a native of Glasgow, and had joined the R.A.F. in the early 1930's. Shortly after his initial training he was posted to the Middle East, doing a rigger course and also being trained in various other aspects of aircraft maintenance. With his enthusiasm, he was eventually given the opportunity of doing a course in flying. He passed with flying colours, and eventually became a member of 27 Squadron.

Jock flew in the Middle East during the Iraqi rebellion, and also in the North West Frontier of India. He had over 3,000 flying hours to his credit, and when I first met him was a Flight Sergeant.

On the following Saturday (1st November), after a morning in Ops room, we were stood down at 1300 with weekend leave. I was in the football team playing Rugby Union, and we were to play a team from Penang during the afternoon. However they did not turn up, so I spent the time on Saturday night and Sunday with Ron Winzar looking at the sights of Georgetown (the large city on the island of Penang). On Sunday, after attending a picture show, we decided to go to the Elysses Cabaret. We were very surprised to see a chap who had travelled on the "Marella" with us to Singapore.

His name was "Tiger" King, and he was with a party of Chinese business associates of his, and quite a few young and beautiful girls. Tiger invited us to join them and we quickly noticed that they had a lot of spirits and other drinks on the table. They set out to drink us under the table, but we had to be careful as we needed to catch the midnight tender back to Sungei Patani.

Tiger came from Sydney but had interests in tin dredging in Thailand, and was in Penang meeting some of his business associates. He invited us both if we could get leave over Xmas and New Year to come to Thailand and be his guests. He gave instructions to his solicitor to contact us, and make all the necessary arrangements. It would have been good, and very pleasant, but unfortunately the Japanese had other ideas.

Whilst at this party, the Chinese business friends of Tiger's gave us the toast of "Yamsing". We did not understand at first, but Tiger explained to us that when a Chinese lifts his glass and gives this toast to you, you must reply also with the salutation of "Yamsing". In giving you this toast he considers that you are a friend. You have the opportunity of returning this by drinking the full glass and showing you return his friendship. If you leave some drink in your glass, he is not your friend. A Chinese custom, and a polite way of either making or not making a friendship.

As one of our hosts gave us the toast, and we acknowledged it as expected, the waiter would immediately replenish our glass. As soon as this was done, another person would repeat the toast. By the end of the evening when we were due to return to the station, Ron and I were really feeling the effects of the party. We just made the ferry leaving from Georgetown with a minute to spare, and bundled ourselves into the station transport tender. We arrived back at the station in the early hours. We thought it just as well that we were not scheduled to fly during the morning.

One of the duties for us on the Station was duty pilot. This was a twenty-four hour duty, involving manning the Duty Pilot Office from an 8 a.m. start. We also had the assistance of a wireless operator, and between us maintained a watch for the full twenty-four hours until relieved. In the days before the balloon went up, we spent many days on duty pilot duties, and I appreciated the time it gave to keep up my diaries, and also to catch up with correspondence.

It also was a good opportunity to get to know many of the chaps in the Squadron. They would call over to the office and talk, wanting to hear something about Australia. They had been away from their home country for a very long time, some for three or four years, and being limited to taking leave in the surroundings of their station, loved to talk about something new.

I had several flights during November, some as a passenger for bombing and gunnery, and also navigating in different exercises. In one particular interception exercise, Tit Willows was to fly the bombing plane and be guided by Operations Room on an interception. Tit was taxi-ing out and testing his flaps when he mistakenly took hold of the undercarriage lever. Too late he realised what he had done, and down went the Blenheim on its belly, ploughing its two propellers into the ground.

There was a tremendous commotion, naturally enough, and Tit was placed on open arrest. After a quick enquiry the charge was dropped. It was deemed that as he had not completed twenty hours flying on the Blenheim, he was still under training. He was still shaken with the incident, but on coming dejectedly into the Mess for dinner that evening, he was greeted with the following ditty, composed by one of the lads, and sung by the members of the mess.

To the tune from *"The Mikado"*.

On a little green hillock down S.P. way,
I spied a short nosed Blenheim which lay,
And I said to that Blenheim, "Oh why do you sit",
"Tit Willows! Tit Willows! Tit Willows!"
"Is it weakness of undercart", I cried,
"Or something gone wrong with your little inside",
But with a shake of its little poor head, it replied,
"Tit Willows! Tit Willows! Tit Willows".

That completely broke the tension for Tit, and he became his old self once again. He also felt so much more relieved the following day when the charge was withdrawn.

On the 20th November, the C.O. returned from a visit to Singapore, with the news that shortly our Blenheims would be replaced with either Beaufighters or Marylands. Either would do, we thought — both would certainly be an improvement on the Blenheims. The only thing that we navigators pondered over was — if it were Beaufighters, would we be retained or be posted to some other Squadron? We need not have been so concerned, as the events of the next few weeks were to prove.

Saturday, 22nd November.

This day, we went into Butterworth to play football, but the game was scrubbed when we arrived, as they could not field a team. We then decided to go in the ferry to Penang, and there met a R.A.A.F. sergeant from Alor Star. In conversation he told me that during the previous Thursday, an aircraft they thought was a German M.E. 110 had flown over their airfield coming from the direction of Thailand. It circled the drome, and then returned in the direction of the border.

I went for a walk during the afternoon, and stopped to watch some Chinese playing badminton. After a while, I was invited in, and our conversation turned out most startling. They were very concerned and informed me that the Japanese would be invading Malaya within the next three weeks. I found that hard to believe, and asked them why they thought that this was the case. They told me that it was common knowledge amongst them. They had their own source of information, and had reported it to the British authorities, but nobody would take any notice of their concern.

They also informed me that there were several Japanese photography shops in Penang who would sell films, and develop and print them at only half the rate that we would pay at our station (where we already had a cut price). These shops would then take a copy of any photo they thought would give information of a military nature, and pass it on to the Japanese authorities. (This was what was known as fifth column espionage or spying for their country).

If any of our personnel took photographs on our station, which could possibly be considered to have information useful to the Japanese, the photographs would be confiscated and censored by the air force or other military command. The Chinese informed me that there were three such photography shops in Penang, and advised where to find them. I was so concerned about this that I purposely visited two of these shops, and the prices quoted confirmed what my friends contended.

When I returned to the Station, I reported to intelligence, and although they passed it on to the higher authorities, it was more than a week before action was taken. By then it was too late, and the people connected with the shops had disappeared just the previous day. Perhaps they had been warned.

Another matter that the Chinese were concerned about was the coming invasion, which they maintained would be made from the North through Thailand. If they were issued with arms they considered they would be able to resist the Japanese invasion or at least do much to hinder their advance. This would also make it much easier for our army to hold them. As it was, they considered that even the Australian army would not be able to hold back the invasion. I ridiculed this idea and the thought that the Japanese assault was imminent, but in later years, I often wondered whether their help should have been enlisted.

During November, we flew sixteen flights ranging from low level bombing and ground firing exercises lasting about twenty-five minutes each to a practice formation flight of two and half hours duration. This flight was very interesting with nine planes flying in formation to Alor Star, returning to Penang and then on to Ipoh and Taiping, before finally returning to Penang and then to base. It was felt that we were becoming operational as a squadron.

On the 26th November, with Jock Kennedy as pilot, myself as navigator, and Sergeant Stout as W.A.G., we proceeded to Alor Star and took part in an army co-operation exercise. They had numerous trucks which were camouflaged, and we were supposed to find them and carry out mock bombing attacks. We found several trucks, and dive bombed them as part of the exercise. We returned to Sungei Patani late in the afternoon.

After returning from Alor Star, we were taken into the town of Sungei Patani and played a game of rugby union against a strong team from the Sungei Patani club. We did well to hold them and were defeated by only 11 to 3. I scored the only try for the Station.

The following day, the station had a visit from a Lockheed Hudson aircraft from Sambaiwang. They were an all Australian crew, and I chatted with one of them. He informed me that because of the episode of the M.E. 110 circling Alor Star, No. 21 R.A.A.F. Squadron was being sent north to Sungei Patani.

They had come to Sungei Patani to carry out all the preliminary arrangements for the arrival of the new squadron. On Monday, 24th November, 21 Squadron with twelve aircraft duly arrived. They settled in at the new quarters, but for a few days the new arrivals had to dine with us, and so we had an extra forty or fifty in our Mess. It was good to meet the Aussies, but I did not know any of them — they came mainly from Victoria and South Australia, and there were only two I met that came from Queensland.

It was certainly very reassuring to welcome the new squadron. However, from what we had been told, we would not have any difficulty in resisting any possible attack from the Japanese. The propaganda expounded to us about the Japanese was that they were not good pilots, could not fly at night, could not fly at great altitude, and so much more bulldust. We had a lot to learn, and we learnt it very quickly.

Wednesday, 26th and Friday, 28th November.

The Squadron was carrying out exercises with the army, doing dive bombing and general reconnaissance. The news was not good, as relations with Japanese diplomats in the United States were grim. Consequently we were on standby alert. The following day, all leave was cancelled, and all crews placed on instant standby, ready to take off at any moment. Extra guards had been summoned at night, and the situation was very tense.

Saturday, 29th November.

I was relieving duty pilot in the morning, and we were to play football against Butterworth in the afternoon. We were to leave by 3 p.m., but leave was cancelled due to the delicate developments with the Japanese diplomats in the U.S.A. All aircraft were placed at the ready, and ground crews worked round the clock to get all unserviceable (U/S) aircraft into a serviceable state. The station was again placed in a state of alert.

I had a telephone call from Don Purdon who was spending the night at Alor Star. Ron Winzar spoke to him for most of the time, but he was able to impart in a roundabout way that their Squadron — No. 60 — had left Rangoon, and was on its way to Kuantan, on the east coast of Malaya. All leave from the station was cancelled.

Sunday, 30th November.

The Station was in a state of alarm but this eased somewhat during the afternoon. The doubling of the guards was reduced to normal, and some leave granted, but with the stipulation that a telephone number had to be provided to allow for instant recall if necessary.

Ginge Hooper was duty pilot, and as he wished to take advantage of the leave situation, I relieved him of the balance of his shift.

All planes had been loaded with ammunition, and all bomb crates filled for instant loading on to aircraft. However, the general feeling was that with the Russians pushing back the Germans on the southern front, and the successes in Libya, the Japs would again back down, and not start a scrap.

We now had orders to carry on all occasions our gas masks and tin helmets. Aircrews had a relatively quiet day, though on alert, but the ground staff were working at full capacity, getting everything into a state of readiness.

Tuesday, 2nd December.

News came today of the arrival of the "Prince of Wales" and the "Repulse", together with a vast squadron of naval ships. It was hoped that their presence would have the desired effect of restraining and stopping the Japanese from any action.

Our crew were shown the results of my photographs taken last week on the army reconnaissance exercise, and they were quite good. We could pick out some of the army vehicles, even though they were camouflaged.

Wednesday, 3rd December.

Seemingly a war of nerves. We were instructed on the use of the tommy gun — just in case we may have need to use one.

Friday, 5th December.

Another quiet day. From that night, all aircrew on battle duty were to sleep in the crew room. This also applied to the duty crews of each aircraft.

Saturday, 6th December.

A game of football had been arranged with Butterworth but was cancelled. All leave was cancelled, and the station placed on alert.

Sunday, 7th December.

I was up early and had a quick breakfast, being duty pilot. I arrived at the watch office before 8 a.m. The news coming through was tense, but nobody imagined that Japan would break the peace and go to war. Being at the watch office all night, I wrote quite a few letters, and also read. We kept receiving news from the Operations Room, and also were asked by the C.O. whether the flare path was out and ready for instant use if required.

We were not placed on full alert, and the lights on the station were left on, there being no blackout. There was certainly no panic, all personnel having the same feeling of optimism. We wondered about the position with the United States — if the Japanese did invade and

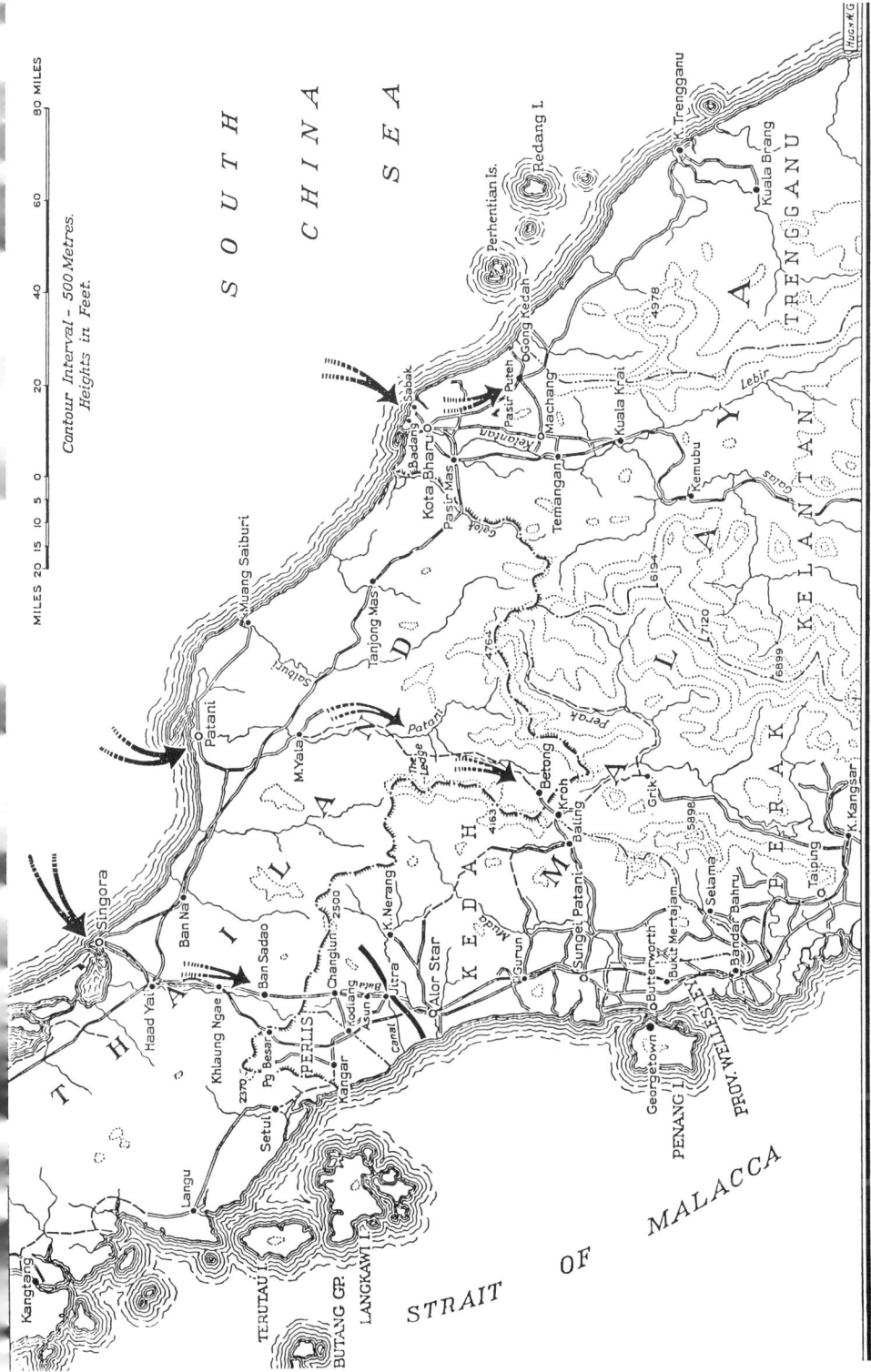

80 MILES

60

40

20

MILES 20 15 10 5 0

Contour Interval – 500 Metres.
Heights in Feet.

S O U T H

C H I N A

S E A

Trengganu

Kuala Brang

Redang I.

Perhentian Is.

Goong Kedah

Pasir Puteh

Machang

TRENGGANU

4978

Kuala Krai

Lebir

Kemubu

Gatas

Sabak

Badang

Kota Bharu

Kelantan

Pasir Mas

Temangan

K E L A N T A N

Tanjong Mas

Golok

Muang Saiburi

Solbuli

Tanjong Mas

6699

7120

Perak

1694

4763

Patani

Patani

M A L A Y

M.Yala

The Ledge

Betong

Kroh

Grik

5898

K. Kangsar

Taiping

P E R A K

Selama

Bandar Bahru

K E D A H

4163

Baling

Sungei Patani

Kulim

Bukit Mertajam

Butterworth

PROV. WELLESLEY

Georgetown

PENANG I.

Gurun

Muda

Alor Star

K. Nerang

canal

Kangar

K.Kedah

Jitra

Asun

2500

Changlun

Kodiang

PERLIS

Pg.Besar

Setul

2370

Khlaung Ngae

Ban Sadao

Ban Na

Haad Yai

Singora

T H A I

Langu

Kangtang

TERUTAU I.

BUTANG GR.

LANGKAWI I.

S T R A I T   O F   M A L A C C A

Huck & G

declare war against us, would the U.S. still remain out of the war, or would they join with us and help us in our cause? We did not have long to wait to find out that answer.

War with Japan

Malaya & Singapore

Monday, 8th December, 1941.

During the previous two days, spasmodic sightings had been made of naval ships with transports moving south through the China Sea. On Friday morning, 6th December, two Hudsons from No. 1 Squadron based at Kota Bharu had sighted convoys moving in a westerly direction and towards the northern section of Malaya. However, a Hudson aircraft on afternoon patrol could not locate either convoy. One convoy had comprised a battleship with cruiser and destroyer escorts and a large number of transports, whilst the second aircraft sighted a comparably large convoy.

During the evening two Catalinas were sent out; later it was confirmed that one was shot down, and the other lost with no details. Whilst the sightings of Japanese convoys so close to Malaya could be considered very grave, the air force was not permitted to attack — the first act of aggression had to come from the Japanese.

The convoy shortly after being sighted had altered course in a north westerly direction. Through the night, one section had moved on to Singora in Thailand, whilst the balance had moved southward to invade the northern section of Malaya in the Kota Bharu area.

Soon after midnight on the 8th December, Indian troops on the sea front at Kota Bharu reported seeing small craft just off the beach. Shortly reports were received of the shelling of beaches by Japanese naval ships. These reports were relayed to Singapore, and by 2 a.m. the Japanese had invaded Malaya, landing in some force. The first blows of the war against the Japanese were delivered by No. 1 Squadron, R.A.A.F., in their Hudsons, bombing and strafing the invaders.

I was duty pilot from 8 a.m. on the previous Saturday morning, and after a good breakfast, took over my writing pad to write home some letters. I expected a quiet day and also an easy night. Going over to the Operations Room, and leaving the airman of the watch in charge, I was somewhat startled to hear of the developments of the previous day, with the Hudsons locating the invasion fleet. I wondered whether the Japanese would make an invasion of south Thailand, consolidating this for a springboard action against Malaya in the near future, or possibly a double invasion plan.

Keeping in touch with Operations Room, I still found time to write my letters. With the Station on alert, there was a general state of tension. The evening came and wore on, with many airmen coming in asking for the latest news and developments. The duty pilot office was very conveniently located, and although we did not have any specific up to date news, it was a convenient meeting room for airmen to gather, talk, and speculate on possible future events. All the squadron personnel were greatly concerned at the possibility of war with the Japanese, particularly as it was felt that we had more than our hands full dealing with the Germans and Italians.

Naturally the atmosphere on the station was electric. Just after 1 a.m., I was called over to Operations Room with others. We were informed by the Commanding Officer, Squadron Leader Fowles, that the Japanese had landed at Kota Bharu. Although war had not been officially declared, nevertheless he deemed this would only be a matter of time. He informed us that No. 1 Squadron was already in action defending their aerodrome, and he expected further news at any time. It was obvious we would be into the fray in the very near future.

I returned to the duty pilot's office, and shortly after this the C.O. rang me asking if the flare path was in position for immediate take off. I replied that I would have it checked, and report back as soon as possible. The team in charge of the flare path immediately investigated the flares, and I was able to report that everything was in readiness for immediate takeoff should that be required.

At about 3 a.m. I was officially informed by Operations Room that we were at war with Japan.

Ops Room also checked again on the flare path. The ground staff were on duty, and engines were being warmed up in readiness. Just after 5 a.m., I was advised by the C.O. to have everything in hand for a dawn take off, with the planes heading for Kota Bharu.

It was 6.30 when the planes lined up for their journey — there were to be nine, but at the last minute one plane (that of Tit Willows) had to drop out as one engine was losing revs. That left eight Blenheims for the raid on Kota Bharu. The aircraft were carrying bombs and were armed to carry out strafing attacks.

Having seen them off, I went down to the Adjutant's Office for the letter of the day, and ran into Tit Willows. He told me of his disappointment at not being able to go with the rest of the Squadron. Whilst we were talking, five aircraft in formation came across the drome. At first we thought that they were long nosed Blenheims — Mk 4, but quickly realised that they were Jap bombers, Army 97 type, known later as Betty bombers.

They bombed the airstrip from about 5,000 feet, and there was no anti-aircraft fire against them. No doubt the anti-aircraft gun crews had not been informed that we were at war with Japan. The bombing was quite accurate, crossing the junction of the two strips, then continuing on towards the administration buildings. One bomb landed in the signals room, killing all five occupants, including a young lad named Stephens, a member of our football team. Many buildings were hit and caught on fire, and a petrol dump was hit.

This raid was immediately followed by another five aircraft, which concentrated on the area of 21 Squadron. Several buildings were destroyed, as well as two Buffalo fighter planes, and another petrol dump was destroyed. This area suffered rather severely and there were many fires and much other damage. It was very disconcerting; we queried where this force was based, being able to bomb us at will and so early on the very first day.

They could not possibly have come from Saigon because of the distance involved, and so had to be operating from Singora or Patani in the south of Thailand, close to the border of Malaya. If that were so and they had come from Thailand, then that country must have been in league with the Japanese.

Our northern aerodromes were within 100 miles of Singora and Patani. This would enable the Japanese to take off from these bases across uninhabited jungle country and attack us at will without any warning. Thus we faced the grim reality of further enemy raids, with our only warning through visual sightings.

As the raid was taking place, two Buffaloes from 21 Squadron took off and managed to get on the tail of the attacking bombers. Due to firing faults we only heard three shots from the guns of the Buffaloes, without any results — rather disappointing for them, and also for us. If they had been successful in bringing down one of the bombers, it would have been a tremendous morale booster to everybody, not just to us at Sungei Patani, but all personnel throughout Malaya and Singapore. The Buffalo fighter was well positioned on the bomber, and the pilot had done a very good job getting there so quickly.

The Sungei Patani aerodrome was quite new, and still in the course of completion. In particular the drainage of the area was incomplete, and this was very important to the future use of the Station. This work was being carried out by coolie labour, with the natives digging the very large drains by hand. The work force was mainly women, who with their small baskets carried the soil away from the area to selected places. It intrigued us to see the women, after filling their baskets, lift them on their head, balance the loads and carry them away. These people would assemble on the site from 7.00 a.m., and commence work at 7.30 a.m.

Whilst so assembled, the Jap bombers came over. Whether deliberately or by accident, several anti-personnel bombs were dropped amongst the hundreds of labourers. They had not been told that we were at war, or to take cover from bombing raids, and the resulting mortality and wounding was terrible. I did not witness it, but was told later by others who had, just how horrible it was. Needless to say, there was panic and a general exodus of the work force from the area, and back to their village. This could have influenced the evacuation of the aerodrome later in the day.

One and a half hours later our planes arrived back at Sungei Patani from their sortie over Kota Bharu. They had been strafing and bombing the attacking ground troops, and felt they had done quite a lot of damage. All aircraft returned, and only one plane was damaged. Several shots went through the fuselage, leaving rather large holes, and another went through the wing, a much larger hole just missing the main spar.

One of the shells exploded into the radio set, and the wireless air gunner sustained small wire shrapnel pieces embedded in his legs. Sgt. Swaffield was the W.A.G. involved, and he did not seek medical attention, but used tweezers to extract the small pieces of wire from his legs. He was still removing these from his legs several days later, but did admit it could have been worse. The formation did not strike any opposition from Japanese fighter aircraft, fortunately, as the Blenheim would have been no match for the Navy O (Zero) if they had been about.

Before the aircraft landed, I had to inspect the landing strips, pinpointing a clear path on the smaller second strip for the landing aircraft, and marking out the bomb craters. The main strip was full of holes and craters and would have been very risky and dangerous for landing. All aircraft landed safely, even though they had to swerve at the end of the strip to dodge a rather large bomb crater.

The crews described the scene at Kota Bharu as one of devastation, with the naval ships having made quite a bombardment of the coastal strip. No ships were seen, all having left the area, but there were plenty of Japs on the foreshore, making headway towards the aerodromes at Kota Bharu.

There was no radar on Sungei Patani, and any air raids had to be sighted visually and warnings given accordingly. We did have some anti-aircraft defence, made up of Bofors guns, and I believe there were some high altitude guns. These were manned by Punjabis, who were rather good with these weapons. They were severely handicapped by the Station not having radar installed to give timely warning of any raids. In addition, our own aircrews were a little on edge that they were not mistaken for enemy aircraft. Coming in to attack from low altitudes, it was a case of the ack ack defence firing first — questions could be asked later.

I was not relieved as duty pilot until 11 a.m., as my relief had been on the raid to Kota Bharu. Feeling hungry, and thinking that there was a lull in activities, I decided to go to the mess and have some breakfast. I was returning to the duty pilot's office to collect my things, and in particular the letters that I had written home, when suddenly the shout went up — more bombers coming.

There they were, coming straight at the drome, in perfect formation, twenty-seven of them, and at a height of about 10,000 ft. As they were dropping their bombs (we could hear them falling), we heard a solitary Blenheim take off, roaring across the strip. We were in a slit trench, heads below ground level, hoping that a bomb would not fall in our trench. We received a real plastering from the raid, giving us a sample of what to expect in the future.

From the accuracy of their bombing, we realised that the enemy had full information about our aerodrome and the surrounding area. This did not boost our confidence and morale, but made us all fear what was in store. I was reminded of my meeting with the Chinese in Penang a few weeks previously.

The workshop area was razed, oxygen cylinders were hit and exploding, hurtling into the sky, and damage to the installations was extensive. In addition, the duty pilot's office suffered a direct hit, and was razed to the ground. In it were all the letters which I had only just written home, as well as all the letters in my satchel from home which I had saved. My diaries were not amongst the letters, being kept in my kit bag. Naturally, there was nobody in the building (all having taken cover), which was a saving grace.

It could be seen that Sungei Patani could not be defended, and so 21 Squadron were told to evacuate immediately to Butterworth. We did not know that this order had been given, but it was very devastating for 27 Squadron personnel to see the other squadron suddenly pack up and leave in such a hurry. In retrospect, this course of action was wise, as the station had no defence to speak of, and with no warning devices, we were just sitting ducks for any Japanese raids.

Shortly after 21 Squadron left, we were told to pack some of our gear, taking only the necessary things, as we would also be evacuating to Butterworth. This would be only temporary, we were informed, as we would be coming back to Sungei Patani in a few days time. Some of us did get back to Sungei Patani, but it was short and swift, and only to collect a few extra things that we considered necessary for our kit.

I decided to leave my blues behind — I didn't like doing this, as I hated to think that some Jap would use them and run round in them. I left the larger kit bag behind. We had been told that we were only leaving Sungei Patani temporarily, and that we should travel light and take only essential things. There were many of us and only a few trucks available to take us to Butterworth. There was not much room, even with our small kit bags. We were also informed that we would be given the opportunity of returning later to collect the larger kit bags. It was all very confusing, almost to the stage of panic.

Thus we left Sungei Patani, rather shaken, realising that what we had been told about the inefficiency of the Japanese and their poor flying ability, and also the false information passed on to us regarding their aircraft, was all just so much hog-wash. With the truth dawning upon us we felt greatly disillusioned, and with this sudden evacuation, the morale of the Squadron was at a low ebb.

Before leaving Sungei Patani, we learnt that the pilot of the plane that took off in the large raid was Sergeant Michael (Tit) Willows. Bombs were falling as he took off, and he was half way across the strip and just airborne when a bomb fell and exploded right under the plane. The W.A.G. was Dusty Rhodes, and he was killed immediately, but Tit lived for about 10 minutes after being taken away from the wreckage. It was a very sad day for us. Tit had missed the first raid over to Kota Bharu through engine trouble, but was determined to take off to attack the bombers.

I took a photo of Tit only a week previously, holding a local monkey. Later I forwarded a print to the "Daily Times" in London, not knowing his parents' address, but expressing the thought that they could be living in Devon. By fortunate circumstances, as was explained by Mrs. Willows, she eventually received the photo, for which she was most thankful. The letters from Mr. and Mrs. Willows are reproduced.

This was our first air casualty, and it did hit us, and brought home the stark reality that war was not a game, but very serious business. We were to be given more examples of this very shortly, and learn more about the enemy.

After a very long day, and not having had a sleep for over thirty hours, I put my head on my kit bag and went to sleep in the truck on the way to Butterworth — about one hour — being awakened when we arrived at our destination. We learned very quickly that sleep was good, and to take it at every opportunity, as there would be so many occasions when we would go long without it.

And so we arrived in Butterworth at about 4.30 p.m.

Letter received from Michael Willows' Father

Telephone
34144
Hours 9.30 — 6
Sat 9.30 — 1

Tortworth House,
92 Queens Road,
Clifton, Bristol, 8.
October, 25th 1942.

Dear Mr. Woodward

I feel I would like to send you a line as well as my wife, to thank you very sincerely for writing to us, it was very decent of you, and we appreciate it very much.

We were terribly fond of Michael and his loss has been a big blow to us. He probably talked to you about us at sometime & we were looking forward to his settling down in Assam again, where he was so happy. However, things don't always pan out as we expect.

We have had quite a nice quiet time here during the last year, but before that Jerry gave us hell. We have had hundreds of raid warnings and about thirteen bad blitzes, one lasting for fourteen hours with a plane or planes overhead dropping bombs at intervals of about ten minutes, a most unpleasant experience. However we ourselves got off alright although there are many houses down quite close to us.

I have been a member of the Home Guard since it was formed, there are nearly two million of us in the Country now, all keen men quite well armed and ready to tackle Jerry if ever he comes over here.

One cannot really grumble at the conditions over here, plenty of food etc. Many things are scarce, of course, but not many real essentials.

The servant problem is very difficult & most people have to do their own house work. This is rather harsh on Mrs. Willows as this is a big house, but she does not mind & it does help to keep her mind off our troubles.

Well Cheerio, and again thank you. It is so pleasing to feel that Michael had such good pals.

Yours sincerely
F.C. Willows

The Letter from Michael's Mother

Telephone
34 144
Hours 9.30 — 6

Tortworth House
92, Queens Road,
Clifton, Bristol 8.
Friday, Oct 23.

Dear Mr. Woodward,

I must start by telling you I am Michael's Mother — & today I have received the snap you took of my boy, & so very kindly sent to us, and believe me it is very precious to us — the last photograph to be taken of him.

The Editor of the Times has been so understanding. He sent your letter to the Western Morning News — a Devon paper. There a Plymouth man saw the enquiry for us — how he knew us we don't know, but he wrote to us sending us the cutting. I then wrote to the Editor & today I have the snap — Oh, thank you so much.

I don't think it could be possible to love a boy more than we loved Michael. It just tore our hearts out to let him go to Assam — but we always counted on having him home, at any rate every 5 years. When the war started I knew in my heart he would go, never the less I was unpatriotic enough to beg him not to — but as soon as the Government allowed it, he went straight to Calcutta and joined up.

We had the fatal cable on Jan 7th, a month after he was killed, and all that time, although we were worrying when we heard of the Japanese raids, we were beginning to think it was all right — & then the terrible news came. I couldn't wish my greatest enemy to go through such agony.

I expect you were great pals — wasn't he good fun — always cheery and bright whatever happened. I expect you knew he was engaged — it all seems so utterly cruel as (without the war) he had such a happy future in store for him.

Michael & I were great pals — he would tell me much more than most boys would tell their mothers, and we had such fun together. Sometimes people mistook me for his sister or girl friend, and he would laugh and love the joke. Now I think I should be taken for his grandmother.

I have another boy, Peter, but alas he has been an invalid all his life. He has a wonderful brain, and hopes to be a writer. My only consolation is that he can't be taken to fight — I loathe war and always have, & I'm afraid this has made me vindictive — I want to punish our enemies.

Will you ever be in England — if so come and see

Michael's Mummie.

Butterworth — Northern Malaya

Monday, 8th December, 1941.

The war with Japan had not finished its first day, and already we had left our station of Sungei Patani and evacuated to Butterworth. This was on the western coast of Malaya, in the province of Wellesley, and directly across the sea within a mile or so was the island of Penang, and its large city of Georgetown.

Immediately we were lodged in an open shed with iron roof and concrete floor, which was to be our future domicile. There were quite a number of these buildings in the area — whether for the use of air force personnel or otherwise, I never did find out. Toilets and ablution blocks were some distance away, but that did not worry us unduly. The administration block and offices were a bit makeshift, being located about 400 yards away.

The quarters were probably intended for the Malayan workers on the Butterworth strip and surrounding padi fields and rubber plantation, but they at least had a roof and were quite acceptable. One very favourable aspect was that the quarters were not too far distant from the sea, and a swim in the briny was always on, and proved very popular. We had to be careful, however, that we did not go too far from shore, as the Jap Zero and other planes were prone to strafe the beach, and any other target considered worthwhile.

There had been quite a lot of activity during the day, and going down to the strip we saw three long nosed Blenheims (Mk.4) from 34 Squadron R.A.F. shot up by the Jap fighters. These Blenheims had been stationed at Tengah on Singapore, and had taken part in the action over Kota Bharu. One plane had been very fortunate as five Jap fighters had caught up with it and shot up its port motor. The pilot landed with his wheels up, as he had no hydraulics, and on stopping, the pilot and observer immediately made a dash for safety.

The W.A.G. had somehow fallen into the tail, and couldn't get out, so the medical officer and his orderly raced out, hacked the tail of the plane open, dragging the gunner out, and pulled and dragged him 50 yards to safety. All this time, the five fighters were diving down and strafing them, and they were very fortunate to escape. Of the three planes, one caught on fire, and the other two were badly shot up. We had no anti-aircraft on the drome at that stage, and the Japanese fighters had an open go. Their aircraft kept attacking until they had no ammunition left, and inflicted much damage. It was terribly demoralising, and all the personnel at Butterworth felt the pangs of defeat.

Tuesday, 9th December.

Second day of the war, and another very black day for us. I had a really good night's rest, missing tea and sleeping for over twelve hours. The only sleep I had had in the previous thirty-six hours had been for an hour in the truck coming to Butterworth from Sungei Patani.

The morning was quiet, but in the afternoon the area around our billet was strafed, and also the beach. We had two Blenheims in the air, and two Buffaloes had just returned from ground strafing the Japs as the enemy fighters came in. The Buffaloes were out of ammunition, and so could not mix it. One got away, and made it south, probably to Ipoh, but the other was shot down into the sea. The pilot managed to parachute out, landing in the sea over towards Penang, and was picked up.

One of our own Blenheims, piloted by the South African, Ginge Hooper, found himself with five fighters on his tail. He wheeled and dived, but couldn't shake them off, but in the process his rear gunner, Sgt. Diss, shot down one of the fighters, which crashed into the sea near Penang. Suddenly Hooper found that he had eight fighters to contend with, and with ammunition running short, made for the coast and crash landed into a padi field. The eight fighters each gave them a burst as they made for the shelter of the nearby trees, and they felt very fortunate to escape.

Fl/Lt Smith, our O.C. ''B'' Flight, was the pilot of the other Blenheim. He attacked a dive bomber, and then altered his attack to another fixed undercart plane, thinking it was another dive bomber. Suddenly he found himself in the midst of seven Army 97 fixed undercart fighters. He made for cloud cover giving them the slip, finally making it back to the Butterworth strip safely.

We noticed six long nosed Blenheims (MK. 4) from 34 Squadron passing overhead on their way back to Singapore. We heard later that they had made a successful raid on Singora aerodrome, landing their bombs in the midst of a lot of Japanese heavy bombers.

It was then that we really copped a belting. Seven dive bombers descended on the drome, but did not do much damage other than creating plenty of holes in the area adjoining the strip. The strip was made of concrete, not very wide, but could withstand light bombing, and also the fragmentation bombs of the type being dropped.

The dive-bombers were supported by twenty-seven Army type fixed undercart fighters. They were looking for our fighter planes, and in between mixing it with our Blenheims and the Buffaloes (21 and 243 Sqdn), they would come down and strafe anything that they could see, and in particular anything moving. After about thirty minutes of strafing, during which they set three of our Blenheims on fire, they left us and made their way over to Penang Island, where they performed aerobatics over Georgetown.

Ron Winzar and I were watching all this from a safe distance on the beach, and decided to go down to the strip and inspect the damage. After looking forlornly at the damage, we started to walk back to the camp when suddenly we heard a shout of warning. We suddenly saw fourteen Navy O Type Fighters (Zero's) about to swoop on the drome. There was no time to get into a slit trench, so we made for a shallow ditch, where we got as close to the ground as we could, and just lay still.

These really gave us a pasting, and set four more planes on fire. Our planes had not been dispersed, which was a pity, as we did not have any to spare. The Navy O fighters were using mainly incendiary ammunition, and we were very relieved when they finally decided to make off back to their base at Singora. Before they departed for base, they went over to Penang Island, and like the fighters before them, gave the inhabitants of Penang a real air show, flying low over the city, diving and looping, watched by the populace of the city.

We heard at night time that the drome at Sungei Patani had been strafed during the day, but the Punjabis had been very accurate with their anti-aircraft fire. They claimed to have shot down five of the fighters who came in flying low and strafing. We hoped it was true.

The ferry was still plying to Georgetown, and during the two days Penang had not been touched. Ginge Hooper was all churned up over his ordeal during the day, so Ron Winzar and I decided to take him into Penang and have a few drinks to cheer him up. We did not have a sergeants' mess in Butterworth, and I am sure that there was no officers' mess. We did not stay long in Penang, leaving early to get some sleep in readiness for the following day, and what it might hold for us.

Whilst at the hotel in Georgetown, we were amazed at the populace being so cheerful, and loud in their praise of the flying qualities of the Japanese during their exhibition over Georgetown during the day. We couldn't help thinking — "How long is this going to last?" We also wondered just what the Japs had in mind, but we could surmise that it would be some ruse, and not too tasty.

Wednesday, 10th December.

We had a very quiet day today, and were left unmolested. This gave us a chance to get on our feet again, after two hectic days. All serviceable aircraft (or rather, all aircraft that could take to the air) were sent down to Tengah (on Singapore Island) to be refurbished. We could ill afford to lose any planes. We heard that seven Army 97's ground strafed Sungei Patani today, and the A.A. claimed to have shot down two of the Jap planes, while a ground staff chap on a Lewis gun held his ground and claimed he also was successful in shooting one down.

Further news from Sungei Patani was that they were trying to repair the damage to the strips. There was a party working on filling in the holes when suddenly fighters appeared. The men took to the truck, and made post haste for cover with a fighter chasing them. Very fortunately for the men, the fighter missed and they got into a ditch, and although strafed several times, none were injured.

Thursday, 11th December.

It was apparent that we would not be going back to Sungei Patani, as the Japanese Army was making steady progress from Singora, and also from Kota Bharu. It seemed that they were also preparing for a landing on the east coast down toward Kuantan. Kota Bharu was being repaired by the Japanese, and already Jap planes were using the three airfields.

We were given the opportunity of going back to Sungei Patani to recover any kit left behind. I brought all my kit to Butterworth except the blues and other excess gear, and wondered just how long I would keep the surplus equipment. On leaving Australia, we were issued with air force blues, and a large quantity of woollen underclothing, scarves, etc. We were also supplied with gifts from A.C.F. (Australian Comforts Fund) and other organisations, generally with the thought that we were going to England or some other cold country. The supplies were very generous, and given with good intentions, but unfortunately did not prove useful.

Returning from our quick trip to Sungei Patani, we witnessed the big raid on Penang. A formation of twenty-seven planes came over, in really good formation, turned and then pattern bombed the business section. The native population came out on the streets to witness the arrival of the planes, no doubt expecting a repetition of the aerobatic display over the previous few days, but they were disappointed and the result was horrendous.

Having bombed the business section, the formation broke away, and in groups of nine, pattern bombed the city again, and then came down to machine gun the area. Having finished their task, they were followed by twenty-four planes which concentrated on dive bombing the shipping in the Harbour. Through the splashes and smoke, not one ship seemed to be hit, though there were some very near misses.

We felt so helpless, being on the beach at Butterworth, and watching the whole of the bombing from beginning to end. The casualties in Georgetown were extremely heavy. We heard that the navy had been called in to assist, and also to work out a scheme of evacuation of the population from Penang. We wondered about this — did the navy have the resources available for this task?

We then heard on the radio about the sinking of the "Prince of Wales" and the "Repulse" — the two capital battleships which had been posted to the Far East. They had ventured out into the China Sea, and were sighted and torpedoed by Japanese aircraft. It was evident from the report that they had had no fighter escort, which left them vulnerable to the Japanese Air Force. That was a bitter pill to swallow, on top of the mauling that we had received, and the retreat of the army from the Thai border down the Malay peninsula towards our old base of Sungei Patani. The news was shattering and most demoralising.

I had lunch, and was told that I would be duty pilot from lunch time, and also that I had to sleep down at the watch office. It was an old ramshackle building with pandanus walls and thatched roof, and not at all strong. A small bomb landed not very far away from the building in the raid on Tuesday, blowing out most of the wall, so it was by then properly air-conditioned. In the event of any raid, the airman of the watch and myself would not be staying in the building but would make for the nearest slit trench. As it turned out, we had a very peaceful day and night, and also managed some sleep, taking a nap in shifts.

The latest news for the day was that Alor Star had fallen, and the Japanese army were making their way down the road towards Sungei Patani. We were also informed that their tactics were to have their troops infiltrate behind ours, keeping well ahead of their main force, working through the jungle and along side roads.

Mostly they were dressed as Malays or in coolie clothing, which was most disconcerting, as we were not well versed in recognising a Japanese from a Malay, or a Chinese for that matter. This posed a great difficulty to ourselves and also the other forces, for if we were to see a person in native dress or similar attire, how would we know if he were friend or foe? The infiltrators were also armed, so we had to be wary that any group appearing to be coolies might suddenly produce arms and use them.

Friday, 12th December.
Raiders were again over Penang today, raiding the town, and setting the fires going again, using mainly incendiary bombs. Dive bombers also came across, picking on shipping in the harbour. Quite a number of ships had already left for Singapore, filled with evacuees. A number of ships were manned by sailors from the Navy — former members of the crews of the "Prince of Wales" and "Repulse", who were saved. It seems that the number lost in the two sinkings was very high.

We followed the progress of one ship which was singled out by a dive bomber for attention. The ship circled, zig-zagged, and varied speed, and did every conceivable thing evasive. The dive bomber used all its bombs without a hit, and then came down at the finish and machine gunned the ship. It was rather spectacular, witnessing the action from the beach, and the audience cheered every time a bomb was dropped — we could see the bomb dropping — and then missing.

Saturday, 13th December, 1941.

I spent the day as duty navigator in the Operations Room. It was a very easy day, handing out maps to different people requiring them.

During the morning three Buffaloes arrived to do a reconnaissance towards Alor Star, where our troops were sorely pressed. Suddenly they saw three Jap bombers with five fighters over towards Penang, so off they went to make combat. One of our Buffs got behind and just underneath a dive bomber — which looked like a J U. 87 — and gave it one burst of the machine gun. It just rolled over and burst into flames and fell into the sea. A fighter soon after suffered a similar fate, whilst a third raced away past Penang with smoke pouring out of its engine, and losing height. Another appeared to be in trouble, and an observation post reported that it had crashed into the jungle. The fighters were Army 97 Fixed Undercart.

I missed the above scrap, but Ron and the other sergeants were most enthusiastic in their description to me at night time, after my sojourn in the Operations Room.

One of our planes evidently got into trouble, diving towards the sea, but the pilot pulled it out (although it seemed to actually touch the water), and all three returned to base at Ipoh. The fighter squadrons operating were 243 and also remnants of 21.

In the afternoon, five Buffaloes were in the air over Butterworth and Penang when suddenly twenty-four Navy O's attacked them. Completely outnumbered, the Buff pilots put on a very good show, losing four planes in the encounter, although one of the pilots was saved. The Japs were seen to lose one of their planes.

Our pilots seemed to be holding their own against the Japs, but were not in the race when outnumbered, and this was usually the case. The Buffalo was able to hold its own against the Army 97 fixed undercart fighter, but was outclassed by the Navy O (Zero).

On going back to my sleeping quarters, I was requested to meet an R.A.A.F. padre. He informed me that he was about to perform a burial service for one of the pilots shot down that day. The padre's name was Padre Shepherd, and he came from Adelaide. The pilot was an Australian, and the Padre thought it would be appropriate if I attended, being a sergeant and a member of the R.A.A.F. I was told the name of the pilot, but did not record it in my diary.

I have since read the volume of "R.A.A.F. 1939-1942", and have found the name Sergeant Oelrich. This somehow rings a bell with me, and also ties in with the circumstances of his being shot down. However, the day recorded in the official volume is different to my date — my diary states the 13th December, whilst the Official History records the 14th. It was quite a solemn ceremony, with several R.A.F. ground staff acting as pall bearers, and the padre and myself being the only Australians present. I felt greatly honoured and mourned his passing.

In the battle yesterday, Fl/Lt. Vigors was shot down after his plane seemed to explode, and parachuted to safety. He was followed down by one of the enemy fighters, who made several passes attempting to machine gun him, but by manipulating the strings of his parachute, he finally came down safely on Penang Island. We were able to witness this feat, which was most remarkable. We also heard later that he was wounded in the fight, and also received burns when the aircraft exploded.

One of the pilots was shot down in a padi field. He commandeered a bicycle from a native, and rode back to Butterworth station.

Sunday, 14th December.

I was duty pilot again, and was certainly getting my share of this work. Still, it kept me busy and was interesting, even though I felt I was in the front line, and the target of any Jap fighter who wanted to do some strafing.

This turned out quite a busy and interesting day, and one which I could never forget. It was also my last day in Butterworth — what an eventful day it was. Duty started at 8.00 a.m., and with the airman of the watch we were driven down to the duty pilot's office. It was still in the same dilapidated state as when I was in the office two days ago — or perhaps had a few more holes than previously, if that were possible.

At 10.30 a.m., over twenty Jap fighters came over near Penang, evidently expecting about five or six Buffaloes of 453 Squadron to be there to take them on. They circled the drome, then flew towards Penang for just on half an hour, came back to our drome, keeping their distance, then flew off, probably disappointed. Our Ack Ack had improved quite a lot, and maybe the Japs had learned to respect it more than previously, as they had lost a few kites to the local gunners. Anyway, they did not come down to the drome to give us a strafing, but kept their distance, which we did not mind.

The news from the north was not good. The enemy had taken Alor Star, and had leapfrogged down the road towards Sungei Patani. The fighting — what there was of it — was for the Sungei Patani aerodrome. The Indian Army was doing a good job, and especially the Ghurkha Company, but jungle fighting was entirely new to them, especially the tactics of the Japanese. Stories were being told of how the Indians would make a stand, then suddenly find themselves being attacked from the rear. They then had to push their way through this line, forfeiting territory which they felt they had fortified and defended well.

We had an air-raid warning about 3.30 p.m. We had been told that we could expect a small flight of Buffaloes from Ipoh at that time, but fortunately they did not arrive. It seemed rather suspicious to us all, as the flight of nine Navy O's were just looking for combat, and certainly would have overwhelmed the small number of Buffs if they had arrived. It pointed to some fifth column work, which we had suspected far too often. The fighters just flew around for over half an hour, and during that time while we took cover (and didn't move once), they kept a sharp lookout but did not attack.

Just after 5p.m., we had a call from the commanding officer. He questioned how we were. He also asked us if we were armed, to which I replied in the negative. He then told me that when the tender came down with our meal, they would bring down some arms, and we could use them if we found it expedient to do so. I asked him what he meant, but he replied that he would contact us later.

Shortly after our meal arrived, and with it a Smith & Weston .38 revolver for me with about 50 rounds of ammunition, and a .303 rifle for the airman. The driver of the truck and his party did not have a clue what it was all about, but told us that they had been instructed to hand over the arms to us. The airman and I had previously thought that we would have a very quiet and pleasant night, and had decided to sleep in shifts, but under the circumstances quickly gave up this idea.

At approximately 10.00 p.m. there was another call from the C.O., informing us that shortly we would receive a visit from a party of riggers and ordinance mechanics, who would be coming down to check three Buffaloes hidden in the trees. We had no idea that they were there — they were certainly well hidden. Shortly after we heard a truck coming down from the quarters, and they shouted to us in recognition. They had been warned that we had been armed.

They immediately moved to the three Buffs and started work on them, and later we heard the engines start up. Evidently these three fighters had been left behind with engine trouble, and had been overlooked somehow or other. Which squadron they belonged to I never did find out. Anyhow they were too valuable to be left behind, and handed over to the Japs. The airmen working on the planes were from our own 27 Squadron, and their knowledge was of Blenheims, not Buffaloes, so they did a good job in getting the planes airworthy.

Within a half hour, the C.O. rang again, checking whether the maintenance men had arrived and found the planes. I assured him that they had, and were working away. He then told me that three pilots would be arriving from Ipoh during the night, and would be flying the Buffaloes out in the early hours of the morning. They would be arriving at varying intervals, and would call out to us in recognition, and we could then escort them over to the planes.

The first one to arrive was a Warrant Officer from 62 Squadron. I think it was W/O Stafford, whom I met later at Palembang in Sumatra; however, I had forgotten the incident at the time and never did check with him. Two hours later, another Blenheim pilot arrived, a pilot officer, whose name I think was Kelleher. At 4 a.m. they were joined by another Blenheim pilot, a flight lieutenant, making up the three pilots to fly out the three Buffalo fighters. They had no experience in flying this aircraft.

I spent the rest of the night with the pilots, and the Flt/Lt. asked the warrant officer his knowledge of the controls. The W/O. answered as best as he could, pointing out that he had only four hours experience on them (the previous four hours). I told them about the condition of the strip; they should keep to the left hand side as there was a large bomb crater on the right.

The riggers passed on what information they had been able to find out about the controls. The three pilots were in readiness to start up and take off at dawn for Ipoh. The Flt/Lt. then thought about the undercarriage — he recognised the lever to raise the wheels, but did not know how to lower them and also whether there was a locking device. Nobody could answer those queries, so it was decided to fly the planes to Ipoh without retracting the undercarts. The whole of the familiarisation of the Buff had been carried out by the three pilots with the aid of a small torch.

At first light, engines were started without any hitches, and the three planes taxied out to the strip. The plane flown by the Flt/Lt. was the first to take off, and immediately went to the right; then on my instructions to keep away from the right hand side, he steered to the left, almost running off the strip before straightening up. He then veered slightly to the left, hitting a rut near a bomb crater, bounced in the air, and eventually became airborne.

The second plane took a longer run, keeping to the centre, and climbing to clear the trees at the end of the strip. The third had quite a bit of trouble, dipping the nose, and then over-correcting, and rocking up and down before levelling out, but eventually getting clear of the strip. The three planes followed one another in a southerly direction and we lost sight of them in the distance, but I did hear that they made their destination safely without undue incident.

After seeing them off (not so safely, but airborne at least), the airman of the watch and I walked back towards the watch office. The van then arrived and picked up the airmen who had worked on the planes, and returned them to the Station. That was just after 7 a.m., and we were not due for relief until 8.00 a.m. It was quite dreary, filling in the time, and we were looking forward to our replacements, the airman saying that he was ready for a good long sleep.

However, when it came to 9 a.m., and they had not arrived, I decided that it was time to ring orderly room, and find out why we had not been relieved. The Adjutant answered the phone, and immediately put the Commanding Officer on. He seemed staggered to think that we were still down on the strip. His first question was — "Have you seen any Japs down there?". I was puzzled by this and asked him "No, should we have?"

His next statement rather shook me; he said that Japanese patrols were on the edge of the drome, and it was expected that their first move would be on the watch office. No time to talk, he said, get going, keep to the side of the road, and have your guns cocked, and be prepared to shoot. A van would be on its way down immediately, but move to meet it.

We certainly moved, walking briskly and keeping a good watch. We were trying to cover each other as best we could, in air force style, wondering just how the army would have carried it out. After about ten minutes, the van approached and we boarded and were taken back to the Orderly Room. The C.O. met us, and his first greeting was — "You both can consider yourselves lucky to be alive, as the Jap patrols were on the far edge of the drome early in the night." I felt like saying to him (but restrained myself), "You might have told us that last night — at least we could have kept a much keener lookout."

He then told us to board the last truck from Butterworth, which was leaving immediately, and he and the adjutant would be following. I was determined to get my kit bags, although the driver tried to persuade us to forget about them and climb into the truck right away.

I noticed a sedan car close by, smeared all over with mud as a form of camouflage. The driver came over and I quickly recognised him as Padre Shepherd. Whilst he had a full car and could not carry any more, he told us both to go and fetch our kit, and he would stay and make sure that the driver of the transport did not leave without us. We both raced to our respective huts, and I collected my small kitbag. We made our way back, very hurriedly, to the Orderly Room, where the truck was waiting. As we arrived, the padre gave us a wave of his hand and made off with his fully loaded sedan, probably to Ipoh, where the R.A.A.F. were stationed.

Thus we evacuated Butterworth, rather hastily, our next stop Kuala Lumpur, and tired out after a most eventful day. It was one of several days in the campaign that will be forever remembered by me, and no doubt shared by my companion, the airman of the watch.

We were both extremely tired, but it was rather difficult to sleep in a very overcrowded truck amongst numerous kitbags, and at the same time keep a sharp lookout for enemy aircraft that might be watching for easy prey travelling along the main road from

Butterworth south. We did see quite a few aircraft on the prowl, and immediately pulled up under the trees to hide.

I heard later that earlier in the morning, many of the evacuation vehicles ahead of us had taken cover when the three Buffaloes which took off from Butterworth earlier in the morning flew over them. They were mistaken for Japanese Army 97 Fighters with their fixed undercarts. The three aircraft flew at considerable risk, as they were flying fairly low, and could very easily have been mistaken for enemy aircraft, and been fired at by our anti-aircraft gunners.

In the evacuation of Butterworth, I felt some satisfaction in that I was part of the exercise of retrieving and saving three of our front line fighters for future operations. All our aircraft, whether fighter or bomber, were considered a valuable commodity. As time went on in the campaign, so many wished —

"If only we had more planes at our disposal."

Kuala Lumpur

Evacuation of Butterworth

Monday, 15th December, 1941.

We passed Taiping without incident, and I am sure that the airmen and I had a sleep on the way. There had been no air alert, and so the truck did not have to pull up and take cover. However, that could not last. Just as we were approaching Ipoh, some enemy bombers were seen overhead, of course with fighter escort; the truck made for shelter at the side of the road.

After the planes had disappeared, we pulled into the aerodrome; they had been heavily bombed. I am not sure by how many aircraft, but it was heavy — and the town itself had also received some bombing. As a result, all the cafes and eating houses in Ipoh were closed, and we missed out on tiffin. However, all the lads just said "Ti Dapa", and on we travelled. It was not long after that we came across a small village where there was an eating house, and at last tiffin was taken.

We arrived in Kuala Lumpur at 7 p.m., and had a bite to eat and a beer at the Air Force Canteen. We were able to camp there for the night, either in part of the canteen or an adjoining building. To make a mattress, a palliasse could be obtained from the orderly room and filled with some straw material. I was too dog tired to care about a mattress, and pulled out my gas mask as a pillow, spread my blanket on the concrete, and within seconds was sound asleep. That concrete was soft enough for me, completely exhausted without a proper sleep for over thirty-six hours.

Tuesday, 16th December, 1941.

I awoke quite early, and found the sergeants' mess close by. I had a good cleanup, badly needed, and then breakfast at the mess.

Shortly after this there was a call for volunteers to drive vehicles down to Singapore. Evidently there were twelve vehicles surplus to requirements, which were needed in Singapore. We were to go in convoy, and as I was the only sergeant I was to be in charge. It sounded easy, but it just did not work out that way.

The vehicles to be ferried down to Singapore were varied, and practically all new. There were two persons for each vehicle. I was in a brand new Ford water wagon truck, with less than 50 miles on the odometer. We were sent off in great form, with my truck at the rear. Within five miles, the one in front of me lost his way, evidently looking at the buildings and the scenery. By the time we realised what had happened, he had gone about twenty miles. We overtook him and then retraced our journey, but did not catch the other vehicles in the convoy at any stage. Coming on dark, we stopped at Segamat for the night, doing in all about 160 miles, including the extra distance because of the wrong road turning.

We found a place that was a rest house for troops. After reporting in, they gave us a meal and bed for the night. This was very handy and much appreciated. This was the area where the 8th A.I.F. Division was located; they were shortly to be called upon to fight the enemy in the defence of Malaya and Singapore. After dinner some army officers turned up, and I had the opportunity to talk with them. They were keen to hear first-hand information of what was happening in the north.

One of the officers was very interesting — he was in charge of a local Malay Regiment which had only recently been formed. They were keen, very loyal, but did not realise just what it was all about. For instance, he said, one Malay had volunteered and after doing some training, decided that he should not have done so, and wanted to return to his village as he had a wife, two children and an old grandmother to look after. The colonel in charge (who in truth was a bachelor) informed the volunteer that he had a wife and three children but his grandmother was dead. This so impressed the Malay that he agreed to remain with the regiment.

The regiment was having great difficulty training the volunteers in the short space of time available. For instance — recently a raid was heading for Singapore at night time, and the planes were passing over Segamat. The water pumping station for the area was operating, and of course could be heard in the vicinity. Some of the regiment on duty proceeded to the pumping station and forced the caretaker and engineer to close down the station for fear that it would be heard by the planes flying overhead, and become a target. It was quite a difficult matter to teach them the correct procedures.

Wednesday, 17th December, 1941.
We decided to leave early for the final part of the journey to Singapore with just the two trucks. Just where the other vehicles were, we did not know; in fact when we delivered our vehicles, only two or three other vehicles had reported in. We never did find out whether they eventually made it — maybe they took more wrong roads on the way, or decided to have a joy ride. In any case there was only one way to go, and that was south towards Singapore, so maybe they did eventually get there.

Pulling out of Segamat, we found that both vehicles needed petrol. First we attempted to get some from the army — no chance of getting them to give us any, so we tried a petrol station run by some Chinese. This created problems, as none of us had any money. To persuade them to fill up our tanks, I said that I would sign for the amount, and they could send the docket to the Adjutant of 27 Squadron, Singapore.

I duly signed the docket for the fuel, and lo and behold three weeks later I had the full amount docked in my pay book. I did not have enough credit in the book to pay for even half of the amount. It took over a week for the Adjutant to be persuaded that what I told him was correct, and have the payment adjusted. That taught me a lesson — never try and book things up, hoping that the air force would duly pay for it, irrespective of how important it might seem.

And so we eventually handed the water tank over to the Transport Depot at Seletar R.A.F. aerodrome. The airman with me went his way — I am not sure where — but I got a lift from Seletar to Kallang which was located on the south side of Singapore, and where our squadron was located.

After reporting, I was taken out to the Rangoon Road School about a half mile or so from Kallang, where most of the sergeants and other N.C.O.'s of 27 Squadron were billeted.

Kallang Airport - Singapore

From 17th December, 1941
to 21st January, 1942.

Our Squadron (No. 27) was stationed at Kallang Airport located on the southern part of Singapore Island. I was told that originally the drome was part of the seafront. It was reclaimed by pumping sand from the area of Singapore Straits, possibly from dredging spoils, and built up above sea level. Before the war, the Empire flying boats would alight in the harbour, and then taxi into the jetty at the sea shore. They were still doing this whilst we were at Kallang, before continuing their journey to London or Sydney.

The landing ramp and jetty were part of the main aerodrome and had been used by local and overseas aircraft. The drome was quite large and although still used as a civil airport, was also now being utilised by the R.A.F., mainly for fighter squadrons.

On the northern part of the island, the dromes of Seletar, Sembawang and Tengah were used by the R.A.F. for some fighter squadrons, but primarily for bombers. Seletar was also used for torpedo operations with Nos. 36 and 100 Squadrons manning Vilderbeeste aircraft. They could not be described as modern aircraft by any means, being biplanes with a cruising speed of about 90 knots, and certainly no match for any of the Japanese fighter planes. Ted Eckersley, Peter Atherton, Bert Cooper and Ken Holmes, all observers, and Jim Axon, Jim Barnes, John Blunt and Arch Buchanan had been posted to the Vilderbeestes when our group originally arrived in Singapore on the "Marella".

On the northern part of the drome at Kallang was a large building, formerly the Airport Hotel. This had all the facilities needed for passengers in peacetime days wishing to break their journey overnight or for longer periods. The administration of the airport was also carried out in this building. On the eastern side of the building was a very high tower, the height approximately equal to a ten storey building. It was from this tower that we had to carry out our duties as duty pilot on a roster basis. A lift was installed from the ground floor of the building to the top of the tower, which was very convenient.

However, when the electricity was switched off (which occurred when an air raid was in progress), it was a long climb to the top on foot. When the air raid siren sounded we were permitted to descend to the bottom, but had to return to the top immediately the raiders left the area. It was often twenty to thirty minutes before the all clear sounded and the electricity was switched on again.

Rather than descend the stairs with the electricity off and then have to climb the stairs again, we decided to stay in the tower and take the slender risk of a bomb being dropped through the top or side of the tower and falling into our office. The odds of this happening were, we felt, very small, and there was not much risk.

At the top of the tower was a balcony which circled the office, and this allowed a full view at any time of any event which might occur on the aerodrome. It was certainly a wonderful view, and we could watch the bombers as they flew over the top of the drome, dropping their loads. Up to the time I left Kallang, the tower had not received a direct hit.

We were housed out in the Rangoon Road School, about a mile from the drome. We dined at the sergeants' mess at the drome, where there was the drink of our choice when we felt like it. Of course, the bar had regulated hours for trading. Transport was provided before each meal to take us from quarters to the drome, and also to return us after the meal. If we decided to stay longer or happened to miss the tender, we had to walk, but this was no problem and quite pleasant.

The distance into the city was about two miles, quite an enjoyable walk, but usually we took the trolley bus which ran regularly and was very inexpensive. At the time no one seemed very worried, and business was being run more or less as usual in Singapore. Most people outwardly showed no sign that there was a war actually raging less than a hundred miles away. Most of the stores were open. Change Alley was in full operation with plenty of bargains, and the Dance Palais was still in full swing. However, the Japanese at this stage were less than 100 miles from the Johore Straits, and advancing quite rapidly down the Malayan peninsula.

24th December, 1942.

I was duty pilot for the day, through to 8am on Christmas morning. I received a Christmas parcel from home the day before, and it was great to receive some real goodies. The mail from home was still coming regularly, with seemingly no difficulties. How long that would last was anybody's guess.

Don Purdon had called out to see Ron Winzar and me the day before. Don came over in the "Marella" with us and was posted to Rangoon with Lex Logan to join 60 Squadron with Mk. 1 Blenheims. They left Rangoon on about the 5th December, and the Squadron came down to Kuantan on the east coast. On the first day of the outbreak of hostilities (8th December), the Squadron went into operations from Kuantan to bomb shipping and troops at Kota Bharu.

Sadly he told us that Lex was in one of the planes that was shot down. Nothing had been heard of them, and it was feared that the whole crew had been killed. (After the war, it was revealed that when the plane had been shot down, the pilot was wounded but had been picked up by a Japanese naval ship. He was interned as a prisoner of war in Japan, but Lex and the W.A.G. had both lost their lives).

Don informed us that the balance of 60 Squadron were leaving by ship from Singapore that afternoon to return to Rangoon in Burma. He looked well, but was happy to leave Singapore.

The news in the papers that day revealed that Sungei Patani (now in enemy hands) had been bombed. We wondered who carried out the action, but had a feeling that it was American Flying Fortresses (B.17) operating from Java. It gave us all a funny feeling to think that our previous station was now being bombed by Allied planes.

The local news was not good, with the Japs still advancing; the only reassuring news was from overseas with Russian successes in their advances against the Germans, and also gains in Libya. If only we could have had some reinforcements of good front line planes, we would certainly have been a lot happier. And I am sure the Army would have agreed with this sentiment.

25th December, 1941.

Having worked until 10 a.m., I asked for and was granted the day off. Jock Kennedy and I decided to go to the City and have the day together. We caught the trolley bus at 10.30, and made our way to the city passing Raffles Hotel on the way. That, however, was not for us, as Jock was a warrant officer — having only just received that promotion — and I was a sergeant, and Raffles was only for commissioned officers.

At the G.P.O. I was pleasantly surprised to receive letters from home. They were two months old but still very welcome, and a lovely Xmas present. From there a visit to Change Alley, where I was looking for a watch and Jock for a belt. However, we could not find anything that suited us, although everything was cheap. Then to the Railway Station office, in the hope that they may have had some of our kit. We both had lost kits and been informed that the railway might have been forwarding lost gear to Singapore. No luck, however.

Leaving the station, we stood on the sidewalk waiting for a trolley bus to town, when a man driving a Chevrolet sedan pulled up. He asked where we wanted to go, offering to drive us there. We intended finding somewhere to have Christmas dinner, and he suggested the Presbyterian Club; they were preparing a dinner for the troops. His wife was helping there. We demurred saying that we could afford to pay for our dinner, but he assured us that there would be plenty, and not to worry, we would be very welcome. They put on a very good dinner with chicken and ham and salad, followed by plum pudding and squash drinks — it was most enjoyable. Before the dinner, we worked up an appetite with a game of table tennis.

There were many places in Singapore that always were open to help the forces, such as the above, N.A.A.F.I. (Navy, Army, Air Force Institute), Y.M.C.A., A.C.F. Anzac Club, Salvation Army, and many other organisations with voluntary helpers. The English women living in Singapore did a wonderful job with their voluntary help, looking after the troops. After leaving the Presbyterian Club we went to the pictures, then called in at the Anzac Club. We had a drink and relaxed in the reading room. I was pleased to pick up a "North Queensland Register", a bit old, but good to read.

We had to leave the Anzac Club at 6, and strolled to the park for a rest. Jock had to be back at camp shortly after, but I decided to stay on, hoping to meet some of the chaps in the Union Jack Club. They did not turn up, and I went to a theatre. Whilst there, the air raid siren sounded, and the audience were warned not to leave their seats, mainly, I think, because of possible panic. The picture continued, but the sound was cut off — why I do not know — perhaps they may have been scared that the bombers flying overhead might hear the noise, and make the theatre a target. However, when the all clear was heard, the sound came on again.

Wednesday, 31st December, 1941.

The last day of the year, and I was duty pilot again. To welcome in the New Year, the airman and I decided we should celebrate. I brought a few sandwiches from the Mess, the airman had a flask of tea, and we settled in to make the most of it. Just before midnight, we had a visit from a Canadian Scot pilot officer — I did not find out where he was stationed or came from.

The three of us welcomed, or rather, saw in the New Year with the tea, which by that time was cold, and some sandwiches. The Scottie mentioned that always previously he welcomed in the New Year with some real scotch whiskey. We assured him that we did not have any such luxury, but he could join us in a cold cup of tea. He was quite a pleasant chap, and we enjoyed it under the circumstances.

During the night, we had two air raid alarms but did not hear any planes. Midnight came and went, and at about 4 a.m., when Scottie thought he would leave us, suddenly the alarm went again. We could hear the plane, or planes, but the noise seemed to be getting less, and we thought could be going away. We were out on the balcony, when suddenly we heard the roar of engines.

There were two planes, it turned out, which had been gliding in from a height. They suddenly opened their throttles and racing straight towards us, dropped their bombs. There was an immediate rush by the three of us to get inside on to the floor. I thought I was there first, but the others assured me later that they beat me by a street.

The bombs missed our tower, but the nearest landed within thirty yards of the hangar, and less than fifty yards from the Airport Hotel eastern wall. The stick of bombs then ran across the road opposite, hitting several native shops, and also a petrol dump of the Asiatic Petroleum Co. It gave us rather a start, but so did many other bombings. One could never get used to them — they were always frightening.

The three northern dromes and also the Naval Base had been the main bombing targets in Singapore up to this stage. The aerodromes at Kluang and Kuala Lumpur had also received quite a lot of attention. As far as the fighters were concerned the Navy O (later termed the Zero) was the most formidable of the Jap planes, whilst the Army 97 with fixed undercarriage was not a match for our Brewster Buffalo fighter planes.

12th January, 1942.
Today was the expected date (providing all went to plan) for our baby to be born in Cairns. Cablegrams and other news were somewhat delayed in those days, so it was likely to be some time before I heard any news from Vera.

All this time in Singapore had been rather monotonous. Ron and I had been trained to be observers (navigators in other words), and not to carry on as duty pilot. I felt so frustrated that I made an application to the Adjutant to be transferred to some squadron where there would be flying duties. The Adjutant seemed understanding, but I wondered if it would get me anywhere. I explained to him that the few planes left in our squadron were being used as fighters; as they did not carry navigators there did not appear to be any position or future for flying duties in the squadron.

Jock Kennedy and I decided to go into the city, where we both had a haircut and then went to the Anzac Club for lunch. It was a very popular place to go and relax, have lunch, and talk to the women volunteers who ran the club. They were mainly Australians and very helpful.

After lunch, I had arranged to visit Mrs. Young and her husband Reg. They were passengers on board the "Marella" on our journey to Singapore, returning after holidaying in Australia. Reg was the superintendent in charge of the Changi Jail, and they were both very friendly. I had rung Mrs. Young and been invited to come to dinner, the invitation being extended to Jock also.

We caught a taxi to the jail, and were shown to their residence. Arriving about 4 pm., they made us very welcome. Reg immediately took us to see his new "dug out" bomb shelter. It was quite elaborate;

the one next door was even more so, but not nearly as compact as the Young's. Quite a number had been constructed for the officers of the institution.

We had afternoon tea which was quite sumptuous and enjoyable. They were very friendly and most hospitable. Two people present at the afternoon tea had been residents of Penang, and the wife treated us to a graphic description of the evacuation from Penang. She was very critical of all that had occurred, and in particular the air force and army and all others who could or should have been assisting them in their ordeal. She did not mention the assistance that was given to all the evacuees by the navy — men who had survived the sinking of the ''Prince of Wales'' and the ''Repulse'' only a week or so previously.

Our hosts, and also Mrs. Farquharson — a friend of Mrs. Young — were most relieved when the pair finally departed. When they left, the whole subject was changed, and it was a very pleasant dinner and evening that followed. Reg Young then arranged transport back to the city, and we caught a trolley bus back to our billets.

Wednesday, 21st January, 1942.

Good news! My application to the Adjutant had borne fruit, and I was called upon to be a member of a crew to go to Tengah and ferry a Blenheim down to Palembang in Sumatra. However, on arrival the plane was u/s (unserviceable) and so we returned to Kallang. At least it was a promising development.

At Tengah we saw some of the damage caused by extensive bombing. They had been the target of a heavy bombing raid just before we arrived. Although only one kite was destroyed, several others suffered damage which would require a lot of work. We saw a Lockheed Hudson lying completely on its back; a large bomb had landed directly in front of it and turned it over. The ground staff were working to get it back on its wheels, and then carry out repairs.

The casualty list was four killed, and many injured. This type of heavy bombing was occurring every day at the three dromes on the northern side (Tengah, Sembawang and Seletar), and so we could expect very shortly the same medicine to be dished out to us at Kallang.

The Japanese Army had made considerable gains driving down the Malay peninsula, and were now less than 100 miles from Singapore Island. The situation was becoming very serious.

Some Hurricane fighters had arrived, being ferried off an aircraft carrier and landing on a drome in the northern part of Sumatra before flying on to Kallang. Already they had been in action with some success against Jap bombers, though they had not yet struck the Navy O. They were expected to hold their own, but no doubt would be very much outnumbered by the enemy fighters.

This was the first day of "blooding" the new fighters in active service in the fight against the Japanese. There was a large raid expected, and Fighter Command made arrangements for a large turnout of the Hurricanes together with a big muster of Brewster Buffaloes to take the challenge direct to the Japanese.

A group of our fighters was to engage the escorting enemy fighters as they approached and then the ack ack was to throw up a heavy bombardment as the bombers crossed the island. As they left, the fighters including the Hurricanes were to engage the bombers. It turned out a real gala day for our fighters and ack ack, with twenty-one enemy planes definitely destroyed for the loss of four of our aircraft. The Japanese had two formations of twenty-seven bombers, and an unknown number of fighters engaged.

Both 488 Squadron and 243 Squadron from Kallang were heavily engaged in this action, and Bert Wipiti, a Maori, was credited with a definite bomber kill. Ginge Baldwin from our own 27 Squadron was also involved flying a Buffalo from 488 Squadron, but in making a beam attack on the bombers received a burst of gun fire into his motor. He was able to glide his plane back to the drome at Seletar, and land it without any further damage. He had persuaded someone into allowing him to fly a Brewster Buffalo, which is worth recounting.

The previous week, Ginge Baldwin was aloft in one of the Blenheims designated a fighter, and cruising along on a roving patrol at about 10,000 feet. He saw six Navy O's just below him, ready to jump another Blenheim flying at about 5,000 ft.

To use his own words, he thought this was rather a poor show, so decided to dive down into the bastards. He engaged the six fighters, and of course they quickly took to him. On the first attack the Navy O's shot away his air bottle, which operated his front guns, so he could not use them again. Next a bullet tore through his port petrol tank, losing petrol but fortunately not catching on fire.

The armour plating protecting the W.A.G. received a cannon shell which ricocheted off through the side of the plane. Another bullet ploughed through one of the ammunition belts from the rear turret being operated by the W.A.G., leaving him firing from one gun.

During the attack, the elevator wires were shot away, and the rudder was jammed, but by using his aileron and trimming tabs, he managed to take the plane out of the dive it was in and gain control. In the meantime, he had entered cloud, and on coming out had lost his attackers. Whilst in the dive, Ginge had called on his W.A.G. to bail out but had received the reply that he would bail out when he saw Ginge bailing out. He was able to limp back to Kallang.

I was duty pilot at the time, and as he arrived and came in to land, I recognised the plane and was surprised at the hairy landing he made. Both his engines were still in action, but with his hydraulics shot away, he just managed to pull up at the end of the runway.

He stopped the engines, and I called him on the two way telling him to get the plane away from the strip. He replied in no uncertain terms, telling me that if I wanted it removed, I could come and do it myself (only more forcefully than that). I then realised that he was in trouble, and called the Ops Room, who organised a tow truck to tow the aircraft away, placing it in a revetment on the side of the strip.

Later in the afternoon, he called into the tower, and apologised for his language, and told the full story. After he settled down, I asked him — seeing that you dived in amongst the six, did you shoot any of them down? His reply to that was that he was sure he had, as only five attacked him after that. His gunner was credited with a kill also, both being confirmed.

I saw the Blenheim the following day, and was it a mess. The ground staff made a full inspection, and counted the number of bullet holes in the plane. Their count was over 120 through the metal parts, and they could not count the number through the fabric parts.

In the meantime, Ginge was left without an aircraft to fly, so he immediately went over to 488 and 243 Squadrons and requested to fly one of their planes. He was very persuasive, and the following day they granted him permission to take one aloft and fly for one hour to get accustomed to it. He did this, and repeated it again the following day, and then went up on the big scramble.

That would have been the 20th January, and it was the largest bomber raid by the Japanese Air Force on Singapore to that date. As Ginge came in to attack the bombers with other fighters, an explosive cannon shell hit the plane, shooting away his hydraulics and holing his petrol tanks. Rather than lose his plane (and realising that if he did, he would not be given another replacement), he glided his plane back and landed at Seletar.

After spending two days at Seletar repairing his aircraft and making it serviceable, he flew it back to Kallang and prepared to go up again. The following day he was paired to fly with another pilot, and they came across six Navy O's and flew into them. They shot down one each, for which they were credited, and then took cover in cloud and lost contact.

There was no doubt that Ginge Baldwin was a good pilot, and as game as you could make them, but we wondered how long his luck would hold out. The ground staff took over his damaged Blenheim, and were determined to repair it, but it did not quite work out that way.

It was about this time that ill feeling arose over the earlier evacuation from northern Malaya of 21 R.A.A.F. Squadron and 27 Squadron (R.A.F.). Perhaps the evacuation was hasty and certainly rushed, almost to the point of panic; nevertheless there was no future in staying on as the defences were simply non-existent. I felt that the sending of 21 Squadron north when they were not fully operational was badly timed, but possibly was carried out as a bluff to the Japanese which did not work out.

Whether as a result of the controversy or not, or merely coincidence, 27 Squadron had a change of Commanding Officer, and Squadron Leader Banks took over the command. I did hear that the same happened to 21 Squadron, but that may have been hearsay. With the controversy that raged, Ron Winzar and I were the target of quite a lot of heckling, being with 27 Squadron and Australians, and we were very pleased when the ill feeling abated.

Palembang - Sumatra

Ferrying Blenheim from Singapore
to Palembang

Thursday, 22nd January, 1942.

Evidently my application for transfer to another squadron had some effect, for on this day I had my first flight since the beginning of hostilities with Japan. With Pilot Officer Kelleher as pilot, myself as navigator and Sgt. Swaffield as W.A.G., we took off from Kallang with two other Blenheims, flying in formation to Palembang. It took us an hour and fifty minutes to reach Palembang.

I had not met P/O. Kelleher before, but he was previously in 62 Squadron and probably one of the pilots who flew a Buffalo fighter out from Butterworth. I felt quite confident in him, as he flew the plane well. It was quite an interesting flight, over the islands close to the coastline of Sumatra. We landed at Palembang aerodrome and were taken into the township for breakfast. We had left very early in the morning, getting away at daybreak from Kallang to avoid possible enemy fighters. They would have liked to have come across us, especially if they happened to be Navy O's (Zeros).

After a good meal of bacon and eggs, we were driven back to the drome at Palembang, and given instructions to fly to another aerodrome which was on the secret list. It was located about forty miles in a south west direction from Palembang aerodrome, and would be known in the future as P2.

We were warned not to mark any route on our map showing where the secret drome was, or make any reference to it in our logs. We were not in any other way to give verbal or written information of the existence of this drome, for fear of it getting into the wrong hands. We were also instructed to remember very carefully our flight to the drome, taking a mental note of all landmarks en route so that we could recognise the direction and location of the site. At the time it all seemed rather mysterious, but the reason became very evident later when we operated from this drome.

On leaving Palembang drome (known in future by us as P1), we flew in a westerly direction until we found a pipe line. This was followed until it seemed to converge on the railway line, which ran from Palembang to the south of the island. Then a road converged on the railway line, and we lost sight of the pipe line which was bringing oil from the Sumatra oil fields to Palembang. This oil pipe line was a very valuable asset, and one which the Japanese wanted very badly for the future success of their war effort.

Suddenly we came across an open field, ringed by forest trees. The trees were quite dense, but without much height. The cleared area was reasonably grassed, but showed no sign of any crops having being grown upon it. The earth was a type of black sand, which allowed the rain to quickly soak through and dry out after heavy rain, providing a good natural drainage. This area was the secret aerodrome to be known as P2.

On the northern end of this field (for that was an apt way of describing it) was a building. It was the only building visible from the air, and also the means of recognition of the aerodrome. We could not see anything else in the way of aircraft, or any installations that could be used — but that was P2. We had to rely on our memory, and print the details indelibly on our mind; we were told that this would be our element of safety. It turned out to be true — ultimately the Jap never did find out where P2 was when it really mattered to him, and he was very much the loser for it.

We landed on the area, and taxied up to the building which we found out was the orderly room, duty pilots room, operations room, and everything that one could imagine. We could not find out much more than that in the limited time. After hanging about for a little while and having lunch, or tiffin as we called it, we gathered our kit and navigational equipment, and were taken back to Palembang, where we spent the night.

After dinner, Ron Winzar and Iggy (Cyril) Donovan (a W.A.G. with 62 Squadron, and one of our travellers on the "Marella"), went with me into the city area of Palembang to a restaurant. We met up with other air force chaps and some Dutch airmen, and had a few drinks and a good talk. Ron and Iggy had been on one of the other planes which accompanied us from Kallang to P2.

Friday, 23rd January, 1942.

After an early breakfast in the mess at Palembang, we were taken to the wharves and boarded the passenger ship, "Kedah". This had plied mainly between Singapore and Penang before hostilities broke out, but had been taken over by the the navy for transport purposes. The ship was approximately 2,200 tons and quite comfortable, with a speed of about 15 knots.

Adjacent to the wharves was an oil distilling plant, with a great number of large tanks of oil and fuel. Smoking was definitely prohibited. We had been on board for about half an hour when we were shepherded below. There was an air raid brewing, with twenty-seven bombers approaching with fighter escort. If the raid had been concentrated on the wharf area, being below in the ship would not have given us any shelter; the whole place would have just

S.S. "KEDAH"

This small ship of approximately 2,200 tons had been taken over by the navy on the outbreak of hostilities. Previously it had been a passenger vessel based between Singapore and Penang. On our first ferrying flight from Singapore to Palembang, we were transported back to Singapore on this ship. She was one of the last to leave before the Japanese overran Singapore.

blown up into a real inferno. However, the raid was concentrated on the aerodrome of Palembang which received another plastering.

The wharf area was left alone and not attacked at all by the enemy forces; their objective, no doubt, was to capture Palembang intact with as little damage as possible and obtain oil supplies for future operations. However, the Dutch were prepared to carry out a scorched earth policy in the face of a Japanese invasion. This did in fact occur, and no doubt denied the Japanese forces the fuel and oil required for their purposes for some time after the invasion. However, these events were several weeks off; the invasion of Palembang coincided with the fall of Singapore, on the 15th February, 1942.

The "Kedah" pulled away from the wharves about 1.30 p.m., and it was most interesting to steam down the Musi River. A very wide river and quite deep, it allowed large ships such as oil tankers to travel up river. The current was very swift, about five to six knots, which no doubt would have kept ship navigators on the alert.

Other sergeants from 27 Squadron who flew down the day before in the same formation were Eddie Edwards and Allan Oliver, both W.A.G.'s. Before long we left the Musi River, and wended our way northward to Singapore. Ron, Eddie, Allan and I settled down together to a game of bridge to pass away the time, and admired the scenery of the islands.

We four were members of 27 Squadron, and Iggy was a member of 62 Squadron which had been stationed at Alor Star. The two were now amalgamated, and known as 27/62 Squadron. Quite a number of 27 Squadron personnel had already left, being posted elsewhere.

The rest of the journey back to Singapore proved quite uneventful — no air raids and no signs of submarines. We were completely blacked out during night time, and had a good rest. The "Kedah" made good speed, and at one stage we were told was travelling at twenty knots.

Late afternoon we entered Johore Straits, passing through the boom, and had a quite impressive view of the Naval Base and the large dock. We travelled to a jetty near the causeway, and alighted from the "Kedah" at a quarter to seven, after a very safe and comfortable journey.

No sooner had we got off the boat, when a very special welcome was extended to us by the air raid siren alarm. However, we did not see any kites, although we heard the ack ack guns on the western side firing (possibly, as one of the lads said, at our own planes that might be flying at that time of night). It did not last long, and the all clear sounded after half an hour.

We had quite a long wait at the wharf, and were really brassed off when the tender finally arrived at 10 p.m. to take us back to Kallang. We were very thankful that the mess was still open, and we were able to have a few beers.

Singapore - Kallang Aerodrome

Upon returning from Palembang Sunday, 25th January, 1942, to Friday, 30th January, 1942.

Raiders were over Singapore on Sunday in two formations of twenty-seven, and their target was Tengah. They certainly knew how to fly in formation, getting up to a good height, about 18,000 to 20,000 ft, and into a perfect "Vic" formation. Apparently these twenty-seven aircraft were from three squadrons with nine kites from each. Occasionally there would be a gap, where our ack ack had possibly been successful in bringing one down. A few days previously, when the Naval Base received a plastering, they had eighty-nine bombers involved, two lots of twenty-seven (with one gap), then two lots of eighteen.

The day we left for Palembang (Thursday the 22nd), Kallang drome had been heavily bombed with two raids of twenty-seven planes. Most of the bombs from the first formation of twenty-seven fell over the road from the drome, doing quite a lot of damage to the Happy World, and starting numerous fires. The bombs from the second formation were right on target (presuming they were aimed at the Kallang drome). One stick of bombs hit a hangar, and badly damaged the building, but fortunately there was very little inside, and in particular no aircraft. Two Buffaloes were set on fire and destroyed and numerous bomb craters appeared along the main strip; these had to be filled in before the strip could be used again.

Apparently there was some delay in sounding the air raid siren, as the bombers were almost overhead when the alarm sounded. As a result the order to the pilots of the fighter aircraft to scramble (the term to immediately take off) was given as the bombs were already falling. Only a few planes got up in time, and that was very risky.

Ginge Baldwin was included in the group to scramble, and as he ran towards his aircraft, one of the riggers had the engine already started as he entered the aircraft cockpit. He took off amidst the dust and smoke of exploding bombs and was definitely seen to get airborne. He made one circuit of the drome and was climbing, but was never seen again. His two riggers immediately commenced running for the shelter of a slit trench as soon as Ginge started his take off, but did not make it, a bomb exploding in their tracks.

Ginge had been quite a popular man in the sergeants' mess. He was very outspoken, but spoke with the courage of his own convictions. He was strong in his criticism of the failures of the higher officers to adequately cope with the present situation, and maintained that we could have been more vigorous in our outlook towards the Japanese onslaught. He set a standard by his own actions, and became an inspiration to 27 Squadron airmen, and also to others at Kallang.

He was an Englishman, a burly type of fellow and ruddy haired as his nickname implied. He joined the R.A.F. in India, having been a tea planter. He was very keen on game hunting, and told us many tales of his exploits in India which, knowing him, I quite believed. He was an excellent shot. At Sungei Patani the aircrew of the Squadron had often gone down to the small arms firing range, and Baldwin always had the best score. The first time we went down we had a sweep, but he won so easily that we all agreed not to bet any more.

He was posted missing at the end of the day, and there did not seem to be any hope of his turning up or being found.

Tuesday, 27th January, 1942.

I received a cable from home to say that a son had been born, and that both were well. Naturally I was most elated, but with the heavy fighting raging in the area, I wondered whether I would be fortunate enough to get back to Australia and be spared to reunite with my wife Vera, and also see my young son. However, I did feel that I now had more to fight for, and so became more resolute to press on and fight for what I thought was right.

The news of the arrival of the baby had taken thirteen days from the date of sending, and came by cable. The delivery of letters from home was now very difficult, and all correspondence to and from the Far East ceased before the end of January, 1942. I wrote a letter home on the 26th January that I had received the cable, and this was the last letter Vera received from me from the Far East.

With the heavy usage of the cable from Australia, a new system was devised whereby numbers for set phrases were instigated. The sender would pick out the number of a phrase to be sent, and only the number would be cabled. At the other end, this would be deciphered and the wording given to the receiver. Four numbers would be allowed for each cable, and with this new system operating, a faster service was provided. For instance, sending a cable either way, the receiver's name would be given followed by numbers such as 44 20 16 10 which could mean "Son is born", "both well", "much love", "wish you were here", and the sender's name. It worked well, and allowed a greater number of cables to flow.

The Japanese onslaught was now moving ahead at a fast rate, and their aircraft were using our aerodrome at Sungei Patani and also others which had been evacuated. This gave them the opportunity of deploying their fighters against us and the army very quickly. With our aircraft being knocked out and the difficulty of bringing in replacements, the Jap certainly had the upper hand. Our army, and in particular the A.I.F. 8th Division, just could not cope with the Japanese advance, particularly without support from our air force.

It appeared that Kallang would soon receive more bombing raids, no doubt because of the fighters located on this side of the island. During the morning, the air raid sirens sounded as we left the dispersal hut, and we saw eighteen bombers headed in our direction. We could tell that they meant business, as they were passing directly overhead.

Soon after we heard the familiar swish of the bombs, and crouched as low as we could in the slit trench waiting for the barrage. I felt a large explosion close by, and further explosions all round us. As soon as the last bomb explosion died away we warily lifted our heads, hoping that there would not be any delayed action bombs, and peeped out over the top of the slit trench.

Two petrol bowsers were on fire; all planes in the dispersal bays had escaped direct hits, but quite a number had been damaged. The large blast that I felt was about twenty-five yards away, leaving a crater twenty-five feet across and eight feet deep. Two other large bombs also landed very close, and just in front of a Blenheim which was in a dispersal pen. The only apparent damage to the aircraft was to the leading edges of both wings which were blown in.

We felt quite relieved when we scrambled out and had a look round, thinking that was it for the day. However, it was only a short respite, for suddenly another air raid alarm sounded. Shortly we perceived a large formation of bombers flying at a high altitude, about the usual height of 18,000 to 20,000 feet. In this formation there were twenty-seven planes. They were approaching from the south east over the sea, where only the ack ack from the aerodrome station and surrounds could fire at them. This flight was only about thirty minutes after the previous raid, so we did not have much of a let up.

This attack dropped its load right amongst us, the bombs being mainly incendiary and anti personnel bombs — somewhat different to those of the previous raid, which were high explosive (H.E.). With smaller bombs, it meant that each aircraft dropped a much greater number than in the previous raid, and this raid had nine more aircraft. Six of us were in the slit trench, which was quite shallow, as were all the slit trenches at Kallang — being about five feet deep, and sand bagged for another two feet above the surface. In actual size, they were about ten feet in length by four to five feet across. Kallang was located on land reclaimed from the sea, and there was always at least a foot of water in the bottom of the slit trench (depending on the height of the tide), which made them even more uncomfortable.

The bombs made an awful noise, and we were relieved when we heard the last of them. Waiting a few minutes, we had a look then climbed outside. Our slit trench was alongside a dispersal bay which housed a Blenheim. One bomb had landed on top of the wall, and threw shrapnel in all directions. On looking back to our slit trench, a piece of shrapnel had torn through a sand bag only inches above where my head was. I had a tin hat on, but I am sure that would not have saved me.

The Blenheim in the dispersal bay was on fire, and exploding ammunition was flying in all directions. This was most ironical, as it was the Blenheim that Baldwin had flown when he caught up with 6 Navy O's some two weeks previously. The ground staff had worked hard to repair and refit the plane, and had just finished and were waiting for it to be test flown. They all assembled in front of the plane, and watched it burn. We all thought that it was probably a fitting memorial to Sgt. Ginge Baldwin.

Another Blenheim was destroyed, as well as two Buffaloes and a Hurricane. In addition two more petrol bowsers caught on fire and were destroyed. Several buildings were damaged including our squadron offices. The afternoon was spent going through the debris, salvaging our flying kits and other gear, and removing them to our quarters in Katong. It was remarkable, however, that the number of casualties was so low, as there were none killed, and only seven injured.

These numbers applied to the station itself, but there may have been more casualties on the outskirts, where bombs had fallen. One Bofors gun had a direct hit but fortunately the crew had taken shelter; it was useless firing their guns, as the aircraft were out of range.

In the first raid, a large lump of soil was thrown into the trench which hit me over the ear. It was sore for a few days, but it was nothing serious. When the same bomb made its crater, it lifted a small Baby Austin car belonging to one of the officers up on the mound beside the crater, leaving it about three feet above ground level. Strange to relate, it was pushed down on to the road, and started without any fuss, apparently no worse for its bomb scare.

Wednesday, 28th January, 1942.
As we did not feel like going through another bombing after yesterday's ordeal, we sergeants decided to stay in our dispersal hut at Katong all day, only going to Kallang for our meals. Thus, after breakfast we were back in Katong with the prospects of an easy day. Katong was located about one and a half miles (2 km) from Kallang, and as there were no military objectives there, other than ourselves, we felt that this would enable us to relax.

However, about 10 a.m. when I was having a shower and clean up, the air raid siren sounded. Not unduly alarmed, we all had a look out, and saw twenty-seven bombers in formation making their way, as we thought, towards Kallang. They were coming from an easterly direction over the sea, and just when we thought that Kallang was in for another drubbing, they altered course, and made for Katong.

We quickly got into a slit trench and saw the bombers go almost overhead, dropping their load. The bombs started landing near the beach and finished level with us, but about 150 yards to the side. The majority of the bombs landed in a poor native quarter of Singapore. I looked out and walked towards the Yock Eng school, which was a first aid post, and noticed that they were becoming busy with people coming in for first aid. I decided to volunteer my services, and Ginge Hooper, the South African, also came with me. They gave us a job of acting as stretcher bearers, carrying injured people in to the school after they were brought in by trucks which went round the neighbourhood.

The casualties were heavy, and were mainly caused by the people not laying on the ground as the bombs came down. All the bombs were anti-personnel bombs, and what the Jap hoped to achieve by dropping this type of bomb in the native quarters was hard to imagine. Most of the injured had shrapnel wounds above knee height, so if they had been laying down, they would probably not have been wounded.

The sad part of it was that so many children were injured. Quite a large number were killed, well over fifty, and more than 300 were wounded. We had a very busy time, and were quite tired out when we finished just after 1 o'clock. We saw some very sad sights which were hard to take, seeing innocent children wounded, and possibly crippled for life.

One particular touching memory was to see a mother carrying her baby child with severe head injuries. The child was dead, but we had to try to pacify her. We took the baby into the first aid station and handed it to the medical officer, but there was nothing he could do.

When we had finished our duties, we asked whether we could be of any further assistance, and were thanked for our efforts. We felt most depressed at what we saw, and could not help but consider the futility of the whole ordeal, the spectacle of innocent people and young children in particular having to endure the pangs of war.

We felt so tired and upset, that after going back to our hut, we got dressed and went to town to the Anzac Club, and had a meal and some beers. We then went to the pictures before returning to our hut at Katong.

Thursday, 29th January, 1942.

We were left alone this morning, but Seletar and Sambawang had their turn for a bombing raid. The Jap now had almost complete monopoly of the skies, without much resistance from the air force. This made it practically intolerable for the army, who were still holding out against tremendous odds.

After tiffin, Fl/Lt. Kentish (from 27 Squadron) called for Sgt Swaffield and myself to get our gear together, and to go out to Seletar to ferry a Blenheim to Palembang in Sumatra. We were to sleep at Seletar, and take off very early the following morning.

Whilst at Seletar I met Bert Cooper, and had a good yarn with him. He told me about the raid by the Vilderbeestes on the Jap invasion of Endau three days earlier. The Vilderbeeste was a Vickers bi-plane, most antiquated, and used for torpedo attacks on shipping. They were also used for bombing, but were certainly no match in this attack when they came against the Jap fighters, coming against the Navy O and also the Army 97 Fighter. Eleven Vilderbeestes were lost out of twenty-two, and although the Jap lost some planes, it was rather disastrous for the R.A.F.

Bert was a navigator in one of the Vilderbeeste aircraft, and gave me a graphic account of the attack, saying that he would never forget the spectacle of so many planes in battle. He said that it reminded him of movies in peace time days, depicting war scenes of the First World War, with hundreds of planes filling the skies, and here and there a plane falling in flames. The only difference in this instance was — this was real. It appeared that there was a real slip-up in providing fighter aircraft cover, with disastrous results.

Seletar had been heavily bombed, and this day was no exception. The whole area was in a mess, though by great efforts the drome was still serviceable, and aircraft could still land and take off. Evidently stores were also still available for servicing and repairs to aircraft.

One of the bombs left a crater (according to Bert) about 40 feet in diameter and 25 feet in depth. That would take a lot of filling, and he wondered whether they should put a bridge over it.

We slept at Seletar, and in this time there were four air alarms, mostly hit and run raids. Altogether, I was told, this made eight alarms for the day. Getting up in the morning, there was an alarm, but it was a reconnaissance plane which circled the island at a great height, going to and fro across the island, no doubt taking photos. The ack ack opened up, but the aircraft was travelling at such a great height and at a speed which made it almost impossible to shoot him down. Our Hurricanes did not take off, as they would not have been able to get anywhere near him. He left a vapour trail in the sky high above, otherwise he would not have been seen with the naked eye.

Palembang - Sumatra

P2 Aerodrome - 30th January, 1942 to 14th February, 1942.

Friday, 30th January, 1942.

We were awake early and airborne from Seletar Aerodrome at 6.55 a.m., bound for the secret drome at P.2. Fl/Lt Kentish was the pilot, I was the navigator, and Sgt. Swaffield the wireless air gunner. We were flying a Short Nosed Blenheim aircraft, Mk. 1., the number being L.8458.

We arrived at Palembang aerodrome at 8.30 a.m., and looked around for the railway line. I suggested to Fl/Lt. Kentish that we should take a westerly course and find the railway, which we should then follow. We found the pipe line, which we mistook for the railway line. We then retraced our course and started again — this time finding the railway line.

Fl/Lt. Kentish was not a bit impressed with me, insisting that we were lost. He was even less impressed when we came to a building just off the line, and I told him that this was P2. I was adamant that this was the place, and that we should land in the large empty field, and then taxi up to that building, which was the headquarters, cum duty pilot office, cum orderly room.

He cautiously started to circle the drome, when suddenly we saw an aircraft, well camouflaged, under the branches of trees. He was then convinced and so we landed, much to his indignation that this should be considered an aerodrome. We reported to the duty pilot, who instructed us to follow a small truck to a spot at the edge of the clearing where the aircraft would be stationed. We then boarded the truck, and were taken back to the orderly room.

Swaffield and I moped around the area for quite a while, and eventually we were taken out late afternoon to our dispersal camp at Gelumbang, a small settlement nearby. Here we were to live under canvas, and we did our best to get the tent organised. There were eight of us in one tent — Jock Kennedy, Staff Stafford, (both W/O.'s), Willy Willmott, Metty Metcalfe, Stan Dent, Iggy Donovan, Clicker Clarke and myself. Jock and I were from the original 27 Squadron, and the rest were from 62 Squadron at Alor Star.

The Squadron, although a combined 27/62 Squadron, was now known as 27 Squadron. It was good to see Iggy and Clicker again. Jock and Staff were very friendly; both were W/O.s, and I think they had been together previously in India or somewhere.

Sunday, 1st February, 1942.

Jock and Staff went down to a meeting with the C.O. during the morning, together with other pilots of the squadron, and they selected crews for flying duties. Jock Kennedy requested having two Australians flying with him, and so I was in his crew together with Clicker Clarke. Staff had his previous crew from 62 Squadron, namely Willy Wilmott and Chicko Hicks. Metty, Stan and Iggy were together, having been in the same crew in 62 at Alor Star.

We stood by for operations for the rest of the day. Nothing eventuated, so we had a quiet day under the main plane (the wing) of the aircraft. We stood by all night, and were relieved at 8 a.m. the following morning. We spent the rest of the day back at the dispersal camp, cleaning up and making ourselves more comfortable.

Tuesday, 3rd February, 1942.

I spent the day hovering around the machines, making myself generally useful — in particular digging slit trenches, just in case the Jap happened to find this drome. If he did, we could expect quite a lot of attention with bombing and strafing. I also assisted the ground staff in cutting down some branches to place over the planes to camouflage and blend in with the forest background.

All planes were placed in an area which had been cleared. The aircraft were then pushed back into this space, and a dense foliage of branches thrown over them. Consequently, from the air it was virtually impossible to notice any aircraft on the ground. The drome had a very large area, and from the control building to the extreme end would have been at least two miles, with a width of about half a mile. From this main strip (for want of a better term), there were three or four tongues of similar but smaller strips, and these were mainly used for the parking of aircraft.

Quite a number of Hurricanes had landed, which were then ferried up to Singapore to go immediately into operations. Evidently they were coming off an aircraft carrier located off the west coast of Sumatra in the Indian Ocean. Someone mentioned that there were fifty of them, but with the numbers of Japanese aircraft available, I feared we would need a lot more than fifty Hurricanes.

Wednesday, 4th February, 1942.

We were a little concerned this morning and in the early part of the afternoon over Staff. He left yesterday afternoon for an operational trip, landing at Singapore, and was then to take off at dawn for a bombing raid. Six Hudsons went first to do over the drome at Kluang, and then the Blenheims were to bomb the aircraft on the ground. Staff had the only Mk 1 Blenheim, and the others were Mk. 4 Blenheims. He returned late afternoon, and told us that he did not take off from Singapore for the raid, as his aircraft developed engine trouble.

I nearly went up to Singapore during the day to bring down another Blenheim from Sembawang. However, it was called off as they were able to get a crew left behind from our own squadron to bring it down to P2.

The news that night was not the best, as the troops had retreated back to the island of Singapore, and had blown up the causeway which connected Singapore to Johore. It now remained to be seen if they could stop the Jap from invading Singapore Island.

We were standing by during the night for operations, as it had been reported that a Jap convoy was sighted south of Singapore Island, and near Banka Island. It seemed as if they were heading towards Sumatra. This would be logical, as no doubt they would wish to put their naval ships in the area to stop any mass evacuation from Singapore, or to prevent reinforcements coming in to assist the beleaguered forces in Singapore. However, nothing more was heard, and we did not have to take off. It seemed, however, that we would shortly be thrown into the fray very heavily, to resist any landing of the Jap in Sumatra.

Eddie Edwards, a W.A.G. from 27 Squadron in the crew that brought the plane down yesterday, gave us some news about Singapore. About two nights ago, two hit and run Jap planes raided Katong, and dropped a bomb about three yards or so from the trench in the sergeants dispersal house grounds. It was a near shave, and the chaps in the trench were thoroughly shaken even though otherwise unhurt.

Thursday, 5th February, 1942.

We were again on standby, but nothing happened. A bit boring on standby — just hanging around and waiting.

Friday, 6th February, 1942.

We were prepared to go out on an operational flight during the day, but it fell through. The plan had been to take off some time during the day, and fly to Packenbaru in the northern part of Sumatra. There we were to refuel, and before daybreak, take off and bomb Kluang in Malaya at the break of dawn, coming back to Palembang. We were quite looking forward to some action, but it was called off for some reason. I did hear that the C.O., Squadron Leader Banks, felt that the distance of the operation would be really testing the endurance of the Mk. 1 Blenheim to its capacity. With the chances of getting back to Sumatra being too risky, it was suggested that the operation be called off.

Saturday, 7th February, 1942.

A programme was drafted out regarding duties. We were to have leave every fifth day, which meant that our crew were to have the next day off. Jock, Clicker and I had everything planned to go into Palembang, and have a good look round the area. I was given the job of assisting Fl/Lt. Kentish in sorting out various maps. We finished one large lot, but there were more to do.

Sunday, 8th February, 1942.

We had quite a good day visiting Palembang. We caught the ration truck and got into the town about 9.30 a.m. Before arriving at the town we had to stop; there was a raid in progress over P.1., with the usual Jap formation of twenty-seven bombers, escorted by Navy O's. We saw a few Hurricanes take off to intercept. It seemed that one of them was lost, as we saw it turn on its back and dive towards the ground. Later we heard that two Hurricanes had gone down, but there were no reports on whether they shot down any of the Jap planes.

We were learning fast, and particularly respected the capabilities of the Japanese fighter, the Navy O. Prior to the start of the war in northern Malaya, we had been told that the quality of their planes was very inferior to ours, even the Blenheims, and that the Japanese were poor pilots. We had a lot to learn.

The ferry took us over the Musi River and into Palembang. We had an interesting day, and called into the Grand Hotel Swartz for tiffin, where we had "Rifs Staefel" — or "Rice Table" in English. This was a delicious dish with rice as the staple food, and then several platters with about fifteen varieties of fish, pork and various vegetables to add to the rice. Then, of course, there were numerous chutneys and other condiments to give flavour to the dish.

We had talked previously about arming ourselves with a knife, a type of hunting knife, in case we were shot down and ran out of ammunition for our 38 revolvers. We had heard about the fate of many aircrew who had been shot down, and when captured had just been shot or bayoneted. We were determined that if this did happen, we would sell our lives dearly. We each bought a knife and holder which we thought would be handy in case of emergency, and which we would carry whenever we were out on operations in the future.

By 2 p.m., we had made our purchases, caught the ferry across the Musi River, and then travelled in the ration lorry back to camp.

Monday, 9th February, 1942.

I spent another day on the maps, this time on my own without any help from Fl/Lt. Kentish, who had taken sick and left for Batavia. It was a standby day, and the rest of the crew and others were in the standby hut, ready to get hold of me in case of emergency.

Tuesday, 10th February, 1942.
Another day was spent on the maps on my own, and they were not yet completely sorted out. I expected to finish them the next day. The news from Singapore was grim, with the Jap having forced a landing on Singapore Island, pushing our troops back. All sorts of rumours were flying round the camp, probably mostly groundless, but nevertheless they did affect morale.

Wednesday, 11th February, 1942.
I finished sorting out the maps today. There were heaps of maps brought in to the Station from various sources and dumped on the floor, with no indication of what they were. Some were army maps, others were used by the air force, and many others were suitable for use in various operations. It was impossible for Ops Room to make use of the maps in the state they were in. Fl/Lt. Kentish evidently was given the job, and brought me in to assist, but I was left on my own to complete the sorting out. It did give me something to do, as just sitting round and waiting for something to happen, particularly under these circumstances, was most frustrating.

We heard news that the Americans had carried out an air raid on Hainan Island, destroying several ships and numerous aircraft. Any news like that was good news, whether for propaganda purposes or not.

We saw quite a number of our planes taking off, Hudsons and Mk 4 Blenheims, carrying out raids on the Malayan mainland, and principally upon Kluang, where the Jap had large numbers of fighters and dive bombers. Kluang is about 60 miles north of Singapore, which placed it in easy range for the Jap fighters to operate over Singapore.

We received quite a number of alarms and witnessed some Japanese planes flying overhead. They knew that the R.A.F. was in hiding somewhere, but just could not locate the place. Palembang aerodrome had been bombed very heavily, almost beyond recognition, but their efforts had been fruitless, as no bombers were located there — only a few fighter aircraft.

Quite understandably, the oil tanks and pumping installations had not been touched, as no doubt the enemy wanted to be able to use these when they captured the place. And it seemed at that stage that it was only a matter of time before this happened.

In between our hiding place (P2) and Palembang (P1) were several areas like ours which were bare and uninhabited, but nevertheless could have been used as aircraft landing areas. To accommodate the Jap and his desire to bomb some place where there were aircraft, some enterprising residents of P2 went to one of these areas with timber, canvas, and other materials. They made up some silhouettes of aircraft, and other features to resemble an airfield. This became known to us as P3.

It was found very quickly, and the area received two visits from Jap bombers. The story when circulated to the camp gave everybody quite a lot of satisfaction, but also the realisation that things could happen very quickly if they stumbled on P2. It made us more alert.

The whole of the area had been placed under the leadership of Group Captain McCauley. He created an air of confidence right throughout the camp; everybody realised that we were up against it, but morale was very high. Everybody was determined to give his all and to show the enemy that he was not the superman he thought he was. How regrettable that the Group Captain was not our leader in Malaya.

To make sure that complete secrecy was observed, all receiving and transmitting from the planes and Operations Room was strictly forbidden, so that the enemy could not get a bearing on the drome. All radios in every aircraft were silenced so that this could be fully observed.

The conditions in the camp were pretty rough, and the meals not the best. Some of the men were grumbling — but on the whole it was being taken in good grace. All seemed to be very determined, however, to give of their best.

The lack of transport was very acute, and we had to walk to our destinations more frequently than not. From the camp, for instance, we walked to the main operations area, and if we were to go down to the aircraft, a distance of about two miles, then we also had to walk. This also applied to the ground staff and maintenance men on the aircraft, particularly if they required some parts for repairs. It was very awkward and inconvenient, but nevertheless so necessary under these trying circumstances.

It is interesting to record the Air Force strength at P2 at this stage (taking the information from the Official History of the R.A.A.F.):-

No.	1	Squadron	R.A.A.F.	16	Hudson 11
,,	8	,,	,,	6	Hudson 111
,,	34	,,	R.A.F.	6	Blenheim 1V
,,	62	,,	,,	10	Hudson & 5 Blenheim 1
,,	27	,,	,,	3	Blenheim 1
,,	84	,,	,,	10	Blenheim 1V
,,	211	,,	,,	4	Blenheim 1V

Our 27 Squadron took over the Mk 1 Blenheims from 62 Squadron, making our strength eight. Two of these aircraft were designated as fighters, two for some reason unknown flew out to Java, and we were left with four aircraft for bombing operations.

It was encouraging to see the two new squadrons with the Long Nosed Blenheims (Mk. 1V) arrive. I ran into one of the navigators from 211 Squadron, Sgt. Brian O'Brien, whilst I was doing the sorting of the maps. Brian was a trainee with me on 10 Course, hailing from Victoria. We had quite a talk, as can be imagined.

A very serious accident, or rather — series of accidents — happened on this night, the 11th February. A raid on Kluang drome in Malaya was planned with the aircraft to take off just after midnight, and after dropping their bombs returning to P2 shortly after daylight. Hudsons and Mk 4 Blenheims were to take part, with the Blenheims taking off first.

The flarepath was laid out and the first of the Blenheims took off. Due to the heavy weather and the wet ground over which they were taking off, and perhaps because of the length of the flarepath and the inexperience of the pilots (they were not long out of training school) three of the bombers crashed just after takeoff. Two crashed just as they cleared the runway, stalling with insufficient speed, and as they crashed, the bombs exploded and all were killed. The third plane crashed into one of the administration buildings, with the bombs exploding.

The whole camp was awakened by the explosion and the noise of the crashes, occurring one after another, and there was nothing that anyone could do to save the occupants of the planes — they were all killed instantly. The balance of the flight took off, and carried out their mission. It was rather a blow, and a gloom came over the whole camp for the following day.

Thursday, 12th February, 1942.

This was a quiet day, and I was able to have a good rest. Resting was most important, because we were sure that we would need all our energy in the very near future.

The main drome at Palembang was still being continuously bombed. We felt that the Japanese thought we were in the adjoining area, with planes well hidden amongst the rubber trees. They had been bombing this area very heavily the last few days, so perhaps the theory was right. However, much to our satisfaction, apart from knocking down and destroying a lot of rubber trees, they were not achieving very much.

A naval convoy had been sighted further up north, just out of range of the Short Nosed Blenheims, and seemed to be heading this way. However, with the filthy weather, our planes were finding it very difficult to locate the convoy or any other shipping, the visibility being down to practically zero.

There was a feeling in the squadron that the Japs had an aircraft carrier in the vicinity, from which they were sending off fighters to use over Palembang. There was another thought that the fighters were coming from Kuching, in Borneo, and using long range tanks. This was a new innovation used by the Japs; the fighters had extra tanks for fuel, which they could ditch and then continue on their ordinary tanks. It certainly gave them a very large range, and a big advantage.

All crews were on standby, waiting for the call to get into the scrap.

Friday, 13th February, 1942

We were up very early at 4.30a.m., and on call for immediate take-off, but nothing seemed to be in our range as yet. The Hudsons and Long Nosed Blenheims were going and coming with great regularity, but they did not seem to be striking anything or finding any targets. Still that would come.

Saturday, 14th February, 1942.

We took to the air with the object of searching for a naval convoy consisting of one cruiser, two destroyers, and nine motor vessel transports. We had four Short Nosed Blenheims, all that were left of our Squadron in P2. With the C.O. (S/Ldr. Banks) in the lead, we set off, getting into formation and carrying four 250 pound bombs. We were also told to bomb any single ship on sight, as it could be remnants of the convoy for which we were searching (presuming that the convoy may have been broken up by previous flights).

We were airborne at 10 a.m., and made for a landmark cape on the eastern coast of Sumatra, then setting course in a direction just south of east for approximately 120 miles. At this destination, we were to alter course south and then make our way back to the original landmark on the coast. Our crew was Jock Kennedy as pilot, myself as navigator, and Clicker Clarke as wireless air gunner. We had radio silence, so could not contact other planes or the base, or even the planes in our formation.

We flew to the extreme of our first leg, and as we turned on the southern leg, I noticed a ship on our beam approximately 5 miles away. I pointed it out to Jock, and he immediately moved forward in the formation, and drew the C.O's attention to it. The C.O. acknowledged the signal, and beckoned us to go down to the attack, with our kite leading and the other planes following. We dived down to the rear of the ship to carry out a mast head attack from the stern, at the same time expecting some anti aircraft defence to be thrown at us.

Jock made a masterly attack, getting down to almost sea level, and then rising to just clear the stern. Our bombs had nine second delay fuses, so that they would explode nine seconds after hitting some object, and our purpose was to drop the four bombs in one salvo.

Just as we were climbing to go over the stern, we saw the White Ensign. Jock had his thumb on the bomb plunger, and it was just as well he noticed the flag. We flew low over the ship, and they were very quick to send us the letter of the day. They were also very prompt in sending the letter of the day to the following three aircraft.

We pulled away from the ship, and reasoned that it was probably a ship carrying evacuees from Singapore. We started to climb, and in doing so lost sight of the other three planes, so were on our own.

In pulling away and gathering height, I mentioned to Jock that we were slightly off track from the original course. I showed him where I considered our position to be, approximately 20 miles south of where we should have been. Jock then told me to give him a course north, to this correct position, and from there we would make our own way back to the coastline of Sumatra.

We reached our northern position, then turned westward and almost immediately came across a convoy of fourteen ships. Our instructions on leaving P2 had been that we were not to bomb any convoy, as they could be ships leaving Singapore with evacuees. The convoy was a motley collection, and we suspected they were Japanese.

We gave them a wide berth, going round them and half way down the western side, when we saw a much larger convoy within five miles also to the westward. We went over to investigate, and in this lot counted twenty-four ships.

We could not see any flags, but decided to fly across the convoy and have a really good look. As we were passing over at an altitude of 5,000 feet, they suddenly threw up a decent barrage at us. We were very fortunate in escaping this, as it was heavy.

Jock broke away, and dropped height, gathering speed. In doing so, I looked out on the horizon and thought that I could see three ships, which very much resembled naval vessels. They would have to belong to the Japanese forces, we reasoned, as there were no naval ships of ours left in Singapore.

We decided to have a look, from a distance, but our pilot first wanted to gain height to be on the safe side. We could see the convoy of twenty-four ships in the distance towards the east, and we were heading towards the naval ships climbing towards 7,500 feet.

Suddenly we looked down, and directly underneath us were six Navy O's, flying approximately on our original course and also at our height of 5,000 feet. Jock threw the Blenheim on its side and dived down to sea level, but the six Jap fighters evidently had a mission and left us alone. It certainly gave us a hell of a fright. We discussed our position, and decided that we should immediately head back to P2, rather than investigate any further. We had radio silence, so could not transmit messages to base. Therefore it was imperative to report the position of the two convoys and also the existence of naval ships in the area.

Whilst on our way back, Jock asked me if I could fly a plane. When I said no, he told me that I had better learn. He placed me in the pilot's seat, and had me making mock landings on the clouds, pulling back the stick and laying off the throttles to simulate a landing.

He said that this was important as in an attack, the pilot could be injured and the navigator should be capable of flying the plane home. He also impressed on me not to attempt to make a wheels landing; make a belly landing, he said, the plane didn't matter but his life did. Thank goodness, this never came about.

When we were passing over the fighters, Jock put the plane into a dive, opening the throttles. The port motor gave a distinct cough and spluttered for quite a few seconds, which gave Jock quite a bit of concern. However we made our way back to base without further incident, keeping a little to the north of P1, and landed after being three hours and twenty minutes in the air.

As we were passing P1, there were quite a few fires round the place. There also seemed to be fires near the oil tanks. We could see a number of aircraft in the distance which appeared to be fighters round the drome. We gave them a wide berth, knowing that they could not be ours.

On getting back to P2, we were greatly concerned to see fires near the living quarters, and generally around the administration block. Our first thoughts were that the Jap had finally found our drome, and made an air attack upon it. As Jock remarked, "It looks as if the b. Japs have at last found P2 and bombed hell out of it".

Jock circled the drome three times at low level, with both Clicker and I keeping a good watch for anything untoward and suspicious. We must have spent ten minutes flying around before deciding that it was safe to come in and land. We made a good landing, and immediately taxied to the operations room so as not to waste time in making our report.

We were really grilled about our findings, and our report on the actual locations of the convoys and in particular the three war ships. Not having actually seen the warships but only their silhouettes, they could not determine the strength of the enemy attacking force.

We had a feeling that the Operations Room and the Intelligence were somewhat hesitant to accept that we, a crew from 27 Squadron, and R.A.F., should be the ones to have found these convoys and the covering naval ships, not having been originally assigned to search for the information. We had been sent out on a search and patrol for a particular assignment, and not for this. However, the information brought back by us could not be ignored.

It was not long before they had three Hudsons in the air to check on the warships. We heard later in the night after two of the three returned, that the naval strength was three cruisers and six destroyers and also an aircraft carrier. Whether correct or not, this was the information brought back to us by Jock Kennedy and Staff Stafford after they had been to briefing for the next day's operations.

It appeared that the Hudsons had run into a real hornet's nest, with fighters taking off from the aircraft carrier and meeting them before they reached the naval squadron. From all accounts, they were considered very fortunate to survive, and able to return to base with their information.

The fires that we saw at P1, and also the fighter activity, related to a major attack by the Japanese in the form of a drop by paratroops on the edge of P1. A regular battle was in place, and the fires were in the oil refinery and oil tanks. This was the beginning of a scorched earth policy carried out by the Dutch to deny oil to the Japanese. By next morning fires were really raging, and flames and smoke could be seen from a long distance away.

The fires at P2 were started by a small group who panicked when the report came through that paratroops had landed at P1. Private and secret documents and several buildings were set on fire, and also food rations and other necessary things that we would need for the following day were destroyed. Fortunately, common sense prevailed, and a gang of airmen extinguished some of the fires.

After our session with the intelligence officers, Jock started the engines of the Blenheim and taxied it to the parking bay, which was at least two miles from the operations room. Our two ground staff riggers, Horan and Burton, were patiently waiting for us, and Jock swung the plane round into position for its next flight, whenever that might be. I'm not sure how Horan and Burton got on for food, and where they slept for the night, but they were there early the next morning ready for our next take off.

Thanks to the cooks and kitchen staff who raced in and rescued the foodstuffs from the fire that had been started, we did have something to eat for dinner that night (not very much) and tea or coffee. Otherwise, we who were flying the following day would have been really hungry.

The two convoys were the main invasion fleet which had eluded all the other aircraft for so many days. It was unfortunate that it was not found sooner, as no doubt our air force could have taken great toll on its strength.

Our squadron was later disappointed and upset that due credit was not given to it for location of the Japanese invasion force. Upon reporting the facts to operations room, No. 1 Squadron, R.A.A.F., were immediately briefed to check on our discovery. They duly found the Japanese force as reported by us, and then were credited with the achievement.

Although 27 Squadron was R.A.F., nevertheless the crew of our plane had a R.A.F. pilot and two R.A.A.F members in the crew. I always thought it was sad that jealousy existed between the two.

Looking at my log book, our flight took off at 10.00 a.m., and we landed 3 hrs. 20 minutes later, so it would have been about 2 p.m.

before we were in operations room reporting our findings. The speed of the convoy would not have been any more than about eight to ten knots, and being in a position about 80 to 100 miles north of the mouth of the Musi River when sighted by us, the convoy would have been in position for invasion soon after midnight.

After parking the aircraft, we discussed why we were not attacked by the group of six Navy O's that we encountered on our patrol, and considered ourselves very lucky to have escaped. We could only advance three possible reasons — firstly, the aircraft may have been assigned to go to P1 to protect the paratroopers being landed at that time. Secondly, when we left the second convoy, we set a course in a south westerly direction. These aircraft had probably come off an aircraft carrier in the vicinity, and they may have been assigned to follow us at a distance and let us lead them back to the secret drome of P2. The fighters were on the identical course and height that we were on as we left the convoy. Thirdly, they did not see us — very unlikely, we were so close to them.

Whatever the case, we were indeed fortunate to have escaped. We would not have been any match for them if they had decided to attack us — even one aircraft would have been enough, but six — it made us shiver to think of it.

It was shortly after this that Staff and Jock were called away to the operations room and briefing for the following day. Our four remaining Blenheims of 27/62 Squadron were to take off just on daylight, on a raid on the enemy invasion forces.

They were briefed that barges of the expected invasion force would be progressing up the Musi River before first light, and that they would have ten miles to travel before reaching Palembang. The convoys were expected to be anchored between the mouth of the Musi River and Banka Island, and the actual composition of the vessels was not really known.

Our force of four planes would be led by the C.O. (S/Ldr. Banks), with the other pilots being Fl/Lt. Dunn and W/O.s Stafford and Kennedy. It was to be left to the discretion of the aircraft skippers to pick out targets themselves, as no doubt there would be many fighters supporting the invasion fleet.

And so arrived the day that has always stood out so much in my mind, and also, incidentally, the day that Singapore fell.

P2 Palembang

The Attack On The Invasion Force

Sunday, 15th February, 1942.

We were up very early, before 5 a.m., and had a scanty breakfast of dry biscuits and cheese, with tea or coffee. That was all that was available after the debacle of the previous day, when a large quantity of the stores including food and other essentials were set on fire, for fear they would fall into the hands of the Japs. Thank goodness our chaps from the mess rescued some of the provisions.

We were taken down to our aircraft, and made ready to take off on the first mission. The bombs were still on the aircraft from the previous day, though the fuses had been altered to instantaneous. It had rained very heavily through the night, and everything was really soaked. These wet conditions and the humidity caused no end of trouble to maintenance of the aircraft in this tropical area.

The starboard engine immediately started up, but trouble was experienced with the port motor. Eventually it started, but just spluttered and would not come up to the revs required. This was the engine that had given us anxiety the previous day. The motor would not pick up, and the other three aircraft were out on the strip waiting. Jock was not satisfied, maintaining that it was unsafe to fly, and so we had to abort the operation, leaving it to the other three. Naturally, we were disappointed — as we were looking forward to having a go at the Japanese Air Force, knowing that there was the element of surprise on our side.

Horan and Burton worked on the motor with Jock, and after about an hour during which time they dried out as best they could all the necessary components, they were reasonably satisfied that it would be right for the next operation.

The three planes reached their targets, bombing loaded barges in the Musi River and then coming down and strafing them. The C.O. saved his fire and decided to strafe the troop barges in the river itself, doing untold damage to them. He sank several barges, and the Japs who escaped his fire would have been thrown into the river.

The Musi River is very wide, and also very deep, and allows ocean liners and large tankers to navigate the forty odd miles from the mouth to Palembang. The chances of survival of those who were thrown into the river from the barges would have been very slim, with the bombs exploding and machine guns firing.

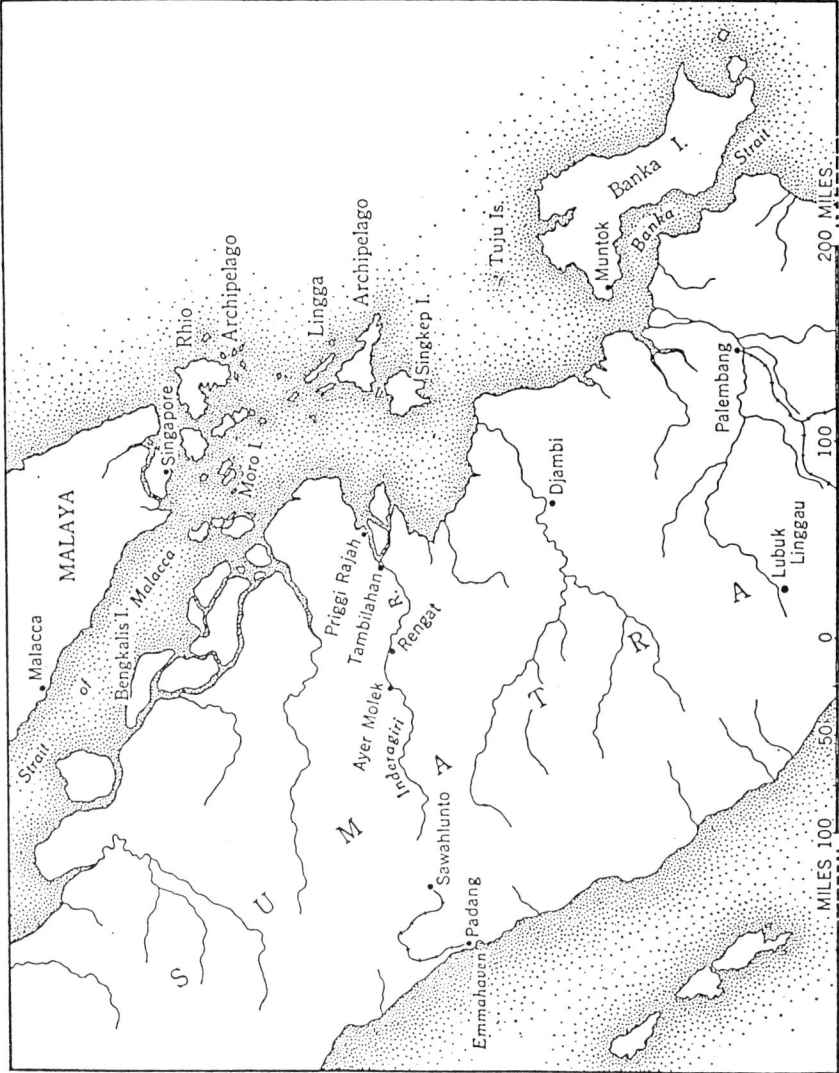

Part of Sumatra and its relative location to Singapore and Malaya.

Normally the current in the river flowed at about six knots, so that it was rather difficult to navigate up river. However, due to the heavy rains, the river was running in light flood conditions, making the task of anyone trying to swim extremely hazardous. In addition, we were told that the river was alive with crocodiles. The enemy casualties from this invasion had to be enormous, and history confirmed this.

The C.O. encountered very intense small arms fire, and his plane was hit in the port motor and through the hydraulic system. On his return to P2 he was not able to lower his undercarriage, and so had to make a belly landing on the drome. He and his navigator were unharmed, but his wireless air gunner, Sgt. Alan Oliver, was shot from underneath through his pelvis, the bullet penetrating up into his body, and he died a couple of hours later.

Our drome was very busy, with Hudsons and Long Nosed Blenheims taking off every half hour, sometimes with fighter protection. The Hurricane fighters carried out strafing on the barges in the river, and from all reports inflicted very heavy casualties. Enemy fighters were in the sky protecting their ships, trying to find the attacking planes, but they seemed to have their work cut out, and the damage inflicted by our aircraft was horrific. Reports came back from the pilots that the river was running red with blood.

It was a foregone conclusion that the Japs would take Palembang by sheer weight of numbers, with only a small band of defending Dutch troops. With at least two aircraft carriers, a vast number of troop ships, and paratroopers, the invasion force was very formidable. However, they struck a very determined defending force.

The Dutch the previous day and through the night had been carrying out a scorched earth policy, and the fires and smoke could be seen from our drome over forty miles away. All other installations of a military nature and useful to the enemy were destroyed, and from the large pall of smoke in the distance, a very fine job was being done. The enemy obviously would have liked to capture Palembang with oil installations intact, but this was mostly denied to them.

About 1 p.m. Jock was brought down to the plane by motor transport (a rare occurrence), and told us take-off would be at 1.30 p.m. At the same time, the majority of our ground staff were being evacuated south by train and road to Oosthaven in southern Sumatra.

There were only three aircraft left in 27 Squadron, and F/Lt. Dunn would be in the lead, W/O. Stafford flying No 2, and our kite in No. 3 position. Jock told us there were still two fighter Blenheims left (where they came from we did not know) which would escort our mission to bomb ships lying off the mouth of the Musi River. We did not see the Blenheim fighters at any stage of the operation — perhaps they got into a scrap, or were merely a mirage to help boost morale. We flew to the south of Palembang to the coast, and then north to the mouth of the Musi River. There we found eight ships, which looked

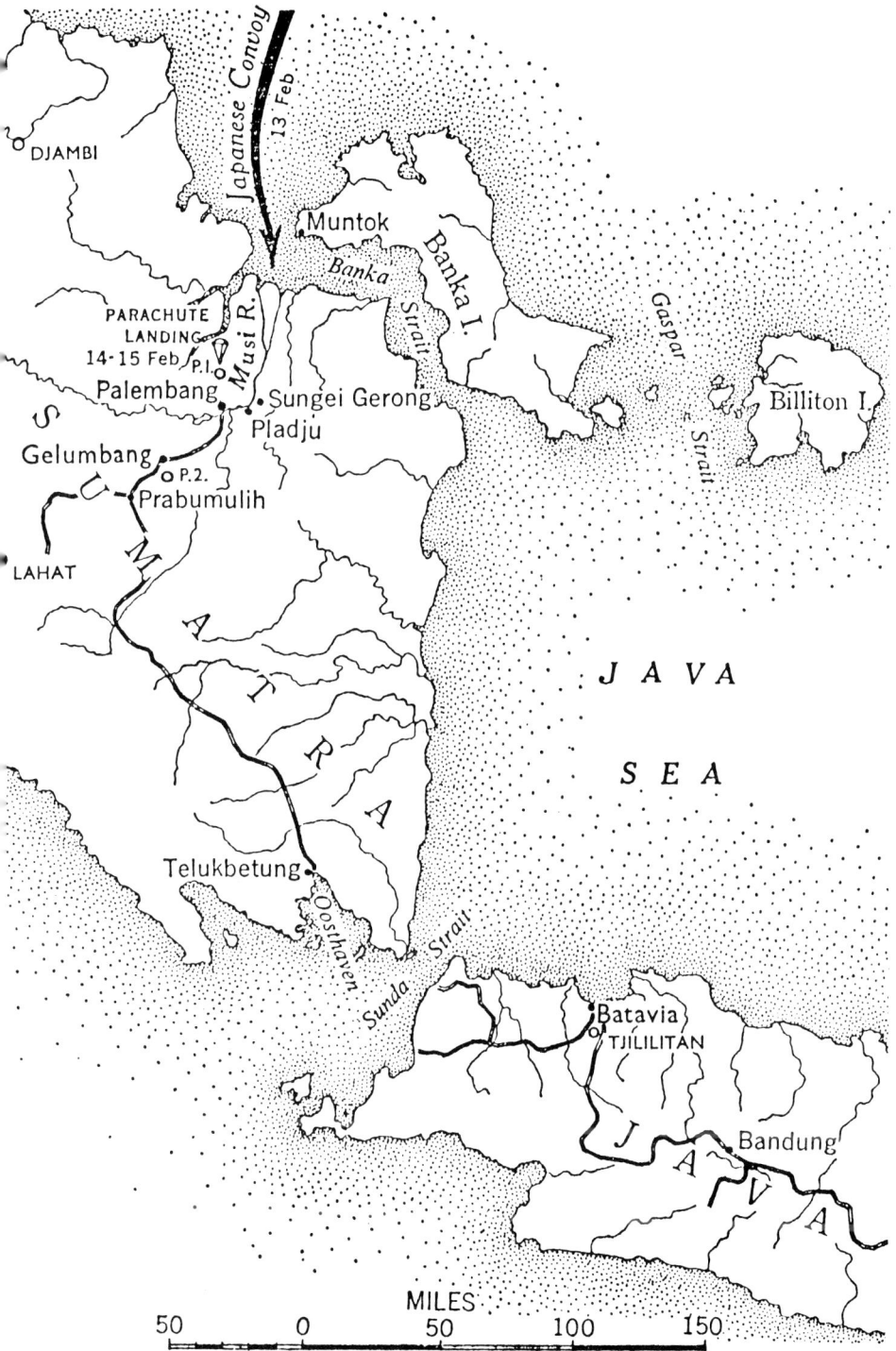

South Sumatra & West Java.

a good target. Flt/Lt. Dunn thought otherwise, evidently thinking that there were better elsewhere.

We went over them and through a heavy anti aircraft barrage, but the leader held his bombs. Off we went again, cruising around, and then made our way further away from the coast towards Banka Island, when we suddenly came across twelve ships, with three cruisers amongst them. In the centre was a very large ship with landing barges spread right round it, and the cruisers in close proximity. This was to be the target, and a worthwhile one at that.

We flew in towards them at between 3,500 and 4,000 feet, with our bombs spreading round the centre of the pack. I was having my attention varied from Clicker in the rear turret calling us to observe the results of his defence against the attacking fighters, and Jock calling on me to watch the result of the bomb drop. All three planes commenced dropping their bombs together, to get a heavy concentration of bombs on the target.

On looking down on the strike, I could count only nine bombs hitting the target, one dropping within a few feet of the stern of the cruiser, whilst the others fell around the large ship and in amongst the landing barges. When I told Jock that I counted nine bombs, he said I must have been mistaken, and we left it at that. One thing we were certain of was that a hell of a lot of damage had been inflicted on the enemy.

Needless to say, there was a very heavy barrage thrown at us, especially from the warships. Flashes could be seen coming from the ships, but we at least were not hit. The leader, Fl/Lt. Dunn, escaped unscathed, but much later we wondered whether Staff in the other aircraft had been hit. Probably the low height saved us, as no doubt they would have been expecting an attack from a much greater height, and their heavy guns were not so effective at our height of about 3,500 feet. Low level guns like Bofors would have been much more effective.

In the meantime Clicker was calling out that there were two fighters on our tail. Just as we dropped our bombs and left the target, going away as fast as we could and singly, one of the fighters, a Navy 95 float plane, made his attack on us. Clicker held his fire, and then let him have it. The fighter's nose suddenly went up and the plane went into an inverted spin towards the sea. He was still spinning at about 500 feet, when suddenly another fighter came in, firing his hardest. Clicker gave him a long burst, and he pulled away into a shallow dive, with smoke pouring out behind. We lost sight of him disappearing in the distance.

Fl/Lt. Dunn pulled away to the starboard, and made a large sweep southward, and eventually landed at base. By the time we returned to base, he had filled his tanks and was taking off to Batavia in Java.

We turned to port, and I gave Jock a course for base keeping away from Palembang and P1. We had been told to avoid P1 and the north of Palembang, as that area was lousy with Navy O Fighters. Suddenly we saw Staff to the north of us, heading towards P1 — the area we had been told to keep away from. The Navy O's were there all right, as we found out.

We edged over towards him, hoping to get his attention, so that he would join us to return to P2. However, he kept at a distance, without altering height or course, and we wondered what was happening. Suddenly Clicker announced that there was a Navy O fighter on our tail, but at a distance. Jock kept muttering and calling for Staff to come and join us, but, of course, there was no inter-plane communication.

Jock then called Clicker and asked him how much ammunition he had left, and received the reply that more than half had gone. We were then well ahead of Staff — he was continuing to just crawl along. Another fighter appeared on our beam, so I gave Jock a course heading for the mountains in the distance, not wanting to take them back to P2.

Suddenly Clicker called saying that there was another fighter on our tail, catching up on us. We had gained height, and were above Staff, and then Clicker called us again that the fighter was diving on Staff, and there were also four others as well. We quickly dived down to just above ground level. We could not help Staff, and made our way back to P2, landing at 3.25 p.m, having been airborne just under two hours.

We did not see Staff and his crew again, and no doubt he was shot down into the jungle of Sumatra. We were all upset, but there was just nothing that could be done to help. Clicker's twin Brownings in the turret had chewed up most of the ammunition against the other fighters beforehand, and the remaining ammunition would not have lasted long if we had been attacked.

We wondered whether Staff might have been wounded and whether his navigator, Willy Wilmott, had taken over the controls. From the way the plane was being handled, it did not seem that an experienced pilot was at the controls. It was just too even a flight, and when the fighters appeared, there was no effort to carry out any evasive action. It was most puzzling.

Arriving back at the Ops Room, we quickly reported our version of events. Clicker was most disgusted — he was only granted a probable and a possible for his two conquests. Because we did not see either of them actually hit the deck, they would not credit him with any definite kill.

Jock was told to leave as soon as possible for Batavia in Java, as it was feared that the Jap would overrun P2 during the night. We were also to take our two riggers, Horan and Burton, who had been patiently waiting for us, hoping that nothing had happened.

We raced away to get our kit bags, and returned to the kite to have it checked and re-fuelled. While doing this, we were absolutely stunned to find that we still had three bombs left in our bomb bay — only one had come off when we did the bombing. So my count of nine bombs was, unfortunately, correct. Nevertheless, the bombing was entirely successful, and the operation well worth while.

We were, however, very sad to lose Staff and his crew. They were all R.A.F. personnel, and I was getting to know Staff and Willy Willmott quite well in the week or so together, and it was rather a jolt to lose somebody from your own tent. They were all previous members of 62 Squadron, based at Alor Star.

We were told to expect a very heavy storm on the way, but we must head to Batavia and not come back to P2. And so we took off at 4. 45 p.m., with Horan and Burton huddled in the bomb bay, minus, of course the three bombs, which they took off and dumped somewhere on P2. It was a bit risky, as the bombs were fused to go off, and so had to be made safe before being taken away from the bomb bays. We had our kit bags also in the bomb bays, and Clicker was in the turret, just in case a fighter came along, though he hadn't added to his already depleted supply of ammunition.

Much later we found out that other crews had been told that if they had difficulty getting through to Batavia, they could return, as it was evident that the enemy would not be anywhere near P2 until at least later in the following day. No doubt this was because of the resistance the Japs encountered in their invasion attack, and the delay in capturing Palembang. With our radio silenced, we could not receive any of this advice on our way.

We had a map of the area, but were not absolutely sure of the location of the aerodrome at Batavia, or of the nature of the country between us and our destination. We headed south of Banka Island, and altered course for Java and on to Batavia. Suddenly we ran into the storm, a big wall of nimbus storm cloud, which built up from sea level to high in the sky. We tried to go underneath the bank of cloud at sea level, but the plane just bucked in the low cloud, jumping dangerously from 300 feet to sea level. Jock managed to turn it round, and ran out of the storm surge, and back into slightly calmer conditions.

During all this time, our port motor was dropping revs., and actually had been doing so from midway through our bombing flight. Jock then tried climbing, getting to 8,000 feet, but the clouds just towered above us. At one stage, we got too close to the edge of the storm, and it was most frightening when lightning raced in front of our eyes, going from one propeller to the other. All this time we were in fierce storm rain. With the faulty engine, Jock deemed it unsafe and unwise to attempt going through the storm, so got away from it as quickly as possible.

These storms, known to us as Sumatras, were recognised as being the fiercest in the world, with a very high ceiling up to 30,000 feet, and a base right down to sea level. Aircraft flying into them were buffeted most severely, and many lost and never heard of again. We had been advised to always avoid getting too close to these turbulent masses when flying in this area.

As time was getting on, we decided to retrace our steps back to the Sumatra coast, and follow it in a southerly direction; maybe there might be some place where we could land. Following the coastline south, there was nothing inviting, only many mangrove lined reaches. We then decided to cross the Sunda Straits to the coast of Java. There was very light rain at this stage, and a course east was set for a place called Serang, which was marked on the map and had a landing ground.

The night was quickly closing in, and by the time the aircraft was over Serang it was dark. Jock fired off a Verey pistol with a green cartridge, hoping that somebody on the ground would respond and turn on landing lights — that was, if they had any. Of course, they could take us for some Jap aircraft, inviting them to give a clue where to drop bombs. There was no response and all our hopes were dashed, and we were on our own subject to God's will from that point onwards.

Having no success we decided to make a course for Batavia, hoping that there would be only light showers over the land. However, this was too optimistic, and after only a few minutes we flew into very heavy and blinding rain. Jock decided to circle the area, hoping that the storm would pass away, and so flew blind in a circuitous path. After circling for quite a while, with conditions not improving, it was decided to force our way out to sea. Jock had checked our fuel position, and estimated that with luck there was a maximum of twenty minutes left, but probably only ten to be on the safe side.

Jock and I discussed the position of parachutes — there was one for each of the crew, but none for the passengers. I wondered whether two could come down on one parachute, but Jock ruled that out as being impossible. In leaving P2, we had not thought of the possibility of having to bale out, and then again extra parachutes probably would not have been available.

The plan decided upon was to fly north, and for me to estimate the time of crossing the coast. Three minutes after that we would descend, hopefully to sea level, and then make for the shore, trusting there would be enough fuel left to get reasonably close to and within sight of the shore. We hoped to be near enough to the shoreline to swim to the coast — rather a wild plan, but this appeared to be the only hope, and we had to take the chance. Our position was really desperate.

We called Clicker on the intercom informing him of our plans, and warning Horan and Burton of our intentions. Clicker had been listening to our talk over the intercom and appreciated the dilemma, leaving it to Jock and myself to decide. The only alternative left to us was to crash land somewhere — but where was our problem.

I pointed out to Jock on the map our estimated position, and set a course north, estimating the time of crossing the coastline. We were within two minutes of that time when suddenly, as if somebody up above had taken pity on us, a gap appeared in the clouds. Reflecting the light of the full moon shining above, a padi (rice) field appeared directly underneath.

Immediately Jock started into a tight turn so as not to lose sight of the clearing, and commenced losing height rapidly. He called Clicker in the rear gun turret to tell him what was happening, and to warn Horan and Burton to brace themselves for a belly landing. We made two quick circles dropping height rapidly from 4,000 feet and keeping within the clear patch. Just before landing I was to turn off the fuel taps, to minimise the danger of fuel escaping and catching fire.

With landing lights on he came in to land, and I turned off the fuel taps; I was not quick enough to get into my seat and belt myself in before he hit the wet ground of the padi field. How fortunate we were to have such a good pilot, and also that our guardian angels had offered a solution. We were most relieved and grateful — it certainly was a lucky escape.

Meeting the ground reasonably gently, we then hit an embankment formed for the purpose of ponding the water, and I was thrown forward on to the bomb sight, which tore the skin off my shins. Apart from that nobody was hurt, and the landing could be considered very good, and reasonably smooth under the circumstances. We all quickly got out of the plane, feeling very thankful to still be alive. Within seconds of landing, the clear patch in the clouds disappeared, and the rain just poured down in buckets.

Being unsure of where we were, we moved around along the embankments, keeping within shouting distance, hoping to find a path that would lead to some type of civilisation. This went on for about an hour when suddenly we saw a car travelling along a road about 400 yards from the plane. We had all been searching in the opposite direction, and were pleased to see it.

After making our way along one of the small built-up walls around the padi field, a pale light suddenly appeared in the distance. We made our way in this direction, and came across a native village. The residents were quite friendly, though very nervous, but could not understand what we were saying. They obviously did not know where we had come from, and whether we were friend or foe. They provided fresh water to drink, which was very welcome. We tried to wash some of the mud off, but soon gave that away, being so dirty from the muddy conditions of the padi field.

We were airborne from P2 at 1645 hours (4.45 p.m.), and were three hours and twenty minutes in the air, which meant that the crash landing occurred just after 8 p.m. We had not had anything to eat or drink since breakfast at 5 a.m., and were hungry and thirsty. We must have certainly looked a sight, five muddy and dirty men in some type of unrecognisable uniform; we could see the funny side of the situation. At least in spite of the state we were in, we felt they did not take us to be Japanese.

We had been over an hour trudging around the walls of the padi field, and then at least another hour in the native village. Suddenly one of the natives, who appeared to be the chieftain, beckoned Jock (whom he probably took to be the chief of our lot), and by signs indicated that he was wanted outside. Not knowing what to expect, Jock asked me to go out with him. The chief came with us, called out, and then disappeared from sight. This was rather bewildering to us, and Jock and I were rather perplexed.

Suddenly a very bright spot light came on from a motor bike. Two persons came running towards us, brandishing guns and covering both of us. Naturally we raised our hands above our heads. The two of them stopped and we were challenged; Jock replied in English that we were R.A.F., and had just crashed our plane nearby.

The leader was a Dutch lieutenant. Replying in English, he asked where we had come from and a few more questions, keeping his revolver on Jock the whole time. Being satisfied, he put his gun away and came forward with outstretched hand and shook hands with Jock.

In the meantime, I was being covered by the Javanese private with a tommy gun pointed directly at my stomach. I called out to the Dutch lieutenant to tell this buggar to take the gun away from my guts. He gave an order, and then both he and Jock burst out laughing. I was the only one who didn't think it was at all funny, as I was on the receiving end. I couldn't help telling them that the private was most reluctant to drop that tommy gun away from me.

We went inside and thanked the natives for looking after us, the lieutenant speaking on our behalf. There was a motor cycle with a side car outside. Leaving the private behind (there was just no room for more than six on the motor cycle and sidecar), with the lieutenant driving and the five of us somehow perched on the pillion seat, the side car and the petrol tank, we made our way about four or five miles to the town of Tjigidon. In any case, I wasn't keen on having that private near me again.

We were taken to the Court House, where a Eurasian man Mr Davies was in charge. Attached to the Court House was the jail, but there were no prisoners inside as all been released. We were given some coffee to drink, and also some Heineken beer, which was really good. We all had a most enjoyable bath, and Mr. Davies arranged for some of the natives to wash our clothes and supply sarongs in which to sleep.

He then organized a large bowl of curry and rice, which we thought was great. None of us had eaten all day, having only a cup of coffee and two biscuits for breakfast at 5 a.m., and not much more the previous night — we were ravenous. The curry and rice was really good, and with the Heineken beer laid on, compliments of the Court House, we had our fill and eventually turned in for the night on top of a blanket in the officers quarters.

Mr. Davies noticed my shins, which were still bleeding and quite dirty from the mud of the padi field. He helped me wash them, and then put some special ointment on them, which he said would keep out all infection, and also heal the wounds. He repeated this next morning, and supplied some extra dressing pads and bandages, and also the large jar of ointment. I was very grateful for his help, and also for giving me all those bandages, which I washed clean and kept using for some time in the future.

We were indeed fortunate to escape with nothing untoward happening to any of us in the crash. It certainly could have been a lot worse, and we couldn't help feeling that we were lucky to have such a good pilot. By this time it was just on midnight, and we were then told the bad news of the surrender of Singapore that morning. It was so hard to believe, as we all thought that some miracle would save the island.

As recorded in my diary — ''Wham, what a day!!! and ending with a crash landing in Java''.

Monday, 16th February, 1942.

We all slept in this morning after our big day yesterday, and we were given quite a good breakfast by our hosts. They certainly went out of their way to look after us, nothing seemed to be any bother to them. We thanked them most sincerely for their assistance.

We decided to go out to the plane and rescue any special items, including our kit bags. The clothes worn the previous day were returned to us, nicely washed and ironed. The police provided a vehicle and a driver, and so we had no difficulty in finding the plane. It was rather a sight to see and there were at least a hundred natives out in the padi field looking at the plane. There were also quite a number of children with them.

We removed the locks from the guns, and also all valuable items, and everything that could be of interest to the Japs when they eventually took this island. There was no difficulty in having these items delivered to the road; all the natives wanted to help carry things out to the police truck. We thanked them, and left them to keep watch over the plane.

They carried our kit bags out to the road, and even loaded all the gear on to the truck, and when we left to return to Tjigidon, they gave us a cheer. What for, we did not know, but they must have thought we were heroes.

We had a look at the track made by the aircraft when we crash landed in the padi field the previous night. It staggered us to find a steel tower beside the beginning of the track. Our starboard wing must have missed it by a very narrow margin. What purpose this tower served we didn't find out, but, had it been hit, we shuddered to think of the possible outcome.

I took the opportunity of taking some photos of the plane, and some of ourselves with a small folding Kodak camera. Much later I had the film developed, and the photographs turned out quite well.

Returning to the police station, we packed the parts from the aircraft into crates supplied from the station. Whilst doing this we were told that the aircraft was smoking, and so Burton and I were taken back out to the aircraft to see whether everything was in order.

Arriving at the site, we found about a hundred people crowded round the plane; the Javanese guard looking after the plane was busy with a dish throwing water over the area from where the smoke was coming. We told the crowd to move back, including the guard, and suddenly flames shot up from the plane. Burton maintained that the batteries had caused a short circuit which started the fire. But probably it was a good thing.

The guard was certainly a sight — with his very nice dark green uniform, and covered with mud just as we were the previous night. I'm afraid Burton and I found it very difficult to keep a serious face over his predicament.

By the time we arrived back at the Tjigidon Court House, Jock had returned from the main part of the town, where he had reported to the Local Resident regarding our aircraft. A message had been sent through to Air Headquarters in Batavia, and we were to catch the train leaving Tjigidon at 3. 30 that afternoon.

We were at the station with our goods when suddenly a van arrived and offered us a lift to Batavia. The driver informed us that this would be a lot faster than the train, which was very slow, pulling up at every station en route and spending long periods at each. He told us that very often the train would take up to eight hours to travel the hundred or so miles. We gratefully accepted the lift, and arrived at Batavia at 5 p.m, reporting to Air Headquarters.

Batavia was the capital of Java, and is now known as Djakarta.

IN RETROSPECT

The 15th February, 1942 will always stand out as indelibly imprinted on my memory.

In the morning our crew's participation in the successful mass bombing of the Japanese invasion fleet on the Musi River at Sumatra.

The evacuation of most of the ground staff of P2 by railway to Oosthaven on the south of Sumatra, and our two riggers patiently waiting for us to return from our bombing operation.

Later came the order for us to evacuate in our own aircraft to Java and our own miraculous survival on crash landing at night.

To cap it all — The fall of Singapore.

What a lucky experience'' — FIRST TIME LUCKY

INVASION OF JAVA MAP

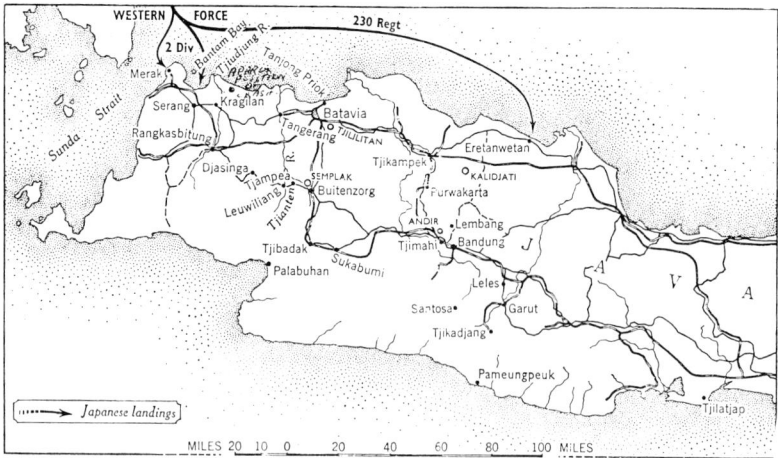

MY FIRST CRASH
*When the Japs invaded Palembang, Sumatra, after bombing them all day,
we finally had to evacuate, and so we took off late afternoon for Batavia.
Running into a heavy storm we forced landed at Tjigidon,
on western tip of Java.*

BRISTOL BLENHEIM MK I
SHORT NOSED BLENHEIM (L 8936)

*The Blenheim lying in the padi-field after crash landing
near Tjigidon. The natives were very curious, probably
the first time they had seen an aircraft, especially in
these circumstances.*

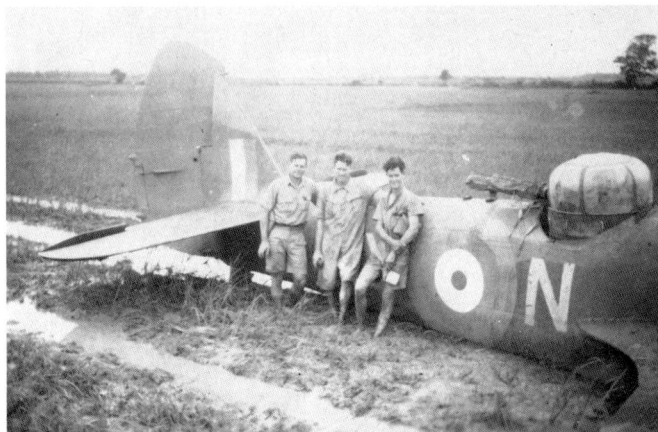

OUR CREW
*W/O John (Jock) Kennedy, (Pilot) Self (Observer) on left,
and Sgt. Gordon (Clicker) Clarke (W.A.G.) on right.*

*Front view of plane — In the background just above "X"
can be seen tower which we just missed coming in to land
(undercarriage up). Did not see it as it was night when we
landed. (Notice Armed Guard standing on the wing).*

"Clicker" Clarke sitting on his turret.
Notice twin Brownings.

Rescuing kit and parts from aircraft. Notice the bent
propellers.

Type of ground we landed in. Known as 'padi' or rice field.

Side view of aircraft.

The crowd of natives around the plane next morning.

Batavia

(now known as DJAKARTA)

Monday, 16th February, 1942.

It was late in the day when we reached Batavia (Djakarta). The van in which we had travelled from Tjigidon dropped us off at a large building that had apparently been taken over by the R.A.F. It was quite imposing, and the front portion resembled the foyer and lounge of a hotel, with the reception desk quite lengthy and wide.

Attending the counter and trying to attend the inquiries of the many new arrivals were young women doing their utmost to maintain some order, and offer help and advice. However, it could be seen that they were most frustrated by the attentions of so many of the men (in particular the commissioned officers) trying to arrange a date with them for the evening. It was, we felt, most disgusting and frustrating to these young ladies, who were doing their best to assist with information.

The core of men at the counter must have been at least six deep. It seemed impossible for the three of us to make our way to the counter; Jock decided that Clicker and I should remain behind the crowd, whilst he pushed his way in to find out the whereabouts of our own 27 Squadron.

It was some time before Jock returned. The information obtained was that the Squadron could be at Bandoeng, but this was not definite. However, he did find out that if we made our way to the Artillery Army Camp, there would be a bed to sleep in, and (most importantly) something to eat. We had no difficulty finding transport to this camp, as there were many different types of vehicles going to and fro at frequent intervals.

We had a sound sleep, awoke early and after quite a good breakfast and a cleanup, strolled around to see if there was anyone we knew. It was a great surprise to meet up with some of the chaps from 27 Squadron, and find that Ron Winzar was with them. It was not long before we found him. He wanted to hear about Palembang, and of course I was keen to hear of his escape from Singapore.

On Wednesday, 11th February, Ron had gone from the N.C.O.'s billets at Katong down to Kallang aerodrome. Finding that there were no duties for him for the day, he was returning to the quarters when a vehicle pulled up alongside him. In the vehicle was Pilot Officer Curtis, a navigator in the squadron, with several others; he asked Ron if he was keen to get out of Singapore. They were on their way down to the wharf area where they had acquired a boat, and this would take them off the island. Ron jumped at the idea, as he was not at all keen to be taken by the Jap — goodness knows what would have been his fate.

Ron asked them to drive back to his quarters at Katong, to get his gear, but they told him that there was no time for that. He could jump immediately into the truck and go with them to the wharf, or else forget about it. Hurry up, they told him, or you will be left behind. With that bidding, and without any more persuasion, Ron hopped up into the truck and off they all went.

They had by some means or other got hold of a type of sampan. Whether they had bought it, commandeered it, or just otherwise acquired it Ron did not know — all they cared about was they had some means of escaping from Singapore. Between them they had collected provisions for about four or five days, and filled kerosene tins with fresh water. The plan was to make their way to the coast of Sumatra, and then follow the east coast down to the Musi River, up to Palembang, and then join the Squadron. However, something went wrong. Perhaps the sampan skipper may have thought better of it, and got cold feet; he told them he would not go, as he did not want to run into Japanese ships along the Sumatra coast.

They all looked around in desperation, and suddenly found a ship, the "Kantor", of about 900 tons. The skipper wanted to take it to Batavia, and needed a crew. The ship had only two on board, the skipper and the engineer, and so the passengers on the ship had to do the stoking and all other tasks. Pilot Officer Curtis was appointed navigator. They had no navigation instruments or charts, but P/O. Curtis had thought of this, and had a chart of the area which he was able to use for the journey.

Curtis suggested to the captain that they should travel at night, and anchor during the day as close as possible to the mangroves on the islands. The ship was a small steamer, but there was no coal on board. They had to rely on wood fuel gathered during the daytime when anchored close to the coast or an island. Fortunately there were several axes on board, which were put into use. Trees were cut down and manhandled to the ship to use in the furnace.

There were many scares from planes flying overhead, but they were never sighted or attacked. They made Batavia on Sunday, 15th February, the day that Singapore fell. On one occasion when they were anchored just off an island — they couldn't get any closer — they saw a formation of twenty-seven planes flying overhead, and breathed a sigh of relief when it passed on. I questioned Ron about the route taken, but in typical fashion he told me that he hadn't a clue; they had made it, and that was the main thing.

Since arriving in Batavia, Ron had been busy visiting equipment stores and getting together some kit. He had, he said, been rather successful, although quite a lot of it was Dutch equipment with a style somewhat different to the R.A.F. Nevertheless, he was quite pleased with the outcome, and also with escaping from Singapore.

About a week after this, Ron left Batavia on board the Orient liner, "Orcades". As I found out later, it was bound for Colombo in Ceylon, now known as Sri Lanka, and then back to Australia.

Shortly after reaching Batavia, our two riggers Horan and Burton separated, and joined other ground staff men from the R.A.F. stationed at a campsite in the area. We did not see them again, and I do not know their fate.

Whilst at the camp, we met up with quite a number of chaps from 27 Squadron, and in particular some who had been on ships that were either bombed or torpedoed. This happened to many of the ships attempting to escape from Singapore. Their stories were rather grim and dramatic, as some of the survivors had been eighteen hours in the water after their ship had been bombed. They considered themselves very fortunate to have survived, been rescued and escorted to Java.

I had a quiet day at the camp, and later in the day decided to go to a picture theatre. By coincidence, I met up with Ron Winzar again. He was with a chap called Steve Day who was working in Batavia as an employee of Burns Philp, and who hailed from Townsville. We had tiffin and a few drinks, and it was quite refreshing to have that time together, and talk of peace time days.

Wednesday, 18th February, 1942.

I saw Jock during breakfast, and decided that with Clicker we should go into the town area again and try to find out some news of the whereabouts of the squadron. The R.A.F. Office did not have any information to give even a clue, so we felt that the best thing to do was to go and look for the squadron ourselves.

We thought that the first place to try would be Bandoeng, and so obtained a rail pass and set off at 2 p.m. This was a really scenic trip, and going up the mountains we were struck by the beauty of the views of the valleys from the train. Altogether we probably climbed over 2,000 feet, and whether we found the squadron or not, just getting on this train and witnessing the scenery of the mountains and the terraced padi fields below was magnificent and gave a respite from what we had been through.

It was dark when we reached Bandoeng, and it was a surprise to find so many air force personnel from the United States of America. Looking for accommodation, we had no difficulty; we were taken out to the Military Academy, where we were made welcome in the N.C.O.'s section. Some of the sergeants invited us to join them for the evening, visiting night clubs and dance cabarets. It was quite a pleasant evening, and so different to what we had experienced at Batavia.

Bandoeng was a really beautiful place, at an altitude of about 2,400 feet above sea level, and with a bountiful rainfall. No doubt it would be a lovely place to live in peace time.

Thursday, 19th February, 1942.

We spent the day at the Academy (what we termed in the R.A.A.F. an air force station). It had an American major as commanding officer. Everything was done on a most lavish scale, almost extravagantly, and it gave us an insight into the U.S. way of fighting a war. They had beautiful limousines, all very new.

The R.A.F. officers attached to them were also afforded some of the benefits and luxuries of the American way of life in this war area. It made us quite envious to think of the way we had to rough it from the outbreak of hostilities, and then see how our Allies fared.

We were told that U.S. personnel were granted a field allowance of four guilders a day to supplement their meals, but we could not find any fault with the meals at the Academy. As a consequence, most of the U.S. troops had all their meals in Bandoeng, whilst R.A.F. personnel ate at the Academy. We wondered what would have been their reaction to the food we were given at P2. However, if they had to put up with a starvation diet for a few days, they would have become like us — eating when we could, how we could, and what we could.

During the day, we found out that the remnants of the squadron were at Kalijati aerodrome, located between Batavia and Bandoeng, and so we obtained rail warrants to our new destination. The U.S. officer in charge of transport insisted also that we should have first class rail passes — the first time this had happened to us. The policy of the R.A.F. was that only officers travelled first class, and that all other ranks travelled second class. We were so wrapped in Bandoeng that we decided to leave our journey until the morrow, and have another look at the city, and in particular the night life.

Our ideas were spoilt, however, by a large air raid on Bandoeng aerodrome by the Japs. This coincided with the return from a raid on some distant target by Flying Fortresses, and the Japanese fighters took a toll on these bombers as they returned. We did not hear how many were lost, but some definitely were shot down. The Dutch had a fighter squadron to protect the drome, but although we did see several dog fights in the distance, and some planes shot down, we were not able to find out full details. We wondered at the time where the Japanese were coming from, especially as they had so many fighters in support.

It was quite confusing, and created great consternation amongst the U.S. personnel, to such an extent that all had their leave cancelled for the night. This also was extended to the R.A.F. in the camp. However, much to the disgust of the R.A.F., the leave of the U.S. troops was reinstated just after dusk, but this was not passed on to the R.A.F.

Java

Kalijati - 20th February, 1942 to 26th February, 1942

Friday, 20th February, 1942.

We left Bandoeng early in the morning and travelled to a railway station near Kalijati aerodrome, having changed trains once en route. Kalijati is located on the northern side of the island, about 150 miles (approx 250 kms) from Batavia. There is a mountain chain running through the centre of the island, with a coastal plain on the north and south coast. Kalijati is about fifty miles inland.

On arrival, we rang the station for a transport, and one arrived soon after to take us to the drome. It was about a twenty mile journey. On the way out — about 1 p.m.— we were given a grand reception, as an air raid was in progress, with a mixed bag of sixteen fighters and dive bombers. Fortunately, being at a respectable distance, there was no danger to us. It appeared that the Japs could do whatever they wished, having air superiority, or practically air monopoly, just as they had in Malaya.

Arriving at the drome, the damage turned out to be slight, with only a few fires from drums of oil that had been hit. In fact, there was really nothing of any great value to be seen at the drome, and no planes in sight. Kalijati was a flying training school for the Dutch, and not a major air base.

Kalijati was being used by the R.A.F. to fly whatever sorties could be mustered with the small number of planes left, comprising the few Blenheims remaining from Squadrons 27, 84 and 211. All Short Nosed (Mk. 1) Blenheims whether fighter or bomber were assigned to 27 Squadron, with no more than four planes altogether, and all in poor condition.

About 5. 30 p.m., after the effects of the raid had died down, we were transported to Soebang, about five miles distant, and billeted in a large residence on an estate owned by the Anglo Dutch Co. This was evidently a substantial company with interests in growing rice, rubber, and other industries. The residence was under the charge of a Mr. Fletcher, but we did not meet up with him; he was absent somewhere in Java acting with a defence force. Thinking about it later, I often wondered whether or not the house may have been the club house for the golf course — it was big enough for that purpose.

A lady by the name of Mrs. Armit, a South Australian, was in charge of the house. There was quite a crowd of us, perhaps thirty or more. She was a very capable person, assisting with information and seeing that we were fed properly. She had quite a number of servants to do the necessary work, and the house was always spotless.

Adjoining the house was a nine hole golf course, and it really set off the whole area. It was, I believe, also the property of the Anglo Dutch Company, and no doubt would have been used extensively by the staff of the company.

We met up with the balance of the 27 Squadron personnel, Fl/Lt. Dunn, Fl/Lt. Kentish and many of the other chaps. There were also some members of 211 Squadron with us — they had flown Mk 4 Long Nosed Blenheims out from Egypt to Palembang via India. It was a case of a little arriving too late.

Saturday, 21st February, 1942.

We went out to the drome and unpacked the box of flying kit salvaged from our crashed Blenheim the previous week. We enquired from the members of 27 Squadron whether any word had been received of Staff and his crew. Nothing had been heard, and it was presumed they had been shot down and lost. It should be remembered that 27 Squadron also included the previous members of 62 Squadron.

Before our arrival at the drome about mid-day, another raid had taken place with quite a lot of damage. Four vehicles and a bowser were destroyed, a hangar hit, and a Hurricane fighter in the hangar partly damaged by fire. We saw the Hurricane, and felt it was a write-off. One of the Blenheims was damaged by gun fire from strafing.

During the night, several Bofors guns had been brought on to the station. They made quite an impression, being credited with shooting down three planes (which were found) and probably a fourth, which disappeared in the mountains close by. Two of the gunners were killed by splinters from the bombs. There were about eight Hurricanes dispersed around the drome under trees, probably being held for some future occasion.

The Dutch troops were rather raw, and would have to mend their ways very quickly to become an efficient fighting force. As soon as a raid was sounded, they all got into vehicles and made their way post haste away from the drome. When the all clear was sounded, they made their way back — that is, if they heard it — and then commenced work again. So much time was lost from the time they left until their return. It was most important for personnel to be present as soon as possible when a raid was over, to clear away any damage or fight fires.

We noticed that there was an absence of slit trenches. This was most unfortunate, as trenches were not only a safety factor from bomb blast and strafing by fighters, but saved a lot of valuable time for workmen. The trenches made it possible to take cover at the last minute, and return to work immediately a raid was over.

Back at the billet I met Brian O'Brien, who was on 10 course with me as a navigator. Brian was posted from Somers (Victoria) Embarkation Depot to the Middle East, and had crewed one of the Mk 4 Long Nosed Blenheims of 211 Squadron to Palembang and then on to Java. Needless to say we had a good talk.

The following day, Monday the 23rd, was a very quiet day, with no raids. As there was no occasion for me to go down to the drome I took the opportunity of walking round the town, having a good look at the golf links, and taking a few photos.

Tuesday, 26th February, 1942.

During the evening, I was informed by Fl/Lt. Kentish that I would be required for flying duties the following day. There were two Mk 1 Blenheims on the drome that were serviceable, and some others that needed parts to bring them into service. Word had come through (whether correct or not, they were not sure) that there were Blenheim spares in Jogjakarta, a town in the southern part of Java and about 200 miles distant from Kalijati.

Fl/Lt. Kentish was to pilot one plane with me as the navigator, and Fl/Lt. Horriban (the officer in charge of maintenance for the Squadron) would act as air gunner in case we ran into trouble. The other Blenheim would be flown by a sergeant pilot with an air gunner, and they would not have a navigator as they would be following us.

I felt quite honoured at being chosen for such an important job, particularly as I had acted as navigator when Fl/Lt. Kentish ferried the plane from Singapore to Palembang (P2) on the 30th January. There had been the confrontation when I assured him that we were at P2, and he insisted I was lost. Perhaps he had second thoughts regarding my ability as a navigator, when he found I was correct.

I studied the map in detail, and called on Jock Kennedy for his thoughts on the route to be taken. It was not easy, as in a direct line there was the mountain chain to be considered, with peaks rising to 10,000 feet or so. We decided on the best route, with alternative ones in the event of bad weather. Everything was all ready for the journey when we left for the drome at 7 a.m. for an early take off, to be clear before a possible raid.

We were picked up in a small bus (about a ten seater) driven by a Javanese private and reported to flying control, expecting to see the two Blenheims close handy. Flying Control did not know where the two planes were, but suggested they could be the two to be seen on the far side at the southern end of the strip. We picked up several ground staff to assist us with the starting of the planes, as well as a Dutch officer, and drove over.

That was the commencement of our troubles. Neither plane could be started; they both had flat batteries, and one plane also had a flat tyre on its tail wheel. It was then decided that only one plane would go to Jogjakarta.

Fl/Lt. Kentish drove back to the hangars to search for another battery, taking with him the other crew, the Dutch officer and driver, and Fl/Lt. Horriban. I was left with three of the ground staff beside the plane we had decided to use. By this time it was just after 9 a.m., the usual time for Japanese aircraft attack.

We were packing our parachutes and my navigation gear into the aircraft, and I noticed the garry returning. All of a sudden there was the noise of aircraft, and, looking towards the north, there were at least a dozen aircraft on their way in to attack. The four of us next to the aircraft decided to make a hurried exit.

The two planes were alongside one another on the edge of the strip, and directly behind them was a type of blady grass about three feet high. About thirty yards away was heavy barb wire fencing for security purposes, so we could not travel far. There were no slit trenches of any kind. Our only course was to hide in the long grass, and pull the grass over ourselves so as not to be a conspicuous target.

All the attacking planes seemed to be carrying bombs. One landed only ten yards in front of our plane, tearing a big hole in the port wing, and also through the fuselage. We could not count the exact number of attackers, as we were frozen in hiding in the long grass; any movement might have been seen by one of the aircraft. All this time the Bofors were belting out a heavy fusillade of fire at them — with what results we had no clue.

Then the strafing started. Our two Blenheims were singled out for special attention, and strafed from the side and then most critically for us from the front. They had to know we were close handy in hiding, because of the gear left in front of the plane. It was nerve racking to hear the bullets tearing through the blady grass around us. The whole show was over in about thirty minutes, when we felt it was safe enough to crawl out of the grass.

Both planes were absolutely riddled with bullet holes, and also damaged by the bomb that exploded directly in front of the aircraft we were to have flown. Petrol was pouring on to the ground from both aircraft, and evidently the attacking planes did not have any incendiary bullets, as otherwise both would have caught fire.

The raid was most successful as far as the Jap was concerned. A Glen Martin and a Blenheim were set on fire, a Hudson received a direct hit and was deemed a writeoff, and our two planes suffered the same fate. We did not hear if the Jap had any casualties from the

Bofors, and did not wait to find out, considering ourselves very fortunate to escape with just a hell of a decent shaking.

Fl/Lt. Kentish came down to the planes in the minibus with the Javanese driver and the Dutch Lieutenant. He decided that we should return to our billets, leaving the ground staff at the drome to help with any rescue work. And so we settled in the bus to return.

During our time in Java, we had heard scathing reports on the conduct of the Dutch residents towards the native population, and in particular troops seconded to the army. We were then to witness a very ugly incident which offended Fl/Lt. Kentish and myself immensely. The Dutch officer gave instructions to the driver to drive to a certain place, which he did, and was told to wait whilst he called on whoever was living there.

Returning to the vehicle, the driver took off, evidently to take us to our billets in Soebang. After about a half mile, the Dutch officer called on the driver to stop, and told us that we could leave the vehicle as we were at our destination. We climbed out querying him; immediately he caught hold of the driver, pulled him out of his seat and pushed him out of the bus with his foot. He then slammed the door, and drove off at a fast pace.

We were absolutely stunned by the act, but picked up the driver who had fallen rather heavily. We spoke to him, but he could not understand us, nor could we understand him. However, he knew we had to go to Soebang, and the three of us walked to our destination, a distance of about three miles.

Fl/Lt. Kentish reported the incident, but there was little the authorities could do about it, other than noting it and hoping that the Dutch officer would turn up somewhere. They suspected that the officer was trying to get his family to Batavia to get them out of the country before the Japanese invasion, and stole the vehicle to accomplish this.

The reports heard by us concerned resident Dutch of Java, and did not apply to the regular fighting personnel. In particular, men of the Dutch air force had come out from England especially to help in this region. They had shown their ability to fly and were particularly keen combatants against greater odds on many occasions. They had flown at Singapore, and were recalled to Java to prepare for its defence when it became evident that Singapore would eventually fall.

I had lunch and was very pleased when Brian O'Brien called on me shortly after, suggesting a walk and swim at the local baths. We had a good talk, and I told him all that had occurred during the morning, and felt much better after getting all those unpleasant happenings off my chest.

During our walk, we came across quite a large pack of monkeys congregated across the road. There would have been at least fifty of them, curiously watching our approach. As we got closer, one of the larger ones in the group, probably the leader, suddenly chased the family away from the road towards the bamboo undergrowth, and then stood his ground and hissed at us. We stopped and glared at him for a minute or so, and he then made off, making sure that his family was away from any harm. It was quite an interesting interlude — the first time we had seen monkeys in Java.

Brian was billeted at a place not too far distant from our quarters, and obtained permission for me to keep him company for dinner. They really put on an excellent meal. I stayed with Brian and met some of the other chaps, and later in the evening obtained a lift back to my quarters.

Wednesday, 25th February, 1942

As there was no occasion for me to go down to the drome, I decided to take it easy and remain at the quarters. There were two raids on Kalijati, one at 9 a.m. and the other at midday. Iggy Donovan, Stan Dent (a New Zealand pilot), and Metty Metcalfe (an R.A.F. navigator), were on duty crew (goodness knows what for, as there were no planes serviceable). They were able to give details of the two raids.

The first was by fighters and some dive bombers, bombing and strafing objects on the ground and also picking on any aircraft that happened to be in the air. On the drome were some Hurricanes manned by the Dutch Air Force, and on this occasion one of these Hurricanes was either returning from a raid or doing some practice landings when the Navy Os came in.

One of the enemy fighters got on the tail of the Hurricane, and followed him in. The Dutch pilot, realising that he had no chance, came in and crash landed his Hurricane. Clambering out of the plane, he ran for his life across the drome for cover. The Navy O pilot quickly turned and could have strafed him but instead flew over and virtually gave him a wave. The planes then continued their strafing of the drome.

At midday, sixteen heavy bombers in three flights of six, five and five came across the drome and carried out a formation bombing attack. It was quite unusual to see such a formation, as previously the Japanese were always so meticulous in having flights of twenty-seven or groups of nine. Whether they were experiencing losses and having difficulty in keeping up the normal strength was hard to say, but we hoped that was the reason.

Thursday, 26th February, 1942.

We were informed that we would be leaving on the first stage of our evacuation of Java. We were supposed to depart by motor transport at midday, but it was 3 p.m. when the trucks arrived. We called in at Kalijati and gathered some flying gear, which confused us. We had a final glimpse of the drome, and really apart from some burnt out aircraft and destruction of the hangars, the damage was more or less superficial. It appeared the Japs wished to have it left that way, as they would want to use the facilities as soon as possible after taking over, which no doubt was going to be within a very short space of time.

Leaving Kalijati, we were taken by truck to a railway siding nearby, to await the arrival of a train. The crowd kept increasing as further trucks arrived with air force personnel. To while away the time, some of the members commenced a concert, which was most enjoyable and helped bolster morale.

It was 8 p.m. when the train arrived, and the carriages were quickly filled by personnel from the station. Altogether there would have been more than three hundred, all air force. The train was blacked out, no doubt for security reasons, and being night time, we did not know just where it was heading.

We finally arrived at our destination at 4. 30 a.m., a place called Tjilijap, which turned out to be a port about midway on the south coast of Java. There was a walk of one and a half miles from the railway siding to the docks. We wondered what type of ship would be there to evacuate us from Java. My gear was a bit awkward to carry, and when a native boy kept pestering to carry some of it, I gave him a parcel. It cost forty cents but it was well worth it.

House in Soebang, Java where we were billeted.

Group outside our house. From left: Fl/Lt. Kentish, self, — , Tom Williams, Fl/Lt. Dunn, Stan Dent, Charlie Cam, — , 'Metty' Metcalfe.

SOEBANG — JAVA

Golf course

Golf Club House

**STREET SCENES
IN SOEBANG**

Evacuation from Java

S. S. "Kota Gede"

Friday, 27th February, 1942.

After being on the train all night and reaching our destination Tjilijap at about 4.30 a.m., we half marched and strolled with our kits and other luggage to the wharf area. Our ship, the "Kota Gede", was tied up at the wharf; it was a cargo vessel of about 4,500 tons, with two holds, fore and aft, separated by the bridge, and no sleeping accommodation for passengers like ourselves. We did not know where we were going and when, but would find out in time.

Breakfast was tea with army biscuits (and were they tough!). This was to be our main diet for the next ten days. I suppose we were most fortunate to have even that luxury — it could have been worse, but how much worse we could not visualise. At that time we did not foresee the fates of those who became prisoners of war for four years.

We boarded the vessel at about 8 a.m., and made ourselves as comfortable as possible on the deck around the rear hold. As the day wore on, more personnel arrived. Instructions were to go down into the hold and place our luggage there, selecting a bedding spot for the journey. We took our gear down, but it was frightfully hot. We made our way back to the top deck again, leaving the kits behind in the hold.

Tied up alongside was a large United States ship named the "Abbekirk". Occasionally troops crossed our ship to board the American vessel — some Australian but mostly Americans. The "Abbekirk" was a large cargo vessel, in the vicinity of 15,000 to 18,000 tons.

She appeared to be well armed with several heavy guns and quite a number of machine guns on her decks. No doubt there would have been many more machine guns hidden from view and ready to be used. The ship could probably have been classed as an armed merchantman.

The "Kota Gede" was Dutch and had a four inch gun mounted on the rear deck, and a Lewis machine gun on either side of the bridge. With that armament we did not feel very secure from enemy attack, whether from the air or from a surface naval vessel or, worse still, a submarine. We certainly would have been an easy mark, and could only trust that the good Lord would be on our side.

Jock, Clicker and I were together, and determined that we would stay that way, and not be parted in the event of anything happening. By about 2 p.m. the ship was very crowded — almost chock a block — yet still more men were coming aboard. It was quite evident that the ship would be very much overcrowded and congested, and that it would be a most uncomfortable journey.

We watched those coming aboard, partly from curiosity and also wondering if we would see anybody we knew. Towards late afternoon we spotted Iggy Donovan, Stan Dent and Metty Metcalfe. We called out and suggested they come and join us, which they did, and this was to be our group, six in all, for the journey.

Iggy, Stan and Metty were all members of 62 Squadron from Alor Star, and had come over to 27 Squadron when the two squadrons were amalgamated at P2 because of the shortage of planes. The previous day at Soebang, the three had been allotted duties on the Kalijati drome. Returning to their billet late afternoon, everybody had vanished. On further inquiries, they were told that the others had left by train for Tjilijap. They quickly decided not to miss out on this opportunity of evacuation from Java.

By some means or other they acquired a vehicle, and driving through the night arrived in Tjilijap not long before the "Kota Gede" pulled out from the wharf. It was rather a tortuous journey, as they had to find fuel and also make sure not to take the wrong road. As it turned out, they could have joined us at the railway station where we spent five hours. However, communications were not the best at the time; in fact they were virtually non-existent.

Soon after this, about 2.30 in the afternoon, there was a real fright when a Jap reconnaissance plane flew directly over the ship at a height of about 5,000 feet. It just had to see all the ships in the harbour and the activity, and there was no ack ack defence at Tjilijap to send the plane on its way. Fortunately for all on board, it was a reconnaissance kite and not armed, though the information it would take back to base could mean trouble the next day.

The "Abbekirk" alongside pulled away just as the reco kite flew over, and headed out of the mouth of the harbour and dropped anchor. We left soon after and joined her, anchoring about 400 yards away. Later, the convoy was joined by several more ships from the harbour, and altogether, by dusk, there were fifteen ships. They were of all sizes, with the "Abbekirk" the largest, the "Kota Gede" next in size, and the balance, a motley lot, much smaller, and no doubt much slower.

All the ships started moving at about 6 p.m., with the American ship in the lead, and the balance of the ships in convoy. We heard through the pipeline that the destination was Fremantle in West Australia. This seemed to be confirmed as the convoy appeared to be travelling in a south easterly direction. We then went down into the

LINING UP FOR MEALS

*We were evacuated from Java (from Tjilijap) on 28.3.42 by the "hell ship"
— "Atmark II" — S.S. "Kota Gede" — a Dutch cargo ship of 4,500 tons. There
were over 2,500 on board. We beat the Japs by 12 hours — as 12 hours after
leaving they had blockaded the port — Yes! we were lucky to have this ship
to get out on.*

rear hold, and estimated the total number in there would have been
well over a thousand people. Naturally, being just below the equator,
it was very hot and humid, the air was most stifling, and it was to
prove that way for the rest of the journey.

About 9 p.m. or maybe just after, Jock remarked that the ship
seemed to be shuddering, as if travelling at a much greater speed. We
thought the same, and surmised something unusual was occurring.
The following day the Dutch gunnery officer in charge of the four
inch gun on the rear poop informed us that there had been a very
large naval battle the previous night, somewhere near the Sunda
Straits (the passage between Java and Sumatra).

This was the battle in which the Australian light cruiser, H.M.A.S
"Perth", and the United States cruiser, the "Houston" took on the
Jap fleet. Both the Allied ships were sunk, but inflicted heavy damage
on the enemy.

It would appear that this Jap force was coming through the Straits
with the intention of blockading Tjilijap, and probably looking for our
convoy. Thanks to the action of the "Houston" and the "Perth", we
were saved from annihilation. We found out next morning that during
the night the "Kota Gede" had broken away from the convoy. She
headed south west and much later west, towards Colombo in Ceylon

(now known as Sri Lanka). At the time of the action, we would have been within 150 nautical miles of the Sunda Straits.

I was told by the gunnery officer on the rear poop deck that the normal speed was about ten knots, but during the night the ship had been moving at about thirteen knots. This also applied all the following day, to place as much distance between us and any searching aircraft operating from Java or Sumatra. In the early part of the morning we passed within a hundred yards of a floating mine, which was not seen until it was on our beam. Evidently it was one that somehow or other had broken away from its moorings — whether it was one of ours or the Japs we did not know.

Life on board ship was harsh and rugged. Many innovations had to be made; many things we would have liked were just not going to be available. Some of the facts we just had to face were the following:—

If we were to be attacked and the ship sunk, there were only five lifeboats, each probably catering for no more than forty or fifty men. Also there were two rafts, probably holding twenty men each. There were no lifejackets that we noticed, and certainly none in our section.

There was a 4 inch gun in the rear and two Lewis machine guns on the side of the bridge for protection. The ship could virtually be classed as defenceless.

For such a crowd, there was insufficient sanitation available in the ship itself. Even if it had been much larger, this would have been a problem. Full credit had to be given to the Captain and crew for the construction of toilet facilities over the side of the ship, with salt water showers running on the side of the deck at the rear for washing oneself after toilets and also for showering.

Fortunately, the seas were relatively calm for the whole nine days at sea, otherwise it would have been very awkward to climb the steps on to the improvised toilet seats over the ship's side.

Eating created a problem for such a large crowd, with few suitable facilities available. There were three meals a day — tinned bacon with two army biscuits for breakfast, biscuits (again two only) with margarine and jam for a snack lunch (if you felt like it) and maconachie stew (made and canned in England) and two army biscuits for dinner at night. All were served cold, though a mug of hot to warm tea was always available. It was not a very sustaining diet, but it sufficed, and we were grateful to have that much.

Most of the personnel possessed a plate or dixie, mug, knife, fork and spoon. If they hadn't, they could always borrow from their friends. Breakfast commenced at about 6.30 a.m. finishing at about 10. 30, with the dinner starting at about 3.30 p.m. and continuing till all were served. The eating procedure meant large queues, stretching from the front of the ship into each of the holds and through to the point at the rear of the ship where the food was served. At all times of the day, meal queues were in evidence.

S.S. "KOTA GEDE"
View of bridge — notice life boat swung over side.
There were five of these.

A Dutch officer leaning against our only gun.

A large gang of volunteers did the serving, with many others opening the tins. Everything came out of tins. As each was emptied, it was put in a drum on the side of the deck, and when all the drums were filled, cans were spread alongside the drums on the deck. After dark all drums were emptied with the tins being thrown overboard, and the decks hosed down. The reasoning behind this was that if the tins were thrown overboard as they were emptied, they could create a trail and be a possible target for any searching submarine.

Full marks had to be given to those who organised the eating, and coped with such a difficult problem.

The number on board was about 2,500, plus! All of the complement were Air Force personnel, and it was roughly estimated that forty per cent of those on board were aircrew. The commissioned officers were in the deck quarters, whilst all other ranks were in the holds or on the decks. It was impossible to freely move round the ship, and the only movement was joining the queues for meals.

With such a number, it was impossible to provide for any type of amusement or recreation. After finishing a meal, the general rule for everybody was to return to one's place of bedding and rest. Reading was very difficult, and the light in the holds very dim — only enough virtually to make one's way. This was a cargo ship, and did not have any library or reading matter.

There was no such thing as life boat drill. If we had been attacked and no doubt sunk, the resultant abandonment of the ship would have been chaotic. With five life boats and two life rafts, there would have been little hope of survival. All we could do was hope for the best and trust that we would eventually make Colombo.

With such a crowd, it was only natural there would be some sickness to contend with. The rear poop area was designated the sick bay, and the medicos did their best to cope with those who required attention. There were no drugs available, and the doctors seemed to have very little in the way of instruments. Some died, two being buried at sea in one day — the fifth day out from our starting point. There were also others, how many I did not know.

I witnessed one of the funerals; the body was placed on a wide plank over the side of the ship at the stern, and covered with the Union Jack flag. The padre recited the funeral service, and at its conclusion, the engine of the ship was thrown into neutral and the propeller stopped. The end of the plank was raised and the body slipped from under the flag and fell into the sea. We all looked in awe at the sea, as the body fell away, and it was quite solemn and impressive. Just as suddenly, the ship's engine started, the propeller set in motion and we were again on our way.

Parades were held at various times in the holds of the ship. Each hold had about four floors, and the access from floor to floor was by ladder. It became quite an ordeal for those who were weak from sickness and exhaustion to move from the lowest level to the top twice a day for food, and as a result many let themselves get very weak and ill. It was quite a common sight to see many of the men have their meagre rations of a meal on the deck, then obtain an extra meal for a friend in the hold who was too weak to climb.

It was also quite difficult to get some of the men who were ill — in particular those in the lower part of the hold — to climb up the ladders to the deck and report to the sick bay. The way that the men assisted those who were sick and in trouble was really wonderful, and illustrated the splendid camaraderie that existed within the ranks, especially under such difficulties. The medical staff and doctors were exemplary, and did an excellent job of assisting the sick, visiting those in the holds and elsewhere who could not make it to the sick quarters.

On Thursday, the sixth day out from Tjilijap, there was great alarm when a submarine surfaced within half a mile of us. As soon as she was seen our only rear gun swung round, but fortunately did not have to fire as she was identified as a friendly British sub. We on the deck heaved a great sigh of relief when she was recognised, or rather, when she acknowledged that she was friendly. Apart from that, we were fortunate in not sighting any other ship on the whole voyage.

Some rain fell during the journey, and as some of the chaps did not like getting wet, they made for the hold. This was the chance to claim their place on the rear deck, in exchange. The rain was quite warm and Jock, Clicker and our group took over this deck space; it was very refreshing to breathe in fresh air again.

On this day, the doctors in the sick bay called for volunteers to hold down a man who was suffering from appendicitis. They did not have any chloroform, and feared they might have to carry out an emergency operation. They kept him in the hospital bed and made him comfortable, hoping that the ship would make Colombo without having to proceed with the operation. This happened, thankfully, and he was one of the first to be transferred on to the transport outside Colombo Harbour on our arrival.

We made Colombo on Friday morning, the 6th March, and the "Kota Gede" anchored outside the harbour. That was the eighth day at sea, and we were most elated at sighting land once again. The Captain called the authorities to send out ferries and launches to take the sick ashore. In due course these arrived, and at least one hundred patients were sent ashore. In some ways it was surprising that there were not a lot more than that. The very ill ones were taken first, then the not quite so sick, leaving the V.D. cases (and there were quite a few of them) till the very last.

The gunnery officer (with whom our group had become quite friendly), informed me that there was some controversy with the authorities about our entering Colombo. As soon as the sick were taken off, orders came for the "Kota Gede" to proceed to Bombay.

Apparently the shore authorities considered there were insufficient facilities in the area to cater for the large crowd on board, and instructions were issued for the ship to proceed on its journey. Bombay was a city on the western side of India, a distance of at least 500 miles (800 kilometres) from Colombo, and the voyage would have taken another two to three days.

The captain was quite concerned with this order, which he considered would be very detrimental to the health of those on board. It was evident that many of the men were feeling the effects of the previous eight days. The gunnery officer was summoned to the bridge by the captain, and on returning invited us to have a fresh water shower. Apparently the fresh water supply had now been connected to the pipes that fed into the showers, replacing the salt water. After a period of enjoying freshwater showers, this was suddenly turned off, and salt water again connected and pumped into the showers.

The captain then sent a message to the shore authorities that he had checked the fresh water, and found that the supply was low and quite insufficient for the voyage to Bombay. Being so desperately short of water, he would need to come inside the harbour to replenish supplies before proceeding on to any other port. And so we were given permission to enter Colombo harbour at dusk on Friday 6th March, having been anchored outside for over six hours.

As we entered, a large convoy left the harbour apparently bound for Australia. There were several large troop ships amongst them, and how we envied the men aboard. One of the ships looked very much like the "Orcades", the Orient liner. Still, there was a strong feeling of relief to have at least escaped from Java.

We anchored in the Harbour, with many other ships near at hand. No large wharf area could be seen, and we were beginning to wonder whether the ship would be going on to Bombay. The journey had been very trying, not only physically but also mentally. Everybody on board had felt the strain not only of the eight days on board, but also the events over the previous three months. Another three harsh days at sea would have been very difficult to endure.

We spent the night on board, anchored in the harbour of Colombo. Everyone went on short rations for breakfast the following morning, expecting that we would be taken ashore to a camp and fed. However, the day passed on, and discontent began to arise.

Late in the afternoon, an announcement was made that all Australians on board should fill in a form. On it were quite a number of questions, such as classification, home address, and previous squadron. Then in alphabetical order, we were called and told to collect our gear, and descend the gangway to be taken by a harbour ferry to a small jetty. Those of the R.A.F. were to follow immediately after.

We were given a week's pay, and also the balance of monies due for the Netherlands East Indies allowance, amounting to 1.8 guilders a day, obtained for us by General Wavell, the G.O.C. (General Officer Commanding) for the Far East. All this money was converted into Ceylon currency, and I finished up with just over 200 rupees. That seemed an enormous sum — a rupee was worth only one shilling and six pence (fifteen cents), but it could purchase quite a lot in Ceylon.

There was much uncertainty about our future movements. In filling out the form during the afternoon, no indication was given whether all Australians were returning home, but Iggy and Clicker were sure this had been suggested.

After all we had been through together, it was hard saying good-bye to Jock who was separated along with the R.A.F. chaps. He gave me his home address in India, but somehow I mislaid it. I felt sure that one day we would meet again, but this was not to be.

After landing at the ferry wharf, a truck took us through the town to a railway station. There a train was waiting to transport us to a transit camp. We had scarcely eaten all day; most of the lads indulged in food available from native shops, and drank quite a lot of hot beer. I bought some tins of sardines and bread to eat on the train, most enjoyable after our starvation diet on the boat.

Quite a number of the chaps were violently ill on the train. They may have eaten native food which did not agree with them, or the hot beer may have had some influence. On reaching our destination, many needed medical attention. Some had to be put in hospital with food poisoning, but recovered very quickly the following day. Still, the thought that we had survived the journey from Java, and possibly were on our way back to Australia, was great medicine.

Our train was headed for the town of Galle, on the very southern point of Ceylon. It was not a very fast journey with the train stopping on many occasions for natives to either board or get off. Four hours later, we stopped four miles from Galle at an R.A.F. rest camp. The camp was only a short distance from the railway; we were escorted to a hut and given a palliasse to be filled with straw for a mattress. By that time it was 4 a.m., and it was not long before all were sound asleep. The sick with food poisoning had been taken to the Hospital Quarters.

Next morning, after a fresh water shower and a good breakfast, we had a look around Boosa Camp. It was a well laid out site located on an area which was previously a race course. The buildings were soundly built, on low blocks with timber floors and attap roof, and only recently constructed. The facilities were very good with stoves and cooking area, and the dining room excellent. Coconut trees abounded, and across the road in front of the camp was a track leading down to the beach, which was ideal for swimming. We were there for only five days, and really enjoyed our salt water swim, with a good freshwater shower to follow.

Apparently this camp had been built for Italian prisoners of war, but had been inspected by Red Cross officials and condemned as such. The facilities had then been taken over by the R.A.F. as a rest camp. It was the best rest area I experienced in the whole of my time in the air force.

On my first morning I ran into Pilot Officer Curtis. He had been an observer with 27 Squadron, and had escaped from Singapore to Batavia in the "Kantor" (recounted earlier). He was able to tell me that Ron Winzar had left the previous Friday (the day we arrived in Colombo) on the "Orcades" for Australia.

The town of Galle with its ancient Fort of Galle Face was within four miles. There was a regular native bus (or garry, as it was known) going past the camp to Galle. We spent some time in town buying items and gifts to take back to Australia. There was always a sneaking doubt that something might crop up and we would be posted elsewhere; we were delighted five days later (Thursday, 12th March) to be advised that we would be leaving the following day on our way back to Aussie land.

Whilst at the camp, I spent much of my time with Brian O'Brien, whom I had trained with on 10 Course, and met up with again at Kalijati in Java. Brian had been a member of 211 Squadron with Mk IV Blenheims, which had been flown out from the Middle East through India and Burma to Palembang. Several planes were lost on the way, and they also suffered many casualties in Sumatra and Java. With Brian was another Australian, Greg Manson, also a member of 211 Squadron. The three of us spent a lot of time together in Galle, and Galle Face; it was intriguing to see the old fort which dated back to the early sixteenth century.

I often wondered what happened to the other fourteen ships that left Tjilijap with us on Friday, 27th February, 1942. I found out their fate at a chance meeting with a man from Oklahoma named Charles Clark, who was attending a Rotary Assembly for Incoming District Governors at Boca Raton in Florida in 1975. Charles told me that he was in Australia during the war, and also mentioned that he landed in Fremantle in West Australia in March, 1942.

Charles was a captain paymaster, and was stationed at Bandoeng with a Flying Fortress squadron of the United States Air Force. When I told him that I had been in Java, and had left in a ship called the "Kota Gede" from Tjilijap, he was very interested. He told me that he walked across the "Kota Gede" to go aboard the "Abbekirk", which was to escort the convoy to Fremantle. He knew that the "Kota Gede" had broken away from the convoy during the first night, after the news of the naval battle in the Sunda Straits; they had heard sometime later, though not confirmed, that we had made Colombo.

He then told me of the torrid time they had on their way to Fremantle. Starting off with fifteen ships, they moved through the night at a very slow speed so as not to lose any of the very small ships. With the "Kota Gede" moving away, they had thirteen ships to look after.

Not long after daylight, Japanese bombers attacked them with bombs and strafing. Several of the smaller ships were hit and sunk. There was little that the "Abbekirk" could do to help, as she was under constant attack from enemy aircraft. This continued all day with a constant stream of bombers coming from various airfields, pressing home their attacks on the ships in the convoy.

The attack continued the following day with long range bombers. It was a case of survival, so the ships dispersed to make it more difficult for the enemy planes to locate them. By the following day, they were out of range of the aircraft, but then had to survive submarine attack, which took its toll on the slower smaller ships.

By this time, the "Abbekirk" had completely lost contact with the remainder of the ships in the convoy, and made Fremantle on the 6th March. They feared that all other ships had been lost, but two days later one limped into port. Whilst it was never confirmed officially, he thought that there may have been another ship which survived. If that were so, it meant that of the fifteen ships which originally left Tjilijap, only four made their way to safety.

And so ended what was probably the last organised (?) escape from the Far Eastern theatre. Of the estimated 2,500 air force personnel aboard the "Kota Gede" probably a third were aircrew — pilots, navigators, wireless operators, air gunners, all fully trained. It was a risky journey, but as it turned out, well worth while, as all who escaped were immediately able to go into active service again.

GALLE FORT
*South of Ceylon
(now Sri Lanka)*

*Sgt. Observers Greg
Manson and Brian
O'Brien. Members of 211
Squadron flying from
Egypt to Palembang.
G.O.H. Hotel in Galle Fort.*

Fort Galle — constructed in mid 1600's.

Street scene at Galle.

Gateway to Fort.

Homeward Bound

Friday, 13th March, 1942.

Friday the 13th may have been considered a bad omen to start a journey, especially one homeward bound, after all the trials and tribulations of the past four months. However, we were going back to Australia, and nobody thought of or was worried by any such superstition. During the morning we were transported with our luggage by train to Colombo, ready for our return home.

We were concerned about the type of ship waiting for us. If it was the "Kota Gede" or a ship of similar size, that would have to be the last straw. So, on the journey to Colombo, this was the main topic of conversation.

On arriving at the jetty, all eyes were on the ships in the harbour to see whether there were any large ones amongst them. One stood out, but we could not discern its name. It was natural therefore when the ferry started embarking the men, to eagerly watch where it finished its journey. However, there were just too many ships for us to see where the first batch had gone. When the ferry came back for its next load, we asked the ferrymen where we were going, and the name of the ship. They did not understand our language, and just smiled. It was most frustrating.

Our curiosity was satisfied, however, when we embarked onto a large ship, the "Stirling Castle". On climbing the gangway to the deck, we greeted each other with a tremendous amount of relief and immense satisfaction. The "Stirling Castle" was a ship of about 25,000 tons, and had been fitted out as a troop carrier.

After the war I was reading through my diaries and noted that on our way to Singapore on the "Marella", we passed the "Stirling Castle" on the North Queensland coast. We had all admired her lines, and thought how thrilling it would be to travel on her. Little did I think at the time that only five months later I would be taken back to Australia on her, after so much activity in the Far East. However, such is life — wouldn't it be dull if we knew exactly what would happen in the very near future?

The ship lay at anchor all night in the harbour, with other air force and some army personnel arriving for the voyage back to Australia. The following afternoon we drew anchor, and set off on the journey home. Soon after clearing the roads or channel, a battleship joined us — the old "Malaya" from the First World War. We were escorted by her and two cruisers and several destroyers until just on dusk. It was an impressive sight and a real confidence booster, sorely needed after the battering that most of us had received over the previous few months.

About 5.30 p.m. we noticed that the "Stirling Castle" started to lag behind the escorting naval ships, until the distance was about two miles. Suddenly the ship started to gather speed, which increased to at least twenty-five knots. The naval ships then altered course forming a lane with two rows, allowing us to pass through the centre. It was a magnificent sight, with the sailors lining the side of their ships waving, and ourselves returning the salutations. All the ships were sounding their sirens, a message bidding farewell, and a pleasant and safe journey back to Australia.

Most of the troops were from the R.A.A.F., but there were some A.I.F as well. In all, we estimated that there were approximately 800 on board the ship. Quite different, we thought, having 800 on a 25,000 ton passenger vessel compared to over 2,400 on the 4,500 ton cargo vessel, the "Kota Gede".

We left Colombo on 14th March, heading for Melbourne, and arrived there after fourteen days, on 28th March. The first few days the ship seemed to travel in a south sou-westerly direction, then changed course to south easterly, getting very low in latitude towards the Antarctic Circle. It became very chilly, and those who ventured on deck always had a blanket or two wrapped around themselves to keep out the cold wind. Practically all had discarded or lost our woollen clothing in the tropical climate of Malaya, and the blankets were welcome. Later we turned east, then nor-east, coming up the western coast of Tasmania through Bass Strait to Melbourne.

About half way through our journey, heading towards the colder latitudes, we came across the albatross. They were magnificent birds, gliding and circling round the stern of the ship day after day, never appearing to flutter their wings. What they did at night time — whether they alighted on the sea or continued flying — we just did not know. From early morn to late afternoon there were always several with us, as if to maintain guard and keep us company.

Just after daylight on Saturday, 14th March, land was sighted outside Melbourne. The "Castle" entered Port Phillip Bay and berthed at the wharf just after 8 a.m. By that stage, breakfast was eaten and bags packed, though most did not have a great amount of luggage. The number of R.A.A.F. personnel would have exceeded 500, probably nearer 600, and we disembarked at 10.00 a.m.

We were then to witness some fine organisation from the R.A.A.F. administration. Trucks in profusion took us out to Ascot Vale, and in the next five hours we had filled in all the necessary forms, and been given a thorough medical and dental examination. We had also visited the equipment store, and been issued with new clothing replacing all the equipment lost during our term in the Far East. Our pay was brought up to date, which was most appreciated, and we were issued with rail passes to our home towns for fourteen days disembarkation leave.

Staff were supplied to answer any queries, especially about conditions in our country over the previous few months. This was very helpful, but we all were very keen to be on our way home. A telephone service was also provided at no charge for anybody who wished to ring home. All agreed that it was very pleasant to have such efficiency in the R.A.A.F., especially after all the difficulties experienced in the Far East; we also wondered how long this could last.

For my part, I rang home but could not get through to my wife. She happened to be in Sarina, having been evacuated from Cairns, but I got a hurried call through to her brother. I caught the 6.40 p.m. mail train to Sydney, had time there to ring Cairns, and then caught the mail train first to Brisbane, and then on to Cairns. All this had been arranged from Ascot Vale, and they had to be complimented on their efficiency.

Reaching Sarina, just south of Mackay, my wife was at the railway station with our young son, and they were able to join me on the train back to Cairns. Also at the station was Mary Cooper, the wife of Bert Cooper. I was very surprised and shaken to learn that she had not received word from Bert since he was in Java. She had heard that he had left Singapore with his Squadron, but no further news.

Nos. 36 and 100 Squadron on the Vildebeestes were in the eastern part of Java, near Sourabaya; we were not in touch with them whilst we were at Kalijati. It came as a great surprise to me to hear that they had not been evacuated from Java, but then there was no communication between the squadrons in that area.

It was now presumed that Bert and other members of 36 and 100 Squadrons on the Vildebeestes (including Ted Eckersley, Peter Atherton, Jim Barnes and John Blunt) had not escaped, and were prisoners of war. This turned out to be the case.

Whilst on the railway platform at Sarina, in the excitement of our reunion and talking to Mary Cooper and other friends, the signal was given by the guard for everybody to board the train. In all the confusion, Vera and I had not brought our baby son John on board. I was on the spur of pulling the cord to halt the train, when our pride and joy was hurriedly passed to us from the friends nursing him on the station. It was a great feeling being reunited, and the rest of the journey on to Cairns was very pleasant.

Part 2

From the Bostons to the Liberators

Sandgate Embarkation Station

After arrival in Melbourne on the "Stirling Castle" on Saturday, 29th March, 1942, everyone was given leave and then instructed to report back to the embarkation depot in the state where they lived. I was given two weeks leave plus travelling time from Melbourne to Cairns, with a further two days added for the time to travel back to Brisbane and out to Sandgate Station.

Sandgate is a township some fifteen miles north of Brisbane, on the coast. On 16th April, I arrived back from leave and escorted my wife and baby out to Coorparoo, a suburb on the southern side of Brisbane. An aunt of mine lived there, and had been kind enough to invite Vera to stay with her.

Route marches, drill and other time wasting duties were the order of the day at Sandgate, and the men did not take kindly to these. We badly wanted to get posted to a squadron, and back into action once more. It was not long before most had received a posting, but I was one of the last to leave Sandgate. Two months after arrival, and really brassed off with the inactivity, I inquired of the Adjutant if there had been some oversight. He had no word of a posting for me, but promised to make inquiries.

The very next day I received a call from Orderly Room and was told to report immediately to 22 Squadron, stationed at Richmond inland from Sydney.

There had been one interesting incident during my time at Sandgate. In early May (1942), coming back to the Station at night after leave and entering the sergeants' mess, I was told that an American Flying Fortress plane had landed during the afternoon on spare ground beside the camp, next to the Hornibrook Highway. Nobody believed the story, which sounded very far fetched, but our informers were most insistent that the story was true.

Early next morning, we were absolutely amazed to find out the story was correct. The Flying Fortress plane (B. 17) was bogged in the soft ground next to the huts on the station.

Evidently six planes had been flying to Amberley from New Caledonia or thereabouts. They had struck heavy rain and a severe tropical thunderstorm a hundred miles or so off the coast. With visibility down to zero they could not maintain contact, and split up hoping to locate a landing ground.

We believe that one aircraft landed at Amberley, whilst others landed at various places on the coast as far south as Coffs Harbour.

This particular plane circled low over the coast near Sandgate in very nasty weather. Seeing the buildings, the pilot assumed that it was a military site, and decided to try to land on the area beside the huts.

The area had recently been reclaimed with red soil; with heavy rain over the previous days, the ground was a real quagmire. The cleared area of land was less than 1,000 yards, and if the ground had been hard, the aircraft could not have pulled up before running into a building. With the soft soil it pulled up quickly, stopping with the wheels bogged to their axles. Miraculously nobody was hurt, which was most fortunate.

The pilot must have switched off the engines when landing, as there did not seem to be any damage to the propellers. There was no sign of them being bent in any way. After the plane was dragged out, the engines were started and responded quite well. It was quite astounding that the plane could have come out of it with no sign of damage.

By the time we got down there, quite a crowd from the station had congregated. The area was cordoned off with rope and patrolled by American military police. No civilians were allowed into the area, though they would have had a view of the plane from the Highway. The M.P.'s were letting everybody know, bellowing at the top of their voices as only United States M.P.'s can do, that no cameras were allowed; anybody caught with one would have it confiscated, and charges laid.

That was a real challenge, which we R.A.A.F. sergeants took up. I had a small folding Kodak camera, which could be concealed quite easily in my great coat. With four of my fellow sergeants, we made our way to a good position as close to the aircraft as we could, and in the front row of the large crowd. Two stood in front, and the other two beside me; when we thought the M.P.'s were not looking, the two in front opened up and I quickly took the photo. It is shown here after all these years.

Three days later, with fine weather and the area drying out a little (though still soft), a large gang of U.S. air force and army personnel had dragged the Fortress out of the bog. It was their intention to attempt to fly the aircraft to Amberley. Everyone thought that the chances of the plane taking off were very slight, and we were not going to miss the opportunity of watching the attempt.

The plane was lightened, and fuel drained from the tanks, leaving only sufficient to fly to its destination. The engines were started, and thoroughly warmed up and checked. They were then revved up seemingly to their maximum. With the aircraft straining to go, the brakes were released, ropes holding the plane were cut (flying in all directions) and the aircraft started to gain momentum.

There were only three crew aboard, two pilots and the engineer. After about a hundred yards, the pilot attempted to lift the plane,

The U.S. Flying Fortress (B.17) which force landed beside the Sandgate I.T.S. Depot in May, 1942.

but it lifted only slightly, and seemed to stall. It fell back to ground, fortunately landing on to galvanised roofing iron which had been used to get the plane out of the bog. The plane then bounced back into the air, and although not really airborne, fell back and almost touched the ground. However, it gathered momentum, skimming the ground, and to everybody's amazement and relief, became airborne. A great cheer rang out from the crowd assembled, but suddenly this turned to a horrified gasp.

During all this time, the plane was veering to the left, and we could see that it was travelling dangerously close to the overhead electricity wires on the side of the highway. The wing of the plane missed them, but the margin must have been only inches. The crew were lucky, and certainly had guts to even attempt such a dangerous takeoff. A tremendous cheer arose from the crowd assembled, and the aircraft made a circuit before wending its way south west towards Amberley.

22 Squadron

Richmond to Port Moresby

July to December, 1942.

On being posted to 22 Squadron at Richmond, just west of Sydney, my wife quickly made arrangements to come with me, accompanied by our young son, John Douglas. His second name came from General Douglas MacArthur, the United States general, who had returned from the Philippines and was in charge of the forces in the Pacific area. It was the first week in July, 1942. We arrived in Sydney the following day, and Vera stayed with her father who had a flat in the city.

I made my way to Richmond; reporting to Orderly Room I was told that I had been absent without leave for three weeks. However, my explanation of not having received the notice of posting at Sandgate was accepted, and nothing more came of it. This type of incident often happened, and was not confined solely to the air force.

The sergeants' quarters, where I was given a room, were very comfortable. I wondered what aircraft had been allotted to the squadron; finding that these were Bostons aroused my curiosity, as I had not heard of them before. My fears were unfounded. The Boston (known as the A. 20) had proved itself in the Middle East, being used quite extensively there by the R.A.F. and known as the Havoc. The plane was American, made by the Douglas Curtis Corp.

The Bostons carried a crew of three, all located in separate compartments with the only communication by intercom. The pilot had a great view of his surrounds in the front upper part of the aircraft, the navigator was in the front or nose of the plane in virtually a perspex shell, whilst the W.A.G. was in the mid upper part of the plane.

The aircraft had a tricycle undercarriage, with a nose wheel and two main landing wheels under the wings. We were warned that it was somewhat hazardous for the navigator in front if the plane came in for a belly landing, but fortunately this did not happen whilst I was with the squadron.

The W.A.G. had a turret with twin Brownings, whilst the aircraft had five guns firing forward. The plane cruised along at a steady 240 miles per hour, and could carry a bomb load of 4,000 pounds or more.

Within a few days of arriving at Richmond, I had my first flight as a passenger with Fl/Lt Vern Morgan, the O.C. of "B" Flight, on a low flying bombing exercise. A few days later, I flew with F/O Claude Sladen in formation flying, which took only an hour.

I was then called on to fly with the C.O., Sq/Leader Bell, on a flight to Laverton on the outskirts of Melbourne. Returning the following day, it was found that my intercom was on the blink. The C.O. told me not to worry; he knew the way back to Richmond, and I could sit back and enjoy the scenery. It was most interesting, and we were back in Richmond in just under two hours, which was quite fast for those times.

By the beginning of August crews had been formed, and I was allotted to a crew with Jack McMaster as pilot and captain. I was the navigator and Jim Larkin the wireless operator/air gunner. The squadron was immediately placed on operational search patrols off the New South Wales coast. Japanese submarines were very active in the area, and several Allied ships had been lost in the past few weeks.

Each day, six to nine of our Bostons would take off on patrols. They carried out a creeping line ahead search out from the coast for a distance of approximately three hundred miles, and then a similar exercise on the adjacent area back to a landmark on the coast. This would be repeated in the afternoon, getting back to base just on dusk. The area under patrol was from Moruya just north of the border of Victoria, to north of Newcastle. The same patrol would be carried out the following day by other crews, and repeated again and again for over three weeks.

By the middle of September the coastal patrols had eased off, and the squadron was preparing to move north. We all hoped that we would be moving to Port Moresby for operations in New Guinea. On 14th September our crew was chosen to fly out from Richmond. Led by Fl/Lt. Ken MacDonald, with extra fuel tanks installed, three planes flew in formation to Charters Towers in five and a quarter hours.

It was very exacting flying, in fact almost hazardous; the leader took us very low, just skimming trees. On approaching valleys, he descended to just above tree top, not thinking of the aircraft on either side. We all felt very relieved to eventually reach the Towers.

We spent the following month between Charters Towers and Townsville, with some local flying. It was rather frustrating, as we were given no indication of what was happening. By mid October, most of the planes had been sent south for modifications. At the same time the navigators and spare air crew had boarded a small cargo ship, and were sent on to Port Moresby. It took three days to reach our destination; we were very cramped, the ship was dirty, and it was most unpleasant. It reminded me of the "Kota Gede".

That was the last the navigators saw of the Bostons, much to our regret. In the squadron, I met Tony English, Arthur Cleland and Cliff Dunn, and later they were posted to Cairns to join the Catalinas.

The Bostons were sent south, and the nose compartment previously used by the navigator was altered to construct a solid mounting for four machine guns of .5 inch calibre. These, with the other five Browning .303 machine guns all firing forward, made the Boston a really formidable strafing aircraft; in addition it was still capable of carrying its full capacity of bombs. When the aircraft of 22 Squadron became operational at Wards Strip in Port Moresby, then later at other bases, they made a great impact on the enemy.

At our new camp site at Port Moresby, we were very disappointed and disgusted at the equipment allotted. The tents, sleeping bags, and other gear were torn and most inferior, and with few mosquito nets, we were looking forward to a very unpleasant time. This applied to all ranks, officers, sergeants and airmen.

Having put up with this for a week, and with everybody grouching, one of our sergeants gathered us together with a bold plan to improve conditions. It was rather wild and risky and we talked about it for some time, but in the end decided to give it a go. It was too dicey for officers to come into it, but the airmen were taken into our confidence, and were to be the receivers at the camp site.

That day the sergeant had been down at the wharves at Port Moresby, and had observed a Liberty Ship unloading top class camping gear and cooking equipment. The Americans always had good equipment, and Aussie gear was second rate by comparison.

He noticed that the cargo was being unloaded on to large trucks, and without being checked was being driven away by Negro drivers. As the loaded truck arrived at the fence around the wharf area, the driver looked round for someone to guide him to his destination. Often there was a wait of five to ten minutes before someone came, climbed into the truck beside the driver, and instructed him where to take the truck for unloading.

The plan was for the sergeant to be present on the wharf during unloading from the ship. When he saw some "suitable" goods he would pass on a signal to another sergeant conveniently placed. A gang of us were to be waiting at the entrance to the wharves; one would enter the vehicle beside the driver, and instruct him to drive out to our camp at Wards Strip.

The goods would then quickly be unloaded, and the truck directed back to the wharf, where the sergeant would get out and disappear. Back at the camp site, selected goods would be reloaded on to one of our trucks, and taken into a nearby hiding places, for collection when the heat wore off. I was not one of the ringleaders, but was quite prepared to act as one of the guides of the truck to the campsite. It was really good fun, and well worth the risk.

BEAUFORT BOMBER
This Beaufort aircraft landed on the aerodrome at Richmond, N.S.W., in May 1942. The observer on the aircraft was Sgt. Ken Holmes, who had trained with me on 10 Course.

It all sounded so crazy, but it worked; we must have guided at least fifteen heavily laden trucks out to our camp. There was quite a lot of unnecessary and useless gear unloaded, and this was left at the campsite. We guessed that the U.S. military police would eventually catch up with us, looking for stolen equipment, and this was where our officers came in. The Squadron would be happy to return gear that was not badly needed.

Sure enough, three days later the M.P.s arrived. The officers talked to them and showed them the equipment that had ''inadvertently'' been delivered. They apologised for the mistake, and got the airmen to reload the unwanted gear on to the trucks. This made the military police quite happy; they had been successful in their search.

We soon put the borrowed camping gear to use, and the rest of our time in the squadron was much more comfortable. The G.I.s from neighbouring camps knew what had happened, and thought that it was well thought out and executed. Our commanding officer was Wing Commander Bell, and our squadron became known by the Americans as ''Ali Bell and his 400 Thieves Squadron''.

In the mid 1970's I was in the United States, and talking to a group of Americans who had been in New Guinea during the war. The conversation got round to various incidents from that time. One asked what squadron I was in at Port Moresby; he was quick to ask —

22 Squadron Bostons (A20)
Flying in formation — Richmond Aerodrome
to Charters Towers

BOSTON — A.20

In Charters Towers — Jack McMasters (Front) pilot, Jim Larkin (Top of Aircraft) wireless op/air gunner.

In Charters Towers — Jack Woodward (nav.) and Jack McMasters (pilot).

"Wasn't that the squadron that we dubbed the Ali Bell and his 400 Thieves Squadron?" So our action must have been well known.

The members of 22 Squadron with their Bostons were outstanding. Although the navigators had to leave the squadron before they went into battle against the enemy in New Guinea, nevertheless we were all very proud of them. My previous pilot, Jack McMaster, was awarded the Distinguished Flying Cross, and there were many similar awards. Bill Newton was a very distinguished and popular pilot, and for his outstanding exploits was posthumously awarded the highest honour that could be bestowed, the Victoria Cross.

The squadron was experimenting with 20 lb fragmentation anti personnel bombs. Fl/Lt. Vern Morgan (the O.C. of "B" Flight) went up to practice bomb a shipwreck at the entrance to Port Moresby harbour. Because of the speed of the plane, the bombs hit against one another in the slipstream, and exploded underneath just after being released. The aircraft crashed into the sea with fatal results — it was a tragic accident.

Whilst awaiting a decision about our future posting, several of us took the opportunity of hitch hiking up past Roana Falls to the mountains and the Kokoda Trail. The Japanese had advanced to this point before being repelled by the A.I.F. and the militia battalions.

We were stopped several miles from the actual front, but it was interesting talking to some of the army chaps who had been up the trail. We were very much impressed to observe the Salvation Army, the Red Cross, Comforts Fund, Y.M.C.A. and many other organisations so near the front line, offering and serving tea and eats to all and sundry, and rendering advice and assistance.

The navigators were all without crews, and had to wait until early December before receiving a posting. I was most elated with mine — to 11 Squadron flying Catalinas, stationed in Cairns. What a wonderful posting that was — I could hardly believe my good fortune. It also meant that I would probably be home for Christmas and the New Year — what a pleasant thought!

I was fortunate in obtaining a flight from Port Moresby to Cairns in an Empire flying boat, arriving home just a couple of days after receiving my posting. I was to report to my new squadron by mid December.

And so on to 1943 — what would it bring?

22 SQUADRON CAMP — NEAR WARDS STRIP
PORT MORESBY

We also found a windmill, which we erected over a well dug out by our sergeants.

*22 Squadron sergeants in front of tent. ('Acquired' from the U.S. Stores).
Self with Doug Frith and Keith Pritchard.*

Another view of our tent and occupants.

Keith Pritchard having a bath after a hard day's work.

Wilson's residence at Myola.

*Doug Frith and Self.
Background Roana
River.*

Our group, with the army officer and the two natives.

*Two of the
fuzzy-wuzzies.*

Prior to leaving Port Moresby in December, 1942, Doug Frith and I were out walking one day in the region of the harbour, and came across this Catalina hull, amongst the coconut trees.

The number was A 24-7, and it had been strafed and sunk by the Japanese on a raid in February, 1942. It was subsequently towed to the shore. After some parts were taken from the hull, it was left abandoned in its position amongst the trees.

11 Squadron - Cairns

Catalina Flying Boats

It was on approximately the 10th December, 1942, when I was notified of my posting to 11 Squadron, based in Cairns with PBY flying boats, known as Catalinas. I had to report to the new squadron by the 15th of December, 1942, and arrangements were made to fly down the following day. This allowed a few days at home with the family, which was very acceptable.

This squadron and its C.O. had a very good reputation, and were held in high esteem. The Catalina flying boat, commonly known as a "Cat", had an excellent record, and the squadron was recognised as being very efficient.

Both 11 Squadron with its sister Squadron No. 20 were stationed in Cairns, and their operations interwoven. Their main duties were reconnaissance patrols and the escort surveillance of ships in convoy. They carried quite a bombload, and their endurance was remarkable. Capable of carrying 8,000 pounds of bombs, it was not unusual for the aircraft to stay aloft for more than fifteen hours. Each squadron had its own commanding officer, with Squadron Leader (S/Ldr.) Frank Chapman the C. O. of 11 Squadron, and S/Ldr. Atkinson in charge of 20 Squadron.

Reporting to 11 Squadron orderly room on my first day, I was rather taken aback when the corporal requested me to see the adjutant immediately. Most unusual I thought; usually on reporting to a new station, one would be casually informed to keep in touch and ultimately told to report to somebody or other. I was then told the C.O. wanted to see me urgently. I wondered what I had done to warrant such attention — I was not late in reporting, and could not remember having committed any misdemeanour.

I did not have to wait long before being ushered into the C.O.'s Office. Squadron Leader Chapman was a very friendly man, and invited me to sit down at his office table. Perhaps I was very guarded, not knowing what the score was. He really interrogated me regarding my previous experiences, and in particular the episodes in Singapore, Malaya and Java. He was interested to hear about 22 Squadron, and what I thought about Boston aircraft.

I was quite puzzled, and began to wonder just what it was all about, especially after having been with him for about three quarters of an hour. Quite suddenly he asked — "How would you like to join my crew?" I was taken aback, but elated to think that this could happen. I replied I would be very happy to accept, and trusted that he would not be disappointed in me.

I then asked whether I would be moving on to Rathmines to do an Operational Training Course. He said this would not be necessary, as I would be trained under his guidance.

Evidently he was well briefed, for when I asked about accommodation, he knew that I was married and that my home was in Cairns. He also was aware that my wife had a flat in Sheridan Street, and that we had a young son. I could live at home, but he would like a telephone to be available at the flat should I be required urgently. I was pleasantly surprised by the interview, and looked forward to an interesting and friendly time with the squadron.

There was no particular training laid down, but each morning on arriving at the station I was to report to orderly room. If the Adjutant wanted me, I would be informed. Otherwise I was to spend the day in the operations room (which was also the Intelligence Section), finding out as much as possible about the aircraft, the squadron and its operations.

Early in the new year, several other navigators and I went on a fourteen day training course on the Norden bomb sight at Mareeba aerodrome. This was the new bomb sight developed by the U.S. Air Force, which was being used quite extensively in the aircraft of the United States throughout all theatres of war. Evidently the R.A.A.F. were keen to have it installed in some of our Australian aircraft.

The new aerodrome at Mareeba had only been completed within the previous six months, having a long strip which could accommodate large aircraft such as the B17 (Flying Fortress) and B24 (Liberators). An extensive area was set aside for training purposes, in addition to the general buildings associated with an aerodrome of this nature.

Amongst these installations was a very large concrete pad traversed by a tall tower. This was the Norden bomb sight instruction area, constructed to educate bombardiers in its use. Alongside the pad was a large control room which recorded the assimilated readings of height, speed, course and wind strength to be set on the bomb sight. It was very sophisticated. There were about twelve R.A.A.F. navigators on the course, in addition to quite a number of American bombardiers.

We travelled to Mareeba by the new road up the range through Kuranda, which had only been in operation about two years. The drivers had to be careful as it was very narrow. We camped in the American N.C.O.'s quarters, and were very well fed and looked after. We were quite envious of their superior conditions.

The instruction given was very intense and absorbing, and we were very impressed with the accuracy of this new bomb sight. The course lasted two weeks, and although we were not told our scores, S/Ldr. Chapman congratulated me on my report commenting I was very high in the marks allotted. I was quite elated and gratified.

Whilst being impressed with the accuracy of the bomb sight, I was very concerned with the time it took to guide the aircraft over the target. With a Norden bomb sight installed, an aircraft's flight path in an attack was governed by it. With only slight variations of course permissible to offset minor corrections, the aircraft then had to be held tightly on this track. Should evasive action be necessary, it would be most difficult to maintain the bombing run.

I explained this to S/Ldr. Chapman; the time taken by a Catalina with its slow speed between lining up the target and releasing its bomb-load could make it very vulnerable, and create an easier target for enemy anti-aircraft fire. I thought the present C.S.B.S. (Course Setting Bomb Sight) much safer for the Catalina than the Norden bomb sight. He seemed very concerned, and felt that the squadron should give this further serious thought.

My first flight with the squadron was as second navigator with F/O. W.G. White, on the 18th January, flying to Port Moresby, in Aircraft No. A 24 — 17. I was not told very much about the flight, only that the aircraft would be taking off again soon after landing. The aircraft departed with only a skeleton crew immediately after refuelling, leaving myself and others behind in Port Moresby.

I could tell that it was a very secret mission. Many months later, I found out that they had picked up some coast watchers and natives from New Britain right under the noses of the Japs. The aircraft returned during the night and we flew back to Cairns the following day. It was interesting meeting Bimbo White, as we were boarders together at the Brisbane Grammar School many years before; he was in his final year and I only a new boy.

During the rest of January and all of February, 1943, I was not called on for further flying duties, and was told by S/Ldr. Chapman to be patient. However, in early March, I was called into his office and informed that at the end of the week he would be flying on a "milk run", and after that I would be relieving his present navigator. I asked whether I could go on the flight for familiarisation. He refused my request, mentioning that there would be plenty of flying after that which would keep me busy. I did feel disappointed, but had to accept his decision.

At the end of the week, his aircraft took off on the "milk run". This entailed flying from Cairns to Milne Bay on the eastern tip of New Guinea, and after refuelling, taking off and patrolling at night along the northern coastline of New Guinea towards Lae. On this occasion they would cross the Strait between New Guinea and New Britain, and patrol along that coastline towards Gasmata. The Catalinas naturally were loaded with bombs, and if at the end of the patrol nothing had been sighted, some target would be designated for bombing.

When the aircraft was about thirty miles south of Gasmata, a hurried message was received that it was on fire. An immediate alert was issued, and although aircraft and naval ships patrolled the area for several days, no sightings were made. It was then presumed that the aircraft had crashed, with the loss of all nine occupants.

The two squadrons in the station were immediately thrown into a state of shock, and needless to say I was deeply affected by the tragedy. This also meant that I did not have a crew. If I was not allotted to another crew, no doubt I could expect a posting elsewhere.

My flying was not altogether finished in the squadron. During March I was included in two flights involving practice bombing, and a later flight with the new C.O., S/Ldr. Atkinson, carrying out a compass swing. In April, I participated in two patrols on ship convoys, the first lasting nearly seventeen hours, when we patrolled a convoy of United States ships being led by a U.S. naval vessel.

This was travelling from Townsville to Port Moresby. Practically in a direct line on this track is Osprey Reef, which has claimed quite a number of ships over the years. The convoy was making a direct line for the reef, and when only about eight miles or so away, our skipper, F/Lt. Fader, sent a morse signal to the leader, a small United States naval ship, suggesting that they had better alter course.

On receiving the signal, the convoy leader drastically and immediately altered course by approximately ninety degrees, with the convoy following. To see the alteration of that course after receiving the signal was quite amusing. It would not have been so amusing if the convoy had piled up on the reef.

Shortly after this I received a posting to Bairnsdale, to report by the middle of May. I was quite apprehensive and not happy with this, as Bairnsdale had a very poor record. It was an O.T.U. (Operational Training Unit) for Beaufort medium bombers, and the number of air crashes in training exercises over the previous six months was frightening; in particular the night time flying training was really dangerous. Still, I had no option but to proceed to Bairnsdale, and await the consequences.

General Reconnaissance School - G. R. S.

Bairnsdale - R. A. A. F.

It was with mixed feelings that I received the posting from 11 Squadron at Cairns to Bairnsdale Station. News from that area was that the accident rate was too high to be comfortable. However, there were no options open to get out of the transfer, and it was a case of wait and see.

I left Cairns by mail train for Brisbane, then on to Sydney and Melbourne. From that point I caught the train to the Gippsland area, where Bairnsdale is located. On the way, some Air Force chaps from Bairnsdale Station told me it was now a General Reconnaissance School (G.R.S.) There were two aerodromes at Sale, not far from Bairnsdale, East Sale being the Operational Training Unit (O.T.U.), whilst the one at West Sale was an Air Gunnery School (A.G.S.).

I wondered what my duties were to be at G.R.S. On reporting to the orderly room, I was directed to the sergeants' mess and then to the Instructional Staff Room. I was completely amazed and rather bewildered — I had no training as an instructor.

Squadron Leader Bob Dalkin was the Chief Ground Instructor (C.G.I.), and he had quite a task in setting up the new school, due to commence over the coming weekend. The participants were pilots and navigators in separate courses with approximately thirty in each course.

The duration of each course was to be eight weeks, with a fresh intake every four weeks. The main purpose was to acquaint pilots and navigators returning from overseas with conditions existing in the northern part of Australia, these being very different from the European, African and Asian war zones. Also there were new trainees who had just completed their courses in Australia and who would be assigned to reconnaissance work.

I was attached to a group of navigation instructors with Fl/Lt. Stan (Nick) Nicholls officer in charge. Nick was a member of the permanent air force. He had recently returned from England where he had spent most of his time with 10 Squadron (R.A.A.F.) on patrols of the Atlantic in Sunderland flying boats. He was an outstanding navigator and had been decorated with the D.F.C. (Distinguished Flying Cross).

Instructors in our group included F/Lts Cec Bourne and Don Brown, both with overseas experience, and F/O. George Leslie, who had distinguished himself with 11 Squadron on the Catalinas. The commanding officer was Wing Commander Derryck Kingwell, a very respected pilot, a good organiser and a disciplinarian. These qualities were very necessary to get a new station off the ground in such a short time.

Subjects for the navigation course included dead reckoning navigation, astro navigation, reconnaissance, ship recognition and meteorology. Fl/Lt. Nicholls called a meeting to organise a plan of instruction. The only text books on the subject were from the R.A.A.F., titled A.P. 1234 and A.P. 1456, and far too long and detailed for this course. Time was short, and it was decided that we must immediately make up a programme, particularly for the subject of practical navigation, in a condensed form that could be delivered over seven weeks.

In record time, lectures were composed and typed to enable the passing on of information based on the experience of these highly qualified men. W.A.A.F. typistes then created copies of the manuscripts, using hand operated duplicators — rather laborious, but well done. Working late at night, the office staff turned out about eighty copies of the lectures on dead reckoning navigation, which proved very valuable to the instructors.

As a sergeant I was the lowest ranked instructor amongst the group. Nick queried when I had finished my original course; when told it was 10 Course, he wondered if I had been in trouble not to have received my due promotion. I answered that I had just been too busy to check up on it. I was actually overdue for promotion to warrant officer (W.O.). Within three weeks I was a flight sergeant, and three weeks later a W.O. That was a wonderful rank, and I held on to it as long as I could.

The practical navigation exercises were mainly held over Bass Strait, commencing from Lakes Entrance and lasting about three hours. Complete air logs had to be kept, and then checked when the exercise was completed. If there was any query about a trainee's proficiency, this showed up in these logs. If there was doubt about a particular trainee, an instructor had to fly with him on a future exercise and carefully observe and assess the operation. The planes used were Avro Ansons, a very friendly and reliable plane. I was still keen on flying, and always volunteered to participate.

One which I always enjoyed was the flight from Bairnsdale to Sydney, carrying out a small coastal navigation exercise on the way. Landing at Mascot in Sydney, the aircraft would refuel, and then make a reconnaissance of Sydney Harbour taking photographs of ships, docks and important strategic areas. A free night would then be spent in Sydney, and the return flight made the next day.

A refuelling stop was made on the way back at Moruya, on the N.S.W. coast near to the border. Here we picked up oysters ordered before leaving Bairnsdale. There was then a final exercise back over Bass Strait. It was necessary for at least two instructors to accompany the trainees on this weekend flight, and I always volunteered.

Bairnsdale was a very pretty town, located on the Mitchell River. The townspeople were very friendly, and went out of their way to make the lives of the servicemen most pleasant. I was often invited out to the home of one of the Dahlsen partners for a friendly card game of solo along with Col Badham, who had joined the instructing staff shortly after it had started.

The station was very fortunate to have a rowing club in the town. The club was dormant because of the war, but had offered all the facilities of the shed and the rowing boats to the air force. There was a very good eight oared rowing boat, as well as fours and several two oared boats, known as tubs.

Regattas were held at frequent intervals, with the adjoining stations (O.T.U. & A.G.S.) at East and West Sale participating. In addition crews took part from the plant at Fisherman's Bend which assembled the Wirraway, Boomerang and Beaufort aeroplanes. They called themselves Beaufort Division D.A.P.

Before enlisting I had rowed in Townsville, and was offered a place in a four in the first regatta. Afterwards, when several members of the eight were posted, I was invited to row in the eight as bow. This was a wonderful opportunity which I quickly accepted.

Gordon Freeth and Vic Shakespeare, both from West Australia (and I believe King's Cup rowers pre-war), were stroke and seven, and rowing at two was the C.O., Wing Commander Kingwell. On the occasion of my first outing in the eight as bow, the C.O. in number two position turned round and warned me to "keep in time, and do not let that oar hit me in the back". I assured him that I would be very careful not to let that occur.

Rowing was mainly held in the summer months, and there was keen rivalry between G.R.S. and the O.T.U. at Sale. The regattas were mostly held at Bairnsdale on the Mitchell River, but one was on the Henley Course on the Yarra in March, 1944. Shortly after this regatta, Wing Commander Kingwell was posted, and also Gordon Freeth and Vic Shakespeare.

Tony English arrived at Bairnsdale not long after my arrival. We had been together in 22 Squadron on the Bostons, both being in "B" flight. He had been looking forward to operations in that squadron, particularly as he was in the crew of Claude Sladen, a really top line pilot. When the navigators became redundant, he had followed me to 11 Squadron, and then to Bairnsdale. Tony did a full G.R.course, and was then transferred to the instructing staff.

Among our instructors and specialising in ship recognition was Commander Brett Hillier, on loan from the navy. He knew his subject well, and was able to impart so much to our students. Tony English had become very interested in this subject, and on Brett's return to the navy took over this part of the course. He proved an outstanding instructor.

The new C.O. after the transfer of Wing Commander Kingwell was Wing Commander "Red" Green. He notified me that I was to be captain and organiser of the rowing. I was already captain of the football team, though we did not play very often. Another newcomer to the station was Squadron Leader "Doc" Burgess, in charge of the hospital. The C.O. and the Doc were both keen rowers, and immediately came into the crew of the eight.

In October, 1943, I was sent to Melbourne with others for an interview for commission as an officer. On the 1st November, I was granted a commission with the rank of Pilot Officer on probation. Six months later, on the 1st May, 1944, promotion to the rank of Flying Officer was confirmed.

I had enjoyed the sergeants' mess, especially as a W.O. Being aircrew, the mess members were convinced that one had achieved that rank through service, and one was treated accordingly. Coming into the officers' mess as a pilot officer, the lowest commissioned rank, I found the attitude very different. I often gave the sergeants' mess a ring and asked to be invited down for a drink, and found the atmosphere there always so much warmer and more welcome.

I was still flying regularly and checking on those navigators experiencing difficulties with their exercises. On Monday, 29th May, 1944, I was listed for flying. However, the weather was really foul, with a cold front passing through the area and winds reaching up to fifty knots. All flying was cancelled, and re-allotted to the following day.

On the Tuesday, we took off at 12.45p.m. in Avro Anson No. W 1580, with F/Sgt. R. Stinton as pilot, Fl/Lt. S.H. Gowing navigator, Sgt. K. Horne wireless operator, and myself navigation instructor. The take-off appeared to be quite normal, and there was nothing wrong with the engines that I noticed.

Quite a strong wind was blowing at the time, at least thirty knots. It was the middle of winter, and with the cold front having just passed through, the day was bitterly cold.

The exercise was a radius of action, commencing from Lakes Entrance on the Victorian coast. We were approximately twenty minutes and forty miles out from Lakes Entrance when the pilot told us that he was having engine trouble. One motor was about to seize, having burst an oil pipe line, and we were returning to base.

Sgt. Horne on the radio was immediately advised to notify base we were returning, and that message was transmitted. Suddenly the engine with the burst oil pipeline seized and stopped. I was not unduly concerned, as we were flying at 1,500 feet and should not have had any trouble flying home on one engine. However, the scene rapidly changed when the pilot told us that the other engine was dropping revs badly, and that the plane was losing height.

The pilot suggested jettisoning all surplus gear and equipment to lighten the load, and assist the plane to remain airborne. Hec Gowing and I moved to the rear of the plane and commenced throwing surplus items out, but we were still losing height, well out of sight of land. Things were looking grim, and we called to the wireless operator to send out an S.O.S.; he failed to do this, as it turned out.

We were rapidly dropping toward the sea and the pilot then turned the aircraft into the wind — there was no alternative but to ditch. It was rather difficult alighting, with the waves very large and the height from the tops of the waves to the bottom of the troughs being about thirty feet. I thought he made a good landing, first hitting one wave, and bouncing on to the next and ploughing right into it, up near the top. The speed of the aircraft at ditching was down to forty knots.

We quickly got the rubber dinghy out of the plane, and the pilot asked the radio operator if he had sent out the S.O.S. When he replied he did not have time to cipher the message, we all just glared at him in disbelief. I suppose you could not blame him, he was only fresh out of W.A.G. school. The pilot quickly jammed down the radio key, but it was useless.

Meanwhile Hec Gowing and I were out on the wing. The rubber dinghy was inflated, and we were holding on by the wing strut. The dinghy had a rope, which we looped round the stay wire to make sure the wind did not blow it away. The seas were large, at least eight metres (about thirty feet). The wind was howling at a good thirty knots, and it was all very frightening.

The starboard wing had a wire radio aerial, leading from near the wing tip up on to the main fuselage. We decided to stay on the aircraft wing as long as possible, before taking to the rubber dinghy. It was very difficult hanging on to the wire aerial, as the aircraft was diving into every wave; we had to brace ourselves each time the aircraft dived into the following wave. Spray was being blown off the crest of each wave as it came upon us, and it was not long before we were thoroughly soaked. The wind and sea were icy cold, and most unpleasant. We had our life vests on (known in the Air Force as "Mae Wests"), but did not inflate them.

Our aircraft was airborne from Bairnsdale at 12.45p.m., and the time was now 13.30. We kept a sharp lookout hoping that another aircraft might happen to fly near on a similar exercise, but none appeared.

Soon after we had taken to the wing of the aircraft, and it was apparent that it would float for some time, I told the pilot that I wanted to retrieve the aircraft clock as a souvenir. He was handy to the fuselage, and volunteered to do this for me. The clock is now on the wall of my study at home, but even though I passed it on to a watchmaker in Bairnsdale to try to neutralise the salt influence, and have had other watchmaker friends look at it since, it does not go too well, possibly protesting against being taken away from its original mountings.

Fortunately for us, George Leslie was on operations duty at the time, and was watching our progress when the call came in that we were returning to base. He tried to pick us up, and when he could not he decided that we were in trouble. He ordered an aircraft on standby to take off immediately to search, over-riding the opinion of the officer in charge of flying. The latter considered we were probably joy riding and taking our time returning to base. (I was later told that George Leslie retorted — not likely, with Woodward aboard).

He quickly worked out a track for the searching aircraft to the point from which he calculated the message had been sent. Jake Bond was the pilot of the search plane, and very fortunately found us immediately. It was approximately one and a half hours from when we ditched to when we were located. That was a very long drawn out time. With the large seas running, we had begun to doubt if we would ever be found, and it was a great relief to see the Anson aircraft overhead. Just as it flew across, we had the feeling that our aircraft was about to dive and sink. Above us Jake Bond and his crew had a bird's eye view of us deserting the Anson aircraft and clambering into the rubber dinghy. He told me later that he wished he had a camera — it was so dramatic.

The plane kept circling, but there was nothing to be done other than transmitting our position back to base. It wasn't long before he was joined by another aircraft, and then another, until we had four Ansons looking down on us. There was no way of getting a message down, and all we could do was to stay in the rubber dinghy and just wait and hope.

When posted to Bairnsdale I had a dread of the cold winter weather, and always made provision for warm clothing, especially when flying out over Bass Strait. This exercise was no exception, and I was wearing a long sleeve woollen singlet, long john woollen underpants, woollen socks, long Air Force trousers and shirt, and over the top a summer flying suit and fleecy wool lined flying boots.

My companions were not so well dressed for the occasion. Being from the southern states, and more used to the cold weather, they were wearing overalls over ordinary day clothes. Of course they had not been expecting the bitter conditions suddenly thrust upon us, and were at risk with the night coming on.

We had saved one parachute and taken it aboard the dinghy. As night started to approach and conditions became freezing, we opened it and tore it up into pieces. The other three wrapped these around themselves, to try and get some warmth and protection from the elements. It did help a little, but it was still dreadfully cold.

By 4. 30 p.m. night started to close in, and we lost contact with the aircraft flying overhead. The sea was still very rough. We had to continually bail out water, because of the spray driven in with each large wave.

There was no room to move about in the dinghy, which was about ten feet (or three metres) in diameter. With four men sitting down, feet outstretched and overlapping each other, it was rather uncomfortable. We had to sit in that one position until finally rescued. We were also afraid that if we did move very much, a hole might be torn in the rubber. We had a repair outfit for this, and before night set in went through the instructions for mending the dinghy in case it sprang a leak.

Some distress flares were available in the dinghy, and we worked out how to use them (which was not difficult). Night had come, and aircraft could be heard at different times flying overhead. A sea anchor was played out and this no doubt stopped us from drifting too far, but nevertheless the fierce wind was pushing us away from the aircraft flying overhead.

To mark our position, my three crew mates decided we should light the flares to guide the aircraft overhead. I was against this action, as I considered it important to keep the flares to alert any surface craft of our position. However, I was outvoted, and the decision made to fire the flares to guide the planes back.

We had been in the rubber dinghy about five hours. Just on 8.00 p.m., we thought we heard the engines of a boat some distance away. We started shouting at the top of our voices, and then were sure we heard a motor start. We knew that they could not hear us with the wind, and also above the sound of their motor, so preserved our voices until we heard them again.

It must have been twenty minutes later when the motor was heard to come within about a hundred yards, and then stop. We gave a loud and long concentrated hail. This happened four or five times — but unfortunately we did not have any torches or any other light to guide them to us. I couldn't help but think (though it would not do any good to say it) how helpful it would have been to have had a flare at that stage.

Just after 9 p.m. the launch came very near to us — within about twenty yards. We could not see it, the night was so dark with no moon, but we sensed by hearing the motor that it was very close. We shouted out as loudly as we could, but even then they nearly pulled away, and were not sure of our position. Suddenly one of the crewmen shone a torch on us, shouting "There they are" — and the boat drifted down on to us.

We threw the rope line from the dinghy, and the four of us climbed aboard, to our tremendous relief. The crew then pulled the dinghy itself aboard. We had ditched the aircraft at 1.30, and it was over eight hours later that we we taken aboard the launch — the "Lily G.''. We had spent about one and a half hours on the wing of the plane, and six and a half hours in the rubber dinghy. We were very fortunate that they found us — it was just fate, and it would have been daylight before there was any further real chance of being located.

Jack Gray was the owner and skipper of the fishing launch, the "Lily G.'', named after his wife. On board with him were his two sons, and two residents from Lakes Entrance, H. Broome and V. Carstairs. On the way back, I stayed in the deckhouse on top with Jack Gray. Although wet, I did not feel the cold with the woollen clothing I had on. The other three were chilled to the bone, and were taken down below, given plenty of blankets, and placed alongside the engines to try and warm up.

There was no radio on board, and so a message could not be sent to shore. Starting back towards Lakes Entrance, we could see aircraft circling the area well out to sea from where we had been picked up. They continued to do so until after midnight when we arrived back at the Entrance, and word was sent to the station that we had been rescued.

With the wind behind us and following seas, we had a good run back to Lakes Entrance, arriving at the bar about 11.30 p.m. Because of the low tide and the very large seas, Jack thought that taking the launch over the bar was far too dangerous, and considered it safer to wait until daybreak.

The other crew members thought that the three airmen down below were in quite a bad way from the cold, and wanted to make the shore as soon as possible. I was asked my opinion, and went down to have a look at the other three, but considered that the decision must be left to the skipper, Jack Gray.

For more than half an hour, the fishing boat moved back and forth outside the entrance, with Jack not being able to make up his mind just what to do. He still thought it was too dangerous attempting to take the boat over the bar entrance. However, just after midnight he eventually decided to give it a go. He informed the crew, and called on his son to give him full throttle when called upon.

I remained up in the wheel house observing the drama. He moved up and down outside the bar for about ten more minutes, waiting for a suitable wave. Suddenly he turned the boat and called for full throttle. The boat rode the wave well, but suddenly the wave passed by and we lost it. The "Lily G" hit bottom, going almost side on, and the boat got a dangerous list, sitting on the entrance floor. Suddenly, as if by providence, a small wave appeared, lifting us off the bottom, and we rode it over into deep water.

Many years later I called to see Jack. He told me that in all his years of fishing and boating, that was the closest shave he had ever experienced. He added that if that small wave had not appeared, the boat must have capsized, and in that cold water not one of us would have survived.

IN RETROSPECT

30th May, 1944 is a day standing out in my memory, which I can never forget.

Being part of the crew in the Avro Anson stationed at Bairnsdale, in Eastern Victoria, Australia.

Ditching in the sea during the middle of winter in Bass Strait, and then taking to a rubber dinghy.

Standing on the wing of the plane for one and a half hours, and then spending six and a half hours in the rubber dinghy.

Being rescued by a fishing boat, skippered by Jack Gray, and crossing the bar entrance at night time in rough seas, hitting the bottom of the entrance bar.

What a lucky experience — SECOND TIME LUCKY!

* * *

As soon as we arrived at the jetty, word was immediately sent on to the Station. Within fifteen minutes the C.O. and the Doc appeared on the scene. In the meantime some kind ladies gave us sandwiches and coffee.

We made one small stop on the way back from Lakes Entrance. The Doc asked the C.O. to pull up as he had some medicine — a flask of coffee with a good stiff dash of rum. That was good, but when the other three men in the rear seat refused, Doc told the C.O. to really get moving, as they were suffering from the cold and needed urgent attention.

We made good time back to Bairnsdale, a distance of about eighteen miles. The three others were immediately put into hospital, suffering from extreme exposure. The Doc wanted me to go into hospital also, but I preferred to go to my own room after a good stiff scotch. I had a couple of decent nips, and hit the hay at about 2 a.m.

There had been a chapter of accidents at the station following the news that we had been located in the rubber dinghy. An ambulance van was ordered to proceed down to Lakes Entrance to be available if we were eventually picked up. It was a cold wet day, and the driver of the van skidded off the road down an incline, finishing up in hospital. His assistant was unhurt, but the van badly damaged.

Upon this news being received back at the station, another smaller ambulance van was prepared. It also got into trouble, running into a cow that happened to be on the road. Nobody was hurt in this instance, but the van was extensively damaged. This was why the C.O. and the Doc decided they would personally come down to Lakes Entrance in the C.O.'s own staff car.

The following morning I stayed in bed till about 11, and then walked to the hospital and saw the Doc. He asked me how I was, and I told him I was fit — fit enough to play football in the afternoon. He forbade me to play, but I pointed out I was captain of the team and we were playing against Sale. He then said he would come down to the match, and keep an eye on me. What he didn't tell me was that he was bringing a hospital van down as well.

The football match started off in good swing, and after five minutes I got the ball, saw a gap and made for it. The gap suddenly closed, and the next thing I knew I was on the sideline with the Doc leaning over me. I was driven to the hospital, and although I complained, he gave me a needle that really knocked me out. He allowed me out of the hospital the following afternoon.

The papers and the radio had the story of the ditching, and it went around the country very quickly. ''Dramatic Rescue of Air Crew'' was the heading in one of the Melbourne papers. People in Cairns heard about it, and let my parents and wife know about it before I had the opportunity of getting in touch with them to say I was all right.

The Chief Ground Instructor was appointed chairman of the Committee of Enquiry, at which I gave evidence. As soon as I had given my version, I was told to go home on leave for at least a fortnight, which was most welcome. S/Ldr. Murphy was piloting a plane to Sydney on 12th June, and I took advantage of an offer to travel with him to Mascot. (He later became the C.O. of 12 Squadron on Liberators, and we were to be together later on with that Squadron.)

On returning to Bairnsdale, I made an application to England to become a member of the Goldfish Club, which was duly accepted. I was issued with a badge, which I could wear, if I wished, and also a certificate which stated:-

This is to Certify that

P/O J.K. Woodward

has qualified as a member of the Goldfish Club by escaping death by the use of his Emergency Dinghy on 30th May, 1944. and signed by C. D. PETITH

The badge shows a goldfish with a flying wing attached.

Referring to the ditching in Bass Strait, the following news item appeared in the Sun newspaper in Melbourne on the 1st September, 1944.

"On the 31st August, 1944, John Gerald Gray, his two sons Norman Gray and Graeme Gray, Victor Keith Carstairs and Harold Broome received Royal Humane Society Awards at Government House, Melbourne. All received the Bronze Medal, except Vic Carstairs, who already held a Bronze Medal, and he was presented with a Bar to his previous award. The citation was for risking their lives in rescuing four airmen from drowning off the Ninety Mile Beach."

A photograph of the five recipients accompanied the article.

After three weeks leave, I returned to Bairnsdale, feeling reasonably well after the ordeal in Bass Strait. Shortly after my return, we were talking in the officers' mess one night with a couple of chaps from Sale. The conversation was more or less of a general nature, when mention was made of the crash of an Airspeed Oxford on the Bairnsdale drome the previous year, with the loss of all occupants.

It was a great blow to hear that Clicker Clarke had been one of the crew. Clicker had been with me in Malaya, and was in the same crew at P2 in Sumatra and on our fateful flight to Java.

This probably helped prompt my decision to apply for a posting to the north, where I could join a squadron. It was quite obvious that the Japanese could not continue for too long, with the war swinging in our favour; conditions had changed so much from those existing two years previously. I was always keen to get back to the front some time or other and retaliate, returning some of the treatment meted out to us in Malaya, Singapore and Java.

I had a talk with the C.O. and expressed my wish to join an operational squadron, and get back to the front. He was quite sympathetic and promised that he would do his best.

In due course I received notice to report to Bradfield Park in Sydney. From that point I would receive further orders. I was given the impression that the aircraft I would be posted to could be Liberators. I was quite pleased at that, although I did not know too much about these aircraft.

Before leaving Bairnsdale, I had a final successful fling at rowing. A regatta was organised for the 30th September, 1944, on the Mitchell

River at Bairnsdale. Four weeks before the regatta, we were in the doldrums for a crew, and I had to go stroke. That was not at all promising.

However, we suddenly received two good rowers amongst our new postings; one had been stroke for a club in Tasmania, and the other preferred two position. I immediately switched to seven, my favoured side, and we immediately clicked into a good crew. Regatta day came; we won our heat against Sale A.G.S., and then defeated Sale O.T.U. by over three lengths. That was a fitting finale to my stay in Bairnsdale.

I left on the 2nd October, 1944 and travelled to Bradfield Park Embarkation Depot. They had received notice of my posting, to report to Townsville by 16th October. I was given rail warrants, but decided to go out to Mascot aerodrome. I was able to find a lift in a Lockheed Electra to Townsville, and then another by D.C.3 to Cairns, so I was home by night time on the 3rd October. This gave me thirteen days leave before having to report to Townsville.

I was always fortunate in obtaining lifts in aircraft from place to place. When given leave, the time of travel by rail was always taken into account and added to the leave. Rail warrants were issued for this purpose. It was not difficult to find out from operations room if any aircraft were going north or south, and an approach to the pilot was always successful if he had any spare room. Occasionally the ride was a little uncomfortable, but that did not matter very much.

And so I reported to Townsville on 16th October, after a good spell home in Cairns.

"LILY G"

The fishing boat (without its sails) which rescued us from the seas.

News of the rescue from Melbourne papers.

FORCED DOWN INTO SEA

Airmen Rescued From Dinghy

LAKES ENTRANCE, Wednesday.—Four members of the R.A.A.F. had to take to a rubber dinghy after their plane had been forced to come down in the sea 18 miles off Lakes Entrance about 2 p.m. yesterday. All are safe.

Air-Observer Corps officials were notified of the forced landing, and a motor launch operated by the R.A.A.F. Air Sea Rescue Service, and with Mr. J. Gray and his two young sons, and Messrs. H. Broom and V. Carstairs aboard set out to search for the airmen about 4 p.m. The bar was very rough, and the sea choppy, and it was not until 8.30 p.m., after a rough trip, that the launch found the dinghy. The position of the dinghy was marked by parachute and float flares dropped by a search plane. Half an hour later the airmen were taken aboard the launch wet and cold, and suffering from exposure. The return trip was made in about three hours. The bar was safely negotiated again, although a big sea was running, and a landing was made at Lakes Entrance a little after midnight. The rubber dinghy was salvaged.

The rescued flyers were F.-Sgt. R. H. Stinton, Swan Marsh, near Colac (pilot); J. K. Woodward, Q'land; P.-Lt. S. H. Gowing, N.S.W., and Sgt. K. G. Horne, Warrnambool.

DRAMATIC RESCUE OF AIR CREW

18 MILES WEST OF LAKES ENTRANCE

"Lily G" Picks Up 4 Men Afloat in Rubber Dinghy.

ABOUT four p.m. on Tuesday advice was received by the V.A.O.C. at Lakes Entrance that an aeroplane had made a forced descent into the sea about eighteen miles to the westward.

Mr. Jack Gray, in his boat the "Lily G," immediately put to sea. On board with him were his two young sons, Mr. H. Broome and Cr. V. Carstairs, all experienced boatmen. The bar was very rough. This, with a choppy sea, and strong head wind made navigation of the bar very difficult. However, it was negotiated, and the "Lily G" on its mercy trip was set a westerly course.

The night was very cold and visibility was only fair. After about three hours punching into the head wind, the scene of the catastrophe was reached. Parachute flares dropped by aircraft and surface flares marked the position, which was about twelve miles off shore. After half an hour's anxious searching the rescuers were rewarded by hearing cries from the crew of the plane who had taken to their rubber dinghy. A little after nine o'clock the men, with their dinghy, were safely aboard the "Lily G." All were suffering from exposure and cold. The return journey, with a following wind was made in quick time. The bar was still bad but was safely negotiated and a landing was made at about midnight at Lakes Entrance.

The rescued men were practically unhurt. Members of the rescue party were naturally very pleased at the successful outcome of their arduous journey.

It was indeed fortunate that Mr Gray and his companions were available when the SOS was received.

The rescued men were:—
P/O. J. K. WOODWARD (Cairns).
F/Sgt. R. H. STINTON, Swan Marsh, via Colac (pilot).
F/Lt. S. H. GOWING, Willowtree (N.S.W.)
Sgt. K. G. HORNE   Warrnambool

THIS IS TO CERTIFY THAT GOES HERE.

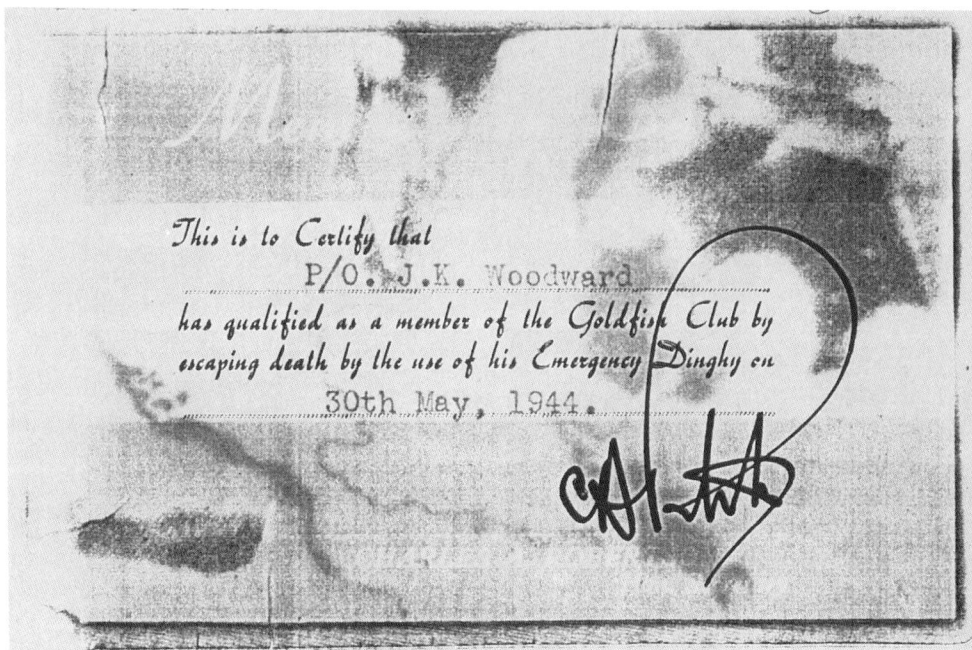

This is to Certify that
P/O. J.K. Woodward
has qualified as a member of the Goldfish Club by
escaping death by the use of his Emergency Dinghy on
30th May, 1944.

R.A.A.F   BEAUFORT

Regatta

HENLEY COURSE

Saturday, 11th March, 1944

SOUVENIR
PROGRAMME

6ᴰ

*Under the auspices of
The Victorian Rowing
Association and by kind
permission of the Metro-
politan Board of Works*

ORGANIZED BY THE EMPLOYEES OF BEAUFORT DIVISION.

Highlights of Beaufort

- Australian Beaufort Torpedo Bombers are playing a vital role in the defence of Australia, and have scored many successes against enemy warships and supply ships with bombs and torpedoes, as well as performing useful wide range reconnaissance work.
- The Beaufort Division operates as a separate entity within the Department of Aircraft Production.
- Starting from an empty office in September, 1939, the organisation produced the first Australian Torpedo Bomber in July, 1941, and reached large scale production in 1942.
- Extensive work in the development of substitutes for materials and parts in short supply, such as rubber, ball bearings, aircraft metals, timber, etc., has been carried out.
- Eighteen Stores, widely dispersed in Victoria, New South Wales and South Australia are required for the storage of Beaufort parts and components.
- The total number of prints of engineering drawings made since the commencement of operations is approximately 1,600,000, issued at the rate of 15,000 prints per week.
- In its administrative offices and six Plants, the Beaufort Division employs over 10,000 persons, apart from thousands of persons employed by contractors. Of total staffs, approximately 35 per cent comprise women.
- Women are employed not only on office staffs, but also in the production plants as riveters, welders, machine operators, bench workers, assemblers, viewers, storeswomen, stock chasers, laboratory assistants, etc.

OFFICIALS:

(By kind permission of the Victorian Rowing Association)

Starter—Mr. K. MACKINTOSH	
Judges	{ Mr. H. T. JAMES
	{ Mr. E. KENNY
Umpires	{ Mr. S. C. STEWART
	{ Mr. W. E. O'BRIEN
Despatch Steward—Mr. W. G. SCATES	
Clerk of Scales—Mr. J. P. RORKE	

ROWING COMMITTEE:

Chairman - J. MULCAHY
Secretary - J. BLAIR-HOLT

COMMITTEEMEN:
E. KERBY
J. CRAWFORD
K. GRANT

COLOURS:

No. 1 O.T.U. EAST SALE	White with red heart
G.R.S. BAIRNSDALE	Light blue
No. 4 R.A.A.F. HOSPITAL	White with red 4
LAVERTON	White with royal blue bands
7 A.D. TOCUMWAL	White with R.A.A.F. Target
BEAUFORT DIVISION	Green

PRESENTATION OF CHALLENGE SHIELD

Donated by Mr. John Storey, Director, Beaufort Division.

To be presented to the unit obtaining the greatest number of points.
4.45 p.m. at Melbourne Boat Shed.

HIGHLIGHTS OF BEAUFORT—(Continued).

- Special measures have been adopted to provide for the welfare of employees, including up-to-date safety devices, internal heating, casualty wards and canteens.
- A Beaufort Squadrons Adoption Fund, financed by voluntary subscriptions, enables the men and women who build Beauforts to care for the needs of R.A.A.F. personnel in Beaufort Operational and Instructional Squadrons.
- In addition to completed aircraft, the Division produces Spare Parts for the servicing of aircraft delivered to the R.A.A.F. in the proportion of one complete aircraft set of Spares for every five production aircraft.
- The Beaufort Division directly controls six large plants in Victoria, New South Wales and South Australia.
- Two Main Assembly Plants - one in Victoria and one in New South Wales - produce completed aircraft from major components assembled by the Area Workshops.
- The Three Area Workshops are annexes to the Railway Workshops in Victoria, New South Wales and South Australia, and were established to produce major components.
- Gun Turrets are produced by the Gun Turret Plant, which is a department of the Beaufort Division.
- Certain important equipment, such as engines and propellors, are supplied by special plants operating as Government annexes, but mostly under the management of private enterprise.
- Thousands of other items of equipment, not hitherto produced in Australia, are now available from hundreds of public and private companies which have turned over their plants to aircraft work.

☞ PROGRAMME ☜

HEATS

NOVICE FOURS

1st Heat—2.30 p.m.

NORTH	CENTRE	SOUTH
7 A.D. TOCUMWAL	**No. 4 R.A.A.F. HOSPITAL**	**G.R.S. BAIRNSDALE**
Stk.—Sgt. Westercott 11st 12lb	W/O. Batcheler 12st 0lb	L.A.C. West 11st 0lb
3 —L.A.C. Pascoe 11., 5.,	F/O. Kelly 11., 2.,	F/Lt. Nicol 14., 0.,
2 —L.A.C. Wright 12., 7.,	F/Sgt. Duncan 11., 7.,	S/Ldr.Burgess 12., 6.,
Bow—F/Sgt. Low 12., 4.,		L.A.C. Corbin 11., 6.,
Cox—		

2nd Heat—2.35 p.m.

NORTH	CENTRE	
BEAUFORT DIVISION	**No. 1 O.T.U. EAST SALE**	
Stk.—M. West 12st 0lb	F/Lt Pearse 11st 0lb	
3 —E. Ekstrom 12., 7.,	F/Lt. Noble 12., 0.,	
2 —L. Comer 12., 0.,	L.A.C. Kelly 12., 0.,	
Bow—S. Toll 12., 0.,	L.A.C. Kilpatrick 11., 0.,	
Cox—C. Frost		

NOVICE PAIRS

1st Heat—2.50 p.m.

NORTH	CENTRE	SOUTH
G.R.S. BAIRNSDALE	**No. 1 O.T.U. EAST SALE**	**No. 4 R.A.A.F. HOSPITAL**
Stk.—F/Lt. Lohan 12st 0lb	F/Lt. Corri 13st 4lb	W/Off. Batcheler 12st 3lb
Bow—F/Lt. Howard 13., 0.,	F/Off. Watt 12., 0.,	F/Sgt. Gadd 9., 0.,
Cox—		

2nd Heat—2.55 p.m.

NORTH	CENTRE	
7 A.D. TOCUMWAL	**BEAUFORT DIVISION**	
Stk.—W/Cdr. Connolly 12st 12lb	E. Tilley 12st 5lb	
Bow—Cpl. Corkhill 12., 12.,	J. Leathom 11., 10.,	
	H. O'Donnell	

OPEN FOURS

1st Heat—3 p.m.

NORTH	CENTRE	SOUTH
LAVERTON	**7 A.D. TOCUMWAL**	**BEAUFORT DIVISION**
Stk.—P/Off. Mackie 10st 0lb	F/Sgt. Tomlinson 12st 2lb	N. Wallace 10st 6lb
3 —P/Off. Keddie 13., 0.,	Sgt. Price 12., 4.,	F/Off. Oldfield 11., 7.,
2 —F/Sgt. Leach 12., 7.,	W/Off. Heterick 12., 13.,	T. Westall 11., 4.,
Bow—F/Off. Woke 10., 10.,	L.A.C. Arnott 11., 8.,	R. Dawson 10., 8.,
Cox—		C. Frost

2nd Heat—3.5 p.m.

NORTH	CENTRE	
No. 1 O.T.U. EAST SALE	**G.R.S. BAIRNSDALE**	
Stk.—S/Ldr. Clarke 12st 7lb	Sgt. Sears 11st 0lb	
3 —F/Lt. Wood 13., 0.,	L.A.C. Summers 10., 7.,	
2 —F/Off. Barraclough 12., 10.,	P/Off. Theelis 10., 7.,	
Bow—Sgt. Hawkes 12., 0.,	F/Sgt. Hanson 10., 4.,	
Cox—L.A.C. Lillicrapp		

FINALS

OPEN EIGHTS

Final—3.45 p.m.

NORTH	CENTRE	SOUTH
G.R.S. BAIRNSDALE	**No. 1 O.T.U. EAST SALE**	**BEAUFORT DIVISION**
Stk.—F/Off. Freeth 12st 4lb	F/Lt. Carrol 12st 7lb	K. Grant 12st 2lb
7 —F/O.Shakespean 13., 2.,	F/Lt. Dobson 7., 2.,	J. Mulcahy 13., 4.,
6 —F/Off. Fortes 14., 0.,	P/Off. Tabe 14., 0.,	E. T. J. Kerby 11., 8.,
5 —F/Off. Gallie 12., 3.,	F/Sgt. Darval 12., 10.,	J. Crawford 13., 0.,
4 —Cpl. Goodall 12., 10.,	W/Off. Lake 11., 0.,	J. Blair-Holt 10., 3.,
3 —F/Sgt. Hassell 11., 4.,	L.A.C. Rankin 12., 0.,	J. Robertson 10., 3.,
2 —W/Com. Kingwell 11., 0.,	S/Ldr. Block 11., 5.,	J. Picone 10., 8.,
Bow—P/Off. Woodward 11., 4.,	Cpl. Zihful 10., 7.,	F. Jessott 10., 7.,
Cox—P/Off. Twiddy		C. Frost

OPEN FOURS

Final—3.55 p.m.

NORTH	CENTRE
Winner of First Heat	Winner of Second Heat.

W.A.A.A.F. FOURS

4.5 p.m.

NORTH	NORTH-CENTRE	SOUTH-CENTRE	SOUTH
No. 1 O.T.U. EAST SALE	**G.R.S. BAIRNSDALE**	**No. 4 RAAF HOSPITAL**	**7 A.D. TOCUMWAL**
Stk.—A.C.W. Stockwell	A.C.W. Bottrill	Sister Scholz	Cpl. Stebbing
3 —A.C.W. Fraser	Cpl. Tuck	S/Sister Doherty	A.C.W. Gant
2 —Cpl. Johns	Sgt. McDonald	S/Off. Bremner	A.C.W. Buckley
Bow—A.C.W. Dodd	A.C.W. Palmer	L/Bdr. Brownless	Cpl. Clysdale
Cox—	P/Off. Twiddy		

NOVICE FOURS

Final—4.15 p.m.

NORTH	CENTRE
Winner of First Heat.	Winner of Second Heat.

SCULLS

4.25 p.m.

NORTH	NORTH-CENTRE	SOUTH-CENTRE	SOUTH
BEAUFORT DIVISION	**No. 1 O.T.U. EAST SALE**	**G.R.S. BAIRNSDALE**	**7 A.D. TOCUMWAL**
E. T. J. Kerby 11st 8lb	Cpl. Swarbrick 13st	F/Lt. Patterson 12st 6lb	L.A.C. Stone 12st 2lb

NOVICE PAIRS

Final—4.30 p.m.

NORTH	CENTRE
Winner of First Heat.	Winner of Second Heat.

2.55 p.m.—

INTER-UNIT W.A.A.A.F. FOURS

Second Heat.

East.—4 R.A.A.F. HOSPITAL.

(White with Red Cross).

Sister P. Scholz (st.).
Sister R. Perger.
Sister J. Rayner.
Sister C. Ryan.
F/Lt. R. Martin (cox).

West.—A.G.S.

Cpl. D. Harding (st.)
A.C.W. A. Parker.
Cpl. M. Dick.
A.C.W. P. Blacknall (bow).

3.05 p.m.—

INTER-UNIT OPEN PAIRS

440 YARDS.   FIRST HEAT

East.—D.A.P.

R. Corser (st.).
T. Westell (bow).
J. Frost (cox).

West.—A.G.S.

Sgt. E. Innes (st.).
W/O. H. Oliver (bow).
L.A.C. K. Fraser (cox).

3.15 p.m.—

INTER-UNIT No. 1 FOURS.

880 Yards.—First Heat.

East.—BEAUFORT DIVISION D.A.P.

R. Hine (st.).
M. West.
E. Tilley.
S. Toll (bow).
J. Frost (cox).

West.—No. 1 O.T.U.

F/O. J. Tennant (st.).
F/Lt. C. McDona'd.
F/Lt. J. Lemcke.
F/Lt. R. Kelly (bow).
W/O. B. Hudson (cox).

3.20 p.m.—

INTER-UNIT OPEN PAIRS

Second Heat.

East.—G.R.S.

L.A.C. Temple-Smith (st.)
F/O. M. Dewar (bow).
A.C.2. Lukins (cox).

West.—No. 1 O.T.U.

F/O. R. Wilmott (st.).
F/Lt. C. Walch (bow).
F/Lt. R. Martin (cox).

3.30 p.m.—

INTER-UNIT No. 1 FOURS.

Second Heat.

East.—G.R.S.

F/O. A. Craze (st.).
F/S. P. Wheeler.
F/S. M. Walker.
F/O. Murray-Prior (bow).
A.C.2 Lukins (cox).

West.—A.G.S.

L.A.C. L. Orbel (st.).
L.A.C. J. Wilson.
L.A.C. R. Wilson.
Cpl. F. Chapman (bow).
L.A.C. K. Fraser (cox).

AFTERNOON TEA

3.50 p.m.—

FINAL EIGHTS DAHLSEN SHIELD.

East.—Winners First Heat v. Winners
Second Heat (West).

O.T.U. 2
G.R.S 1

4.00 p.m.—

FINAL NO. 2 FOURS.

East.—Winners First Heat v. Winners
Second Heat (West).

O.T.U 2
G.R.S 1

4.10 p.m.—

FINAL W.A.A.A.F. PAIRS.

East.—Winners First Heat v. Winners
Second Heat (West).

G.R.S. 3
A.C.S 1
4. RAAF. 2

4.25 p.m.—

FINAL No. 1 FOURS.

East.—Winners First Heat v. Winners
Second Heat (West).

O.T.U 1
G.R.S. 2

4.35 p.m.—

FINAL OPEN PAIRS.

East.—Winners First Heat v. Winners
Second Heat (West).

O.T.U. 2
A.G.S. 1

4.45 p.m.—

FINAL—W.A.A.A.F. FOURS.

East.—Winners First Heat v. Winners
Second Heat (West).

G.R.S 1
4. RAAF HOSP. 2

5.00 p.m.—

PRESENTATION OF SHIELDS
(Near Judge's Stand).

R.A.A.F. ROWING REGATTA

ON THE

Mitchell River BAIRNSDALE

SATURDAY, SEPTEMBER 30
1944

President:
GROUP CAPTAIN J. P. RYLAND
D.F.C.

Secretary:
F/O. R. C. BLUNDSTONE

Committee:
P./L. Chaplain P. Wood, F./L. C. Mc-
Donald, F./L. A. Dobson, L.A.C. R.
Rankin, A.C.W. A. Stockwell

Judges:
W./C. T. McBRIDE PRICE D.F.C.
W./C. J. HEPBURN D.F.C., A.F.C.
S./L. DALKIN, D.F.C.

Starter:
MR. J. L. LANFRANCHI

Umpire:
MR. A. O. YEATES

Commentator:
MR. RAY TODD

Marshalling Officers:
S./L. GEOFF JONES, F./L. RON
PEARSE

PROGRAMME 6d

THE DAHLSEN SHIELD—
is for a series of Six Challenge
Races by eight-oared crews from
R.A.A.F. establishments in Gippsland
and the Beaufort Division of the
Department of Aircraft Production.

THE GIPPSLAND SHIELD
is for competition among the Units
on a points basis—2 points are awarded to each oar for a win, 1 point for
a second. This applies to finals only.

Starting   Starting
Position   Position

1.   1.45 p.m.
     FIRST HEAT SECOND FOURS
East   D.A.P. y G.R.S.   West
Bank   Bank

2.   1.55 p.m.
     FIRST HEAT W.A.A.A.F. PAIRS
         4 R.A.A.F v A.G.S.

3.   2.05 p.m.
     SECOND HEAT SECOND FOURS
       1 O.T.U. v. A.G.S.

4.   2.15 p.m.
     SECOND HEAT W.A.A.A.F. PAIRS
       G.R.S. v. D.A.P.

5.   2.25 p.m.
     DAHLSEN SHIELD EIGHTS
        FIRST HEAT:
       D.A.P. v. 1 O.T.U.

6.   2.35 p.m.
     FIRST HEAT W.A.A.A.F. FOURS
       D.A.P. v. G.R.S.

7.   2.45 p.m.
     DAHLSEN SHIELD EIGHTS
        SECOND HEAT
       G.R.S. v. A.G.S.

8.   2.55 p.m.
     SECOND HEAT W.A.A.A.F. FOURS
       4 R.A.A.F. v A.G.S.

9.   3.05 p.m.
     FIRST HEAT OPEN PAIRS
       D.A.P. v A.G.S.

10.   3.15 p.m.
     FIRST HEAT FIRST FOURS
       D.A.P. v 1 O.T.U.

11.   3.20 p.m.
     SECOND HEAT OPEN PAIRS
       G.R.S. v 1 O.T.U.

12.   3.30 p.m.
     SECOND HEAT FIRST FOURS
       G.R.S. v. A.G.S.
       AFTERNOON TEA

13.   3.50 p.m.
     FINAL EIGHTS DAHLSEN
        SHIELD
East Bank—Winners First Heat.
West Bank—Winners Second Heat

14.   4.00 p.m.
     FINAL SECOND FOURS
Winners Firs Heat v. Winners
       Second Heat

15.   4.10 p.m.
     FINAL W.A.A.A.F. PAIRS
Winners 1st Heat v Winners
       2nd Heat

16.   4.25 p.m.
     FINAL FIRST FOURS
Winners 1st Heat v Winners
       2nd Heat

17.   4.35 p.m.
     FINAL OPEN PAIRS
Winners 1st Heat v Winners
       2nd Heat

18.   4.45 p.m.
     FINAL W.A.A.A.F. FOURS
Winners 1st Heat v Winners
       2nd Heat

    5.00 p.m.
     PRESENTATION OF SHIELDS
       Near Judges' Stand

—— PROGRAMME (CONT'D)

Start 1.45 p.m. —

INTER-UNIT NO. 2 FOURS.
       880 Yards.

        First Heat.

East.—BEAUFORT DIVISION, D.A.P.

     P. Green (st.)
     H. Sloane.
     K. Thomson
     G. Rogo.
     J. Frost (cox).

      West.—G.R.S.

     F/Lt. K. Thompson (st.)
     F/Lt. D. Wilson.
     F/Lt. T. Meldrum.
     F/O. W. Hamilton.
     F/O. K. Twiddy (cox).

Start 1.55 p.m.—

INTER-UNIT W.A.A.A.F. PAIRS.

      First Heat.

East.—4 R.A.A.F. HOSPITAL.

     Sister P. R. Scholz (st.).
     Sister C. Ryan (bow).
     Sgt. K. Corry (cox).

      West.—A.G.S.

     Cpl. Harding (st.).
     A.C.W. Blackhall (bow).
     Cpl. R. Wes.ward (cox).

Start 2.05 p.m.—

INTER-UNIT NO. 2 FOURS.

      Second Heat.

East.—No. 1 O.T.U.

     F/O. G. Downie (st.)
     L.A.C. M. Hodson.
     F/O. J. Wylie.
     F/O. J. Legge.

      West.—A.G.S.

     F/S. J. Dyall (st.).
     L.A.C. J. Giles.
     L.A.C. B. Chirlain.
     L.A.C. L. Prosser (bow).
     A.C.1. T. Wight (cox).

2.15 p.m.—

INTER-UNIT W.A.A.A.F. PAIRS.

      Second Heat.

East.—BEAUFORT DIVISION D.A.P.

     L. Bailey (st.).
     N. Collins.
     J. Frost (cox).

      West.—G.R.S.

     A.C.W. J. White (st.).
     A.C.W. M. Blythe (bow).
     F/O. K. Twiddy (cox).

"Bairnsdale Advertiser" Print.

2.25 p.m.—

INTER-UNIT EIGHTS—DAHLSEN
        SHIELD.
       1500 yards.
(Present Holders No. 1 O.T.U.).

EAST BEAUFORT DIV. D.A.P.
        (Green).

     R. Grant (st.).
     F. Oldfield.
     J. Mulchay.
     J. Crawford.
     R. Dawson.
     V. Rogers.
     T. Westall.
     I. Robertson (bow)
     J. Frost (cox).

      West.—No. 1 O.T.U.
    (White with Red Heart).

     F/Lt. A. Dobson (st.).
     F/O. R. Blundstone.
     Sgt. H. Porte.
     F/Lt. D. Paramor.
     F/Lt. J. Dennett.
     L.A.C. R. Rankin.
     Cpl. T. Swarbrick
     W/O. J. Donoghoe (bow).
     F/Lt. R. Martin (cox).

2.35 p.m.—

INTER-UNIT W.A.A.A.F. FOURS.
       440 Yards.

East.—BEAUFORT DIVISION D.A.P.

     J. Hill (st.).
     D. Knowles.
     K. Powell.
     S. Sutton.

      West.—G.R.S.

     A.C.W. R. Bottrell (st.).
     A.C.W. K. O'Connor.
     Sgt. B. Lowe.
     A.C.W. A. Coe.

2.45 p.m.—

INTER-UNIT EIGHTS

      Second Heat.

East.—G.R.S. (Light Blue).

     F/Lt. N. Powell (st.).
     F/O. J. Woodward.
     F/O. C. Bright.
     F/O. R. Baillieu.
     Cpl. J. Goodall.
     Sgt. F. Penny.
     F/Lt. R. Neville.
     F/S. R. Hassall (bow).
     A.C.2. Lukins (cox).

    West.—A.G.S. (White and Blue).

     W/O. R. Batchelor (st.).
     L.A.C. J. Berry.
     Cpl. A. Smith.
     A.C.1. S. Sullivan.
     L.A.C. S. Moore
     Sgt. J. Crofts.
     F/Lt. J. Bartley.
     Sgt. J. Stewart (bow).
     Cpl. R. Westward (cox).

G.R.S. ROWING CREW REGATTA 8/4/1944
Stroke — P/O Woodward; 7. — F/O Cooper; 6. — Cpl Goodall; 5. — P/O Bailleau; 4. — W/Cdr Green; 3. — F/O Gawler; 2. — S/Ldr Burgess; Bow — F/Sgt Hassell; Cox — A.C.2 Luckins.

EAST SALE DEFEATING G.R.S.

Nadzab - New Guinea

Liberator Conversion - United States Air Force

Reporting to Townsville R.A.A.F. Transit Depot on the 16th October, 1944, I was not a bit surprised to be informed that they knew nothing about aircrews assembling for conversion training for Liberator aircraft. There were several others like myself; we were ultimately told we should have reported to Amberley Station, outside Ipswich.

Accordingly, late afternoon, we were assembled and transported by United States Air Force D.C.3 to Amberley, arriving at night after a four and a half hour flight. There we received the same treatment as at Townsville — they knew nothing about us.

We tried to sort things out next day, but were then told that the station at Maryborough (200 miles away) knew all about our postings. This did not make sense, as it was a training station, but we made our way by rail to that centre. At least they went to the trouble of finding out where we should report — that was to Townsville on the 5th December. In the meantime we could do what we liked, which meant some spare time in Cairns with my wife and two children.

Quite a number of us gathered in Townsville on the 5th December, 1944, and were informed that we would be moving on to Nadzab in northern New Guinea, outside Lae, for conversion training on the Liberator heavy bomber. We had all that day and the next to be together, and during that time pilots were looking round and choosing their crew members.

During my time at Bairnsdale, I had met quite a number of pilots with overseas experience doing the G.R. Course. One was Tony Martin, a flight lieutenant, who had quite extensive experience overseas, particularly in the Middle East. Tony invited me to join his crew, and I was very pleased to accept. So began an association from my air force days which lasted until our discharge over twelve months later, and which has continued to this day.

We gathered our gear the next morning and boarded a D.C.3 for the journey, calling in at Cooktown en route. At Nadzab, we met up with the other members of the course — it was quite a large contingent. Wing Commander John Handbury was the commanding officer, supervising the training unit. For our crew, Tony selected Les Walsh as his co-pilot, Joe Lake as control fire officer and occupying the upper gun turret, and John Osborne as wireless operator. I cannot recall the name of the bombardier.

On operational flights the Liberator carried a crew of eleven. However, for this conversion course, it was deemed necessary to carry only the crew leaders, and the remainder of the crew for our flights from Nadzab were made up of United States airmen.

Nadzab was located in the Markham Valley in New Guinea, inland from Lae. In 1943, when the Allied offensive gathered momentum against the Japanese, Allied paratroops landed on Nadzab and after fierce fighting captured the area which included several airstrips. From these airstrips Allied aircraft were able to operate against the enemy, and give the necessary support to the army in its thrust along the northern coast of New Guinea.

When we arrived at the end of 1944, the Japanese were being contained in isolated areas such as Wewak, and with a large force cut off in Rabaul in New Britain. Both of these places had no aircraft to support them, and relied on the occasional visit of a submarine for supplies.

The principal conversion training was for pilots, to become familiar with the new four engined aircraft. Navigators had little to do; they had to become accustomed to the aircraft itself, its radar, the use of the upper dome for astro navigation, and also the navigation facilities. The Americans treated us very well.

Our first flight as a crew was on 21st January, 1945. We had a local flight for three hours, and this was followed by a ferry flight to Hollandia and return. On the 27th we had a training flight, bombing the Isthmus of Wewak. Each plane was loaded with eight bombs of 1,000 lb. each. The exercise consisted of twelve planes flying over Wewak in formation, peeling off and following each other, and then dropping one bomb at a time from five thousand feet on the narrow isthmus of Wewak.

We were told that Japanese troops were entrenched in tunnels in this area, and that our exercise would give us good training and also hopefully give the Jap a few frights. Just over half way through the exercise, we noticed the aircraft in front of us open its doors to drop a bomb, but did not see a bomb leave the aircraft. In our circuit following the leader, we travelled inland over the base of the mountain, and closely watched the aircraft in front flying with the bomb doors open.

Suddenly a bomb came away, and the doors closed. The bomb landed in the jungle at the base of the mountain, and started a big fire — it had landed on a hidden fuel dump. On returning to base and reporting the incident, we hoped to be sent out the following day to follow up, but this was not to be. The Americans went out in force early and bombed and strafed the area, but could not locate any more dumps. I believe that the fire lasted several days.

We had another bombing exercise, flying in formation over Rabaul, only this time at 15,000 feet. The Japanese evidently had no fighters to send up to attack us, but had good anti aircraft fire. We carried out our bombing on the wharf area, and did not encounter any ack ack fire. We had a bomb release failure, so did not drop our bombs but brought them back home to base. This was the final part of our training and conversion to Liberators.

Whilst at Nadzab, we got to know the Americans quite well. They were always very generous. There was a recreation area, and part of it was measured out as a football ground. Our friends were keen to see a game of Australian football played, and we were pressed to oblige. It was decided that the officers should play against the sergeants. The next thing to decide was — what code — Australian rules or rugby? There were not enough players for a rules game, so rugby league was decided upon.

The officers team (I was made captain) did not have enough players, even with three rules players, so we took two of the sergeants to help us out. There was no grass, and the ground surface was a type of volcanic ash. Needless to say, quite a lot of skin was lost by the players in the tackles.

The Americans turned up in force to watch the game — and was there some barracking! It was estimated that there were over two thousand spectators. There was a tremendous write up in the American Army newspaper, reporting that this game that the Aussies called football made their game of gridiron look quite "sissy". They wanted a return match. We were all very pleased when our postings back to Australia came early, before a repeat match could be arranged.

About ten years later, in peace time days, I was on a sugar cane farm adjoining Cairns which sent cane to the C.S.R. mill at Hambledon. A new chief cane inspector, Alan Kirkby, had been appointed. When introduced he looked hard at me, remarking that he had seen me before. I could not place him, but each time he came to the farm, he kept saying that he had met me somewhere before.

About six months later he said to me, "I am sure that I have now recollected where our paths have crossed". He then asked me if I was at Nadzab in late 1944 doing a course on Liberators. When I said yes, his next question was — "Did you not have a game of football where you were the captain of the officers team?". I was amazed when he told me that he was the Army Captain in liaison at the course, and he was the referee of the football game. He had some photos taken by the Americans, and handed me some copies. These are included with this story.

The first week in February we left Nadzab, flying to Port Moresby. The following day Tony Martin, Les Walsh and I got a lift in a Sunderland flying boat to Cairns. By this time Vera had obtained a rented house on the Esplanade, and there was room to put Tony and Les up for a couple of days.

Then followed a period of frustration. We had three weeks leave, and afterwards were to report for duty in Sydney by the end of February. Tony lived in Sydney, and I got in touch with him, but could not get any satisfaction regarding our future posting. Most of those on the Nadzab training conversion had already been posted, some to Tocumwal, others to Dalby in Western Queensland, with the ultimate destination being 12 Squadron in Darwin.

For the next six weeks, we were stationed at Ascotvale in Melbourne, waiting for the Air Force hierarchy to decide whether we should be posted to a secret force, under the title of 201 Flight, or whether we should be posted to a squadron. By the end of April, it was finally decided that we should join 12 Squadron, based in Darwin. However, it still took until the middle of June before we eventually arrived there.

NADZAB NEW GUINEA CRTC. 13.1.45 FOOTBALL MATCH
Officers v. Sergeants

SERGEANTS   **OFFICERS**

*Jack Woodward, 2nd from right and Tony Martin, my skipper,
3rd from right.*

SCENES OF THE FOOTBALL MATCH

Liberators

12 Squadron - Darwin

After all of the frustration of the previous three months, we finally arrived in Darwin in the middle of June, 1945. Apparently the new Squadron had assembled at Dalby in Western Queensland, and the advance party travelled to Darwin in April preparing for the arrival of the main group. The flying section and the aircraft (Liberators — B 24) arrived one month later in May.

We quickly settled in, three to a tent, with Tony Martin, Les Walsh and myself being together. Our commanding officer was Squadron Leader John Murphy, who had been O.C. of flying at Bairnsdale whilst I was there.

Probably because of my association with Bairnsdale and G.R.S., it was suggested that I should be appointed the squadron navigator. However, conferring with Tony, we disagreed; by tradition, the navigator in the C.O.'s crew should hold this position. So Bob Hatch became the squadron navigator, but I offered to assist on any occasion.

The officer commanding "A" Flight was S/Ldr. Basil Brown, whilst S/Ldr. Bob Russell was O.C. "B" Flight. Our crew was assigned to "B" Flight. Within a week we were on training flights, doing practice bombing, test runs and familiarisation exercises.

The squadron had great difficulty obtaining spares, and the maintenance of aircraft was creating severe problems. This also applied to other Liberators in the area. Accordingly the North Western Area (N.W.A.) put a proposition to the Air Board for an aircraft to travel to Biak, an island to the north of New Guinea, to obtain parts from the United States Air Force.

Air Board responded, and the War Council agreed to a proposal to purchase spare parts under Lease Lend to the value of two hundred thousand pounds. This would not have purchased very much at all. However, it was a starting point.

To supplement the funds provided, the party "acquired" many cartons of various liquids to entertain the Americans with whom they might have dealings. Biak was a forward war zone area for the Americans, and, as such, was considered a 'dry area' for American troops.

NORTH-WESTERN AREA MAP

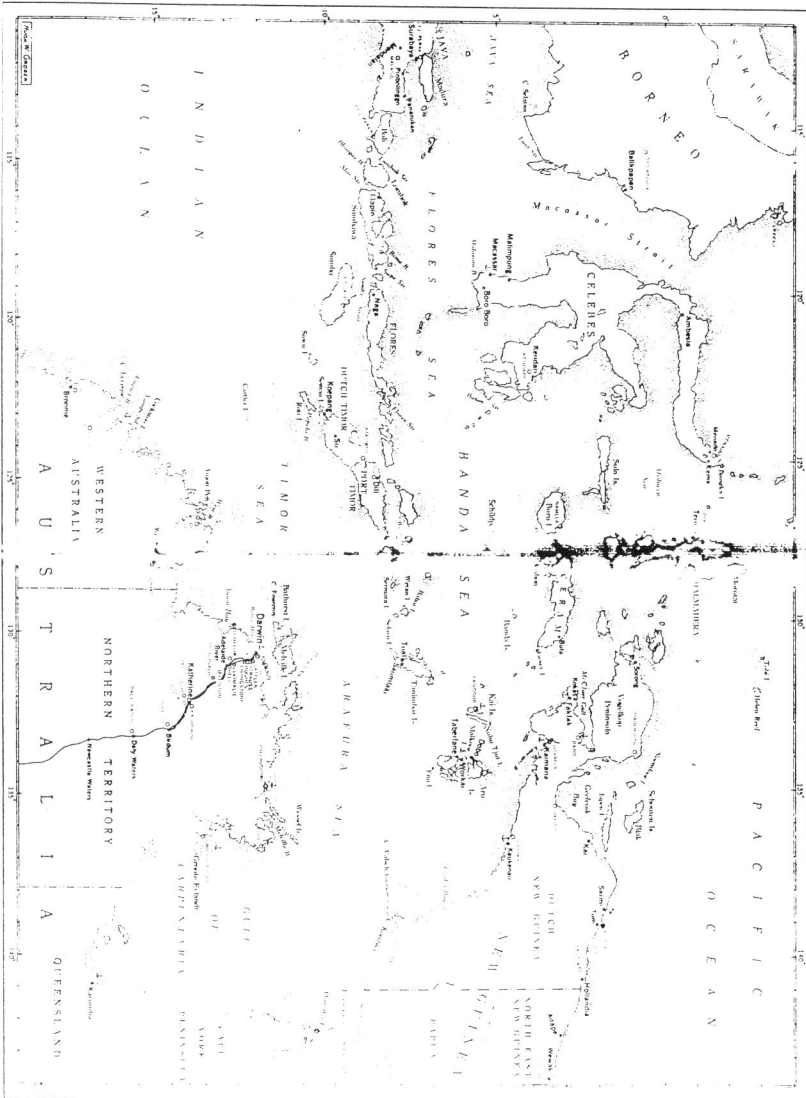

S/Ldr. Bob Russell, O.C. of our "B" Flight, was detailed to fly the aircraft from Darwin to Biak, with a selected group of officers from maintenance. As Bob's navigator was absent on leave, he asked me to take his place in the crew. It was a skeleton crew, with Bob Russell as captain, his co-pilot, myself as navigator, a wireless operator, and the aircraft engineer who was a senior officer from the North Western Area (N.W.A.). Altogether there would have been about fifteen personnel on board the aircraft.

We were to pass over enemy territory, and though the chance of being attacked was minimal, nevertheless the other members in the aircraft were instructed how to man the gun turrets.

We arrived at Biak after a five hour flight from Darwin. Much to the party's consternation, there were several R.A.A.F. service police present on the island. They had recently been stationed at Biak to check R.A.A.F. personnel returning from Morotai and places north, bringing with them items not permitted in New Guinea and Australia. This delayed discussions, until a signal to N.W.A. was put into action, temporarily transferring all the S.P.'s to Lae.

I was not in the party appointed to negotiate the deal, so was given a pass on Biak Island and provided with accommodation. I was also given permission to purchase anything I wished from the G.I. equipment store. Biak was a very large staging camp for the American Air Force; it was a surprise to see so many women on the island performing all kinds of useful operational duties.

It was also amazing to see the variety of goods in stock — so many items were just unavailable in Australia. I purchased quite a number of pairs of silk stockings for Vera, which I eventually was able to send back to her. Items like this were unobtainable at home at any price.

The Americans were most co-operative regarding parts, and were amazed when told of the shortage of spares that existed in our area. They thought that this was not good for the war effort, to which our officers could not help but agree. The number of "war weary" aircraft of all types parked on the side of the tarmac and around the field was staggering. Any aircraft, irrespective of age, which might take time to repair or even service, was liable to be placed in the category of "war weary".

One aircraft, a Liberator, had only recently been flown out from the United States. A fighter pilot, a Colonel, returning from the north saw the plane, and thought he would like to take it aloft as he had flown a Liberator on some previous occasion. He was taxi-ing it in to its parking bay after the joy ride, and made an error of judgment, with the leading edge of the wing tip touching the hangar building, putting a small dent in it. On investigation, it was considered not worth repairing as it was easier to obtain a replacement aircraft than a part, and so it was placed aside with the war weary aircraft.

Nothing had been removed from this aircraft, and our leaders tried hard to persuade them to transfer it to us, as it could have been flown to Darwin in its present condition. They hesitated and finally had to decline, because if the plane had later crashed and a U.S. investigation team found it with a U.S. number and R.A.A.F. markings, it could have created much embarrassment.

However, they did say, help yourselves to spare parts off the aircraft. We returned to Darwin after a week, leaving several of our maintenance men behind. Our plane was loaded with parts, and on our return a shuttle of D.C.3. aircraft was arranged to run from Darwin to Biak for quite some time bringing back urgent parts for our Liberators. The whole exercise was really an eye opener.

The day after I got back, Tony was scheduled on a night navigation exercise, testing out a U.S. system of Loran (Long Range Navigation). Several of our aircraft were involved, and when we returned, all deemed it a flop, fully convinced that Loran was not as reliable as our R.A.A.F. method of D.R. Navigation.

The following day, S/Ldr. Bob Russell was scheduled on a patrol towards Timor, and called on me to join his crew as navigator. Tony protested, saying that the squadron leader was not entitled to call on members of other crews if he had somebody absent. However, I was keen to go, saying that nothing would happen — it was just an ordinary patrol. Tony still protested, saying that this was the type of flight when something could happen.

The date was 30th July, and we were airborne at 5 a.m. We were to fly to the south coast of Timor, and then carry out a creeping line ahead search before heading back towards base. Our general instructions were to look out for what were known as sugar dogs — a term given to slow-moving small Japanese ships which travelled between islands, conveying stores and goods to their troops cut off from regular supply.

The Japanese at this stage of the war did not appear to have any regular warships in the area, but were relying on small ships which had been "acquired" from the native people of these islands. Apparently they felt that these had a better chance of getting through our surveillance. The terms used for small ships of this nature were "sugar able", (sugar signifying ship), a slightly smaller and slower ship called "baker", then "charlie", and the slowest and smallest "dog".

We had a good run out to the coast of Timor, and were on about our fourth leg of the search when we sighted a small ship in front of us. We immediately made a bombing run, and dropped a salvo of three bombs from 5,000 ft. However, the way this ship manoeuvred made me very suspicious. As the bombs left our aircraft, the ship immediately drastically altered course, with a speed of at least twelve knots.

R.A.A.F. Liberator of 12 Squadron.

I called the skipper and warned him that this was not a "sugar dog" — it was just too fast and could turn so quickly. We made three more bombing runs, and dropped all our bombs, with the same result. We then dropped height to 1,500 feet, and strafed the ship side on from our front, lower and rear turrets (which were equipped with .5 inch machine guns). I was staggered to see the tracers hit the ship and ricochet off. I was then convinced that this ship was constructed of steel, with some armour plating, and not the timber of the "sugar dog" variety.

After five strafing runs, during which I again warned that this was not a "sugar dog", a decision was made to go directly over the ship at 1,000 feet, firing from the front and lower guns, to be followed by the rear turret. During these earlier strafing runs, I called the engineer to bring me the camera with the intention of taking photos; he wished to take the actual photographs under my guidance. This was most important to identify the ship later, as the type was definitely unknown to us.

On our last run over the ship, when we were directly overhead and at a point where our guns could not fire, it suddenly opened fire. We were not sure of the calibre of the guns, but later the navy appraised them as being 20 mm. Their shooting was very accurate, and the aircraft was holed in both wings and the starboard tailplane, as well as through the fuselage.

With such an amount of damage, the plane almost went out of control, and the two pilots fought hard to get the aircraft back on an even keel. I immediately called on the radio operator to send out an S.O.S. with our call sign, repeat it several times and then to jam the

Damage to A72-314 STBD aileron caused by light ack while bombing small enemy vessel. — Capt. S/Ldr. R. Russell.

radio key. (I did not want a repeat of my ditching in Bass Strait). I then worked out our position, and the wireless operator again radioed base, giving our call sign, the S.O.S. and our location.

It was at least five minutes (it seemed an eternity) before the pilots were able to achieve some control over the aircraft. Speaking into the intercom, the skipper enquired if anybody had been injured. Miraculously nobody had been hit. He then informed us that the pilots now appeared to have the plane under control. The engines were on much higher revs, and the aircraft was tilted upwards trying to climb.

Normally our cruising speed was 150 to 160 m.p.h., but even with the engines on the higher revs, our present speed was about 90 m.p.h. and only just above stalling. It was impossible to gain height, and never at any stage for the balance of our journey back to base were we able to get above 1,200 feet.

S/Ldr. Russell then called base, telling them of our predicament and requesting help. In spite of the gaping holes in the wings and tail plane, the controls were responding and did not appear to have suffered any damage. Luckily, it also seemed that the attack had missed the fuel tanks. We did not appear to be losing fuel, and still had a good supply left.

We were over 400 miles from base, and the danger was whether the engines could hold out at the greater revs required to keep us airborne for that distance. The return journey would take at least four hours at the air speed we were making.

We received reassuring news from base that the Air Sea Rescue had been alerted. Two Catalina flying boats were about to take off and escort us back. If we had to ditch, they could alight on the sea and pick us up. We hoped this would not be necessary.

Fortunately, the weather was calm, with waves only about three feet high, and this would have been in our favour if we had ditched. All the crew naturally were extremely tense, with both pilots closely watching the instrument panel and in particular the rev. counters and oil gauges. The skippers kept in close touch with base, regularly reporting the condition of the aircraft and our position. The sergeant engineer was also watching the engines and gauges, and moving through the aircraft, peering at the gaping holes in the wings and tailplane for signs of any increase in damage.

All the crew were wearing their life vests (Mae Wests), and the rubber dinghies and other safety gear were assembled handy to the doors in case we had to ditch. Everybody was very concerned, because the Liberators had a poor reputation when it came to ditching. Other aircraft could stay afloat for a while, allowing enough time for the crews to escape into their dinghies or life rafts. Whilst we were not sure how long we would have, generally it was considered that the time from ditching to sinking of the Liberator was less than ten seconds. We hoped that we would not be placed in the position of finding this out.

After two and a half hours flying on our own, we sighted the two Catalinas. They turned about with one on each side to escort us back to base. It was most reassuring to have them with us on this part of the journey. Our total flying time was eleven hours, and the last four and a half had been very tense and trying.

As we approached Darwin harbour, the two Catalinas left us, returning to their base. We crossed the coast, made a very wide circuit to land on our strip, and then taxied back to our parking bay. On alighting from the aircraft, we had a look at the engines; they were white hot, but thankfully had held out. On examination the following day, the ground staff were amazed that the engines had been able to keep going at those revs for that length of time. We all offered thanks to Messrs Pratt and Whitney.

The Liberator had performed magnificently, and the crew had kept calm throughout, without any sign of panic. However, I could not but feel — after we had landed on Darwin airfield —

THIRD TIME LUCKY

We reported back to operations room, and made out our reports. They were very interested in our having encountered a ship with such fire power, speed and manouevrability. They were pleased to receive photos of the ship, which were developed as soon as possible. Our intelligence section could not identify the ship, and so passed on the prints to the navy for their opinion.

The navy were very caustic in their report. It was a decoy ship, armour plated and with guns, specially set up to entice Liberators and other aircraft to attack at low level. Already these ships had had some success, and we could consider ourselves extremely lucky not to have been shot down. When we asked why we had not been previously advised, their reply was that it was up to us to find out.

Two days later our regular crew (with Tony Martin as skipper), was called out on a formation bombing strike on the harbour of Maoe-mere on the northern side of Flores Island, and north west of Timor. The raid was quite a success as far as the dropping of bombs was concerned, but Tony was not happy with the leader. The initial run was good according to our bomb aimer, but was suddenly aborted and called a dummy run. We were bombing from 15,000 feet.

On the first run, the anti aircraft fire was bursting at least four thousand feet below us. However on the second run the Japanese gunners had evidently re-estimated our height and were infinitely more accurate, with their ack ack bursting amongst us. This resulted in some aircraft being hit with shrapnel, but fortunately no serious damage was sustained.

Five days later (6th August) we were again on a bombing strike over the Flores, on the western tip of the island. The target was a Japanese officers' rest camp. There were six planes on this strike, and we carried out individual bombing, using anti-personnel, small H.E., and incendiary bombs. We had been told by intelligence that geisha girls were visiting the camp over this period. This raid was quite interesting, and I am sure we were not very welcome, as we made it very hot for them.

From take off to landing on this strike on the 6th August was ten hours duration, and it was very late in the afternoon when we arrived back in the mess. We then heard the startling news of a bomb of mammoth size being dropped on Hiroshima in Japan. Further news came through that it was an atomic bomb. We had not heard of this type of bomb before, and could only wonder what it was when we heard news of the size of the damage. This was followed up on the 9th by the news of another atom bomb being dropped on Nagasaki, with Japan subsequently surrendering.

With Japan's surrender, all flying came to a standstill. Our squadron had now reached the stage of being very strong operationally, but still it was heartening news to hear of the surrender, and appreciate that the war was now over. Everybody had been looking forward to this day for such a long time.

Our next flight was on the 23rd August, just a fortnight later. We flew to the western side of the Flores Island over the area which we had recently bombed, dropping leaflets advising the native inhabitants and also any Japanese troops of the Japanese surrender, and that the war had finished.

The area covered was the northern side of this island and all the islands eastward to north of Timor. Wherever we saw towns or settlements, leaflets were dropped. It was quite a long flight, with just on ten hours flying. We were unarmed, with only a skeleton crew, comprising the two pilots, navigator, engineer, wireless operator, the bomb aimer in the nose looking out for villages, and three persons in the rear, dropping the leaflets through the rear windows in the doors.

We then had an interesting flight on the 11th September. With a full crew, bombs loaded and fully armed, we flew in formation to Koepang in Timor to cover the landing of our Occupation Army Force. We circled Koepang until late afternoon, before returning to Darwin. We had nine Liberators covering the landing, and with the navy in full force it was a most imposing sight. I am sure that any Jap force in the harbour would not have dared to raise any objection, with all those aircraft and naval ships in attendance.

Two days later, we were called out on another flight — a real mercy flight. There were twelve Liberators involved. Our guns had been stripped from the planes, which meant we could carry much heavier loads. This exercise was to drop supplies to a town on the south coast of Java called Jokyakarta.

The supplies were to be dropped from the plane onto a landing strip just north of the town. We were then to fly on to Cocos Island in the Indian Ocean, where there would be more supplies to be loaded for dropping at the same place on our return flight. It was estimated that each aircraft carried at least six tons of supplies.

Late on the 13th we took off and flew to Truscott Field, near Wyndham. Topping up the fuel tanks, we left at dawn next morning. We had a skeleton crew, with the two pilots, myself as navigator, wireless operator and engineer, and four crewmen to discharge the packages out of the sides of the plane at Jokyakarta. All went as planned, and we were about the fifth plane to fly over the strip.

In line astern and following the leader, we dropped all our packages (some fragile ones with parachutes attached, and others wrapped in blankets) on to the landing strip. We were told that these were mainly medical supplies, baby foods, some clothing, and other items urgently needed by the inhabitants.

When we had finished our dropping runs, the landing strip was a wonderful sight to behold with all the items that had been dropped from the aircraft. It gave us all a great and wonderful feeling.

It brought back many mixed memories to see this place. This would have been the strip we were heading for when I was based at Kalidjati some three years previously, when our takeoff was aborted by the Japanese bombing and strafing raid. I could not help but wonder if I had taken off with Fl/Lt. Kentish and the armament officer in the Blenheim on that day for Jokyakarta, just what would have been my fate — whether I would have been flying on this day in the Liberator.

I also remembered the town of Tjilijap located only about a hundred miles to the west. This was the port on the south coast of Java, which we had headed for in our evacuation from Java on the 27th February, 1942, boarding the Dutch cargo ship, the ''Kota Gede'', and heading for Ceylon.

Accordingly when leaving for Cocos Island, I deviated with Tony's permission along the coast of south Java until we passed Tjilijap, and then set course for our destination of Cocos Island. In looking over towards Java, I could not help but wonder whether I would again meet up with my friends who had been left behind, and been prisoners of war all this time.

It was a good run to Cocos Island, our flight lasting just on twelve hours. On arrival at Cocos, much to our disappointment, we were informed that there were no supplies available for us to take back to Java. However, the following day we were told that supplies were available in Ceylon (now Sri Lanka), but only enough for six planes. The pilots then had a draw to decide who would go to Ceylon. We missed out and so had a break for three days before returning to Darwin. This return flight took us thirteen hours.

During our stay at Cocos Island, we all really enjoyed the opportunity of swimming and surfing. The waves of the Indian Ocean were coming in over the reef, and then seemed to reform into quite a moderate height, allowing us to surf back to the shore. The depth of the water was about waist high. It was a wonderful experience, and our stay was far too short.

Our next flying duties were ferrying ex-prisoners of war who had been brought to Darwin, taking them south to the capital cities. We carried out four such flights to Sydney, with one flight calling in at Amberley near Ipswich and leaving off some P.O.W.'s destined for Brisbane. Another flight was to Melbourne, calling at Gawler, the airport for Adelaide, en route. All our squadron planes were kept very busy on these ferrying duties.

By the end of October, 1945, these ferry flights had finished. We waited for the next eventuality, expecting our posting for demobilisation.

In flying on missions in this area, it had been most impressive to observe the organisation of the Allies to provide operational safety for aircrew. At the stage when the islands north were still under the control of the Japanese, there were numerous points where coastwatchers or patrols were located, or even where the native population could be relied upon. These were closely and frequently monitored at regular intervals.

It was the responsibility of all aircrews, and particularly the captain and the navigator, to memorise these facts should the plane be shot down, or any other eventuality occur. In support of this, maps of the area where an operation was to be carried out were handed to the captain and navigator before each flight. These maps were prepared by the United States Air Force and were on a silk or linen base, and waterproofed.

Another innovation was an escape and evasion kit handed to the captain and the navigator. This was packed into a small tin about six inches by four inches by four inches deep, and enclosed in a canvas pocket on a webbing belt worn round the waist. In this kit were items such as dressings, atebrin and salt tablets, needles and threads, fish hooks, a compass, wax matches, signalling mirror, water bag, and so many other things. Also included was a booklet giving directions for the use of the items, and a small glossary of the language of the area.

Having been in Malaya at the beginning of hostilities when conditions were rough and tough, it was a great and wonderful morale booster to have all these aids and facilities.

At this time I had been appointed secretary of our officers' mess, and a big party had been organised for Christmas Eve. A handy cash balance had been accumulated over the period, when suddenly advice was received from the Air Board that any surplus funds over a certain amount at the end of January would have to be handed over to consolidated revenue, to be used for other purposes. Hence the big party, with food and refreshments being shared with the airmen.

I was pleased with the prospect of returning to civilian life, but nevertheless could not help but think back on the time spent with the personnel of 12 Squadron in Darwin. With the Liberators, we always referred to our crew as our cricket team, due to the number in the crew (eleven). I had made numerous friends, and this fellowship and camaraderie was very evident throughout the squadron, making it a very efficient fighting force.

Having my commission and my previous association with Bairnsdale and General Reconnaissance School, I had a heightened sense of responsibility. I became quite attached to and fond of the squadron. After my discharge, hearing Vera Lynn rendering her song "Goodnight" would bring back pleasant memories of 12 Squadron, as that was the closing song every night on the public address system.

Some were already leaving Darwin, and the squadron, like all others in the forward areas, was gradually winding down, with flying being almost brought to a standstill. The question on everyone's mind was — when will my notice of discharge arrive?

The method of discharge was based on a points scale, according to years of service in the force. My points were high, and I had been expecting notice any day. My posting for discharge arrived on the 16th December, and I looked forward to returning home at an early date.

It was getting difficult to leave Darwin, as aircraft were not flying as regularly as previously. However, on 20th December, a message was received from a Catalina squadron looking for a navigator for the following day, flying to Rathmines via Cairns. Their navigator was joining them in Cairns, and it would be in order for the navigator to end his voyage at Cairns should he wish.

I could not miss the opportunity and quickly accepted the offer. I obtained a rapid clearance, said my cheerios to the mess, and arranged transport to the base of the Catalina squadron (I think it was 43 Squadron). We had a pleasant flight, and arrived in Cairns just ten hours after takeoff. I felt quite elated, but with a queer feeling that I should end my Air Force career flying in a Catalina, and also landing in Cairns. It was very strange!!!

I reported to Brisbane on the 15th January, 1946, and received my discharge after five years and two weeks service in the R.A.A.F. I was overdue for promotion, and was subsequently notified a month later of my promotion to Flight Lieutenant, back dated from the 1st November, 1945.

FRONT OF SECURITY PASS

此の命令を守れ

注意書！

諸君が衷心より身の安全を願ひ、投降兵としての慰安其他の特權を望む場合、以下の指示に從ひなさい。

一、晝夜の別はないが、自分一人で米軍陣地に近づく事。

二、双手を頭上に舉げ、此査證を打ち振る事

三、米軍兵士側より合圖があつたら此の査證を提示し、そして手眞似の命令に從ふ

米軍の兵士は一人殘らず此の査證の所持者を親切に取扱ふ様命令されてゐるが、萬全を期する事は勿論であるが、然し恐れる必要は毛頭ない。

戰線通過査證

本査證ノ所持者ハ自發投降兵ナリ。同人ハ丁重ナル取扱ヒヲ受クベキモノニシテ、最寄リノ司令宵宛護送サレタル後、更ニ戰闘區域外へ後送サルベシ。同人ハ恐ラク英語ヲ解セザルモ、手眞似ニテ命令ヲ受クル用意アルモノトス。右告示ス。

米國軍司令官

米軍は俘虜を優遇する。俘虜
の待遇に關する國際條約の締約
國として、米國は字義通りそれ
を遵奉し、その待遇は米國兵士
に對するものとこ殆んど變らない
以下同條約文を引用すれば

第二條―(俘虜ハ)如何ナル場
合ニモ情義ヲ以テ待遇サルベク
特ニ暴力行爲、嘲罵、或ハ公衆
ノ好奇心ヨリ保護サルベシ
第十條―俘虜ハ、衛生ト保健
ニ出來得ル限リ留意セル建物又
ハ營舍ニ收容サルベシ
第十一條―俘虜ノ糧食ハ、ソ
ノ量質共ニ(拘留軍)基地ニ於ケ
ル兵士ノ糧食ト同等ナルベシ…
……喫煙ハ許ルサル

米軍の俘虜は米軍兵士と同等
の食事を支給されるから、下表
に見る通り日本でいへば東京で
も一流の帝國ホテル邊りで食べ
られるものを毎日與へられる。
以下、米軍兵士每日の糧食
を示すと

魚及び肉類	一三六匁
米及びパン	九五匁
馬鈴薯	七五匁
	八四匁
野菜類	一匁三分
穀類	三五匁二分
果實類	三七匁七分
砂糖	六八匁
牛乳	三六匁
バタ、其他脂肪類	二四匁八分
茶、コーヒー	一七匁八分

SECOND LEAFLET — FRONT PAGE

戦況画報

日本

フィリッピン

レイテ島

カロリン

ボルネオ

セレベス

←モロタイ島

ジャバ

アンボン

ニューギニア

ニューブリテン

チモール

巨弾日戦艦に命中

る海戦で中央フィリッピン方面
聯合軍の地歩は確立此の戦
で日本側は戦艦二空母四巡
洋艦八駆逐艦六隻失ひ米
國側損害は空母三駆逐二
逐護衛艦一隻で
あった。

空母より飛立たんとする戰鬪機

攻撃下の日巡洋艦

REAR OF LEAFLET

タクロバン附近米軍榴弾砲

フィリッ

米軍首脳部フィリッピン大統領に政権を引つぐ

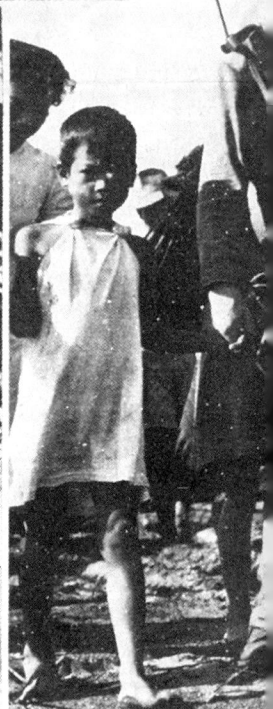

タクロバン飛行場の一隅

軍の進軍

戦況

避難途上の
フィリッピン人婦女子

前進中の米小部隊

KATION

糧抹集積所

戦暇に村落を訪れるオーストラリア兵

レイテ島に

Part 3

Postscript

So far this story has covered my experiences from the time of enlistment with the Royal Australian Air Force in January, 1941 to my discharge five years later in 1946.

I feel that a short resume of the destinies of the other fourteen airmen who travelled on the "Marella" with me to Malaya would form an interesting postscript to my story. Five were taken prisoner of war, five died in their aircraft through accident or enemy action, and four beside myself escaped to see out the duration of the war with the R.A.A.F.

THOSE WHO ESCAPED FROM THE FAR EAST AND SURVIVED THE WAR.

Myself — Jack Woodward	— Navigator
Don Purdon	— Navigator
Ron Winzar	— Navigator
Cyril Donovan	— Wireless Air Gunner
Arch Buchanan	— Wireless Air Gunner

DON PURDON

On arrival at Singapore, Don was posted to 60 Squadron R.A.F., based at Rangoon in Burma and equipped with Mk. 1 Short Nosed Blenheims. He was transported by ship and arrived in Burma on the 2nd November, 1941.

At the end of that month, the squadron transferred to Kuantan on the east coast of Malaya for the purpose of training. At the outbreak of hostilities on 8th December 1941, the Blenheims immediately went into action, bombing shipping off Kota Bharu. Two aircraft were lost in the operation and several others damaged. The Japanese retaliated by bombing Kuantan, extensively damaging other aircraft and the installations. The squadron was then forced to evacuate to Tengah aerodrome on Singapore Island.

They returned by ship to Rangoon before the end of December, 1941, and came under severe attack during the invasion of Burma. The squadron moved to Calcutta in India and reformed, and was then sent to Asanol in Bengal, operating again over Burma. By March 1943, Don had completed his tour after forty-eight operations.

He was then posted as an instructor to a bombing and gunnery school near Calcutta. Not being keen on this, he successfully applied to do a general reconnaissance course at Colombo in Ceylon (now Sri Lanka). He was commissioned on the 31st August, 1943.

On completion of his G.R. course, Don's next posting was to 191 Squadron on Catalina flying boats in November 1943, carrying out convoy escorts, anti-sub patrols and rescues. After this tour, he returned to Australia in March 1945, and completed a course of school administration. With hostilities drawing to a close, he was discharged in August, 1945, with the rank of Flight Lieutenant.

RON WINZAR — 27 Squadron R.A.F.

On his arrival at Singapore, Ron was posted with me to 27 Squadron at Sungei Patani in Northern Malaya and then on evacuation from North Malaya to Kallang at Singapore. I have already recounted his escape from Singapore to Batavia and also his evacuation to Australia on the "Orcades", arriving at Adelaide on the 24th March, 1942, after calling in at Colombo en route.

Ron was posted to Hudson squadrons based at Batchelor in the Northern Territory, operating to the islands north of Darwin. He was commissioned and finished his career as a Flight Lieutenant.

CYRIL DONOVAN — 62 Squadron, R.A.F., & 18 Squadron N.E.I.

Cyril (or Iggy, as he was known to us) was posted to 62 Squadron R.A.F. based at Alor Star. On the day of the invasion of Malaya (8th December, 1941), Alor Star received very heavy bombing raids from Japanese aircraft based at Singora in Thailand. Several aircraft were destroyed and orders were received to evacuate the aerodrome and fly serviceable aircraft to Butterworth, a hundred miles to the south. All other personnel were to be evacuated by road transport.

The following day, their group along with 34 Squadron were to carry out a raid on Singora in Thailand. It was to be led by S/Leader "Pongo" Scarf who took off, but before the other Blenheims could get off the ground, a large force of enemy aircraft arrived and bombed and strafed the aerodrome. Considerable damage was sustained; Pongo Scarf could not see any of the other aircraft, so decided to go alone to Singora. He made it to the target area, dropping his bombs and strafing, but was badly shot up in the process by enemy fighters.

He was severely wounded and his aircraft damaged. Not being able to make base, he crash landed his plane at Alor Star. His two crew were not badly injured, but he was taken to hospital and died that night. For his leadership and valour, he was eventually posthumously awarded the highest honour of a Victoria Cross. Cyril and the squadron felt very honoured and impressed with this award.

By then they had lost the majority of their Blenheims, and those still airworthy were ferried to Singapore. These were later flown to P2 at Palembang in Sumatra and also to Java. Cyril was in Stan Dent's crew who ferried one of the Blenheims to P2, returning to Singapore on the S.S. "Kedah" and later flying another to Kalidjati in central Java.

Cyril evacuated from Tjilijap in Java on the "Kota Gede" to Colombo, returning to Australia on the "Stirling Castle" early in March, 1942.

On his return to Australia, he was posted to No. 18 Dutch Squadron, N.E.I., stationed at Canberra and flying B25 Mitchell bombers. They carried out coastal patrol and were credited with destroying a Japanese submarine out from Nowra, off the New South Wales coast. The squadron mainly had Dutch crews, with some Australian navigators and W.A.G.'s. They moved to Batchelor in the Northern Territory early in 1943, covering the North Western area. Squadron casualties were fairly heavy.

Completing his tour in October, 1943, Cyril was commissioned and was awarded a Netherlands Flying Cross for his work with the squadron. He was posted to Richmond for a radar instructor's course, then to Maryborough in Queensland as a radar instructor, before becoming a gunnery instructor at Sale.

With three others, Cyril was appointed to proceed by air to the United States to attend a radar officers school, so that on return he could instruct in the use of radar being installed in the B24 (Liberator) aircraft. He returned to Ballarat as an instructor and was discharged in January 1946 as a Flight Lieutenant.

ARCH BUCHANAN — Wireless Air Gunner — 100 Squadron.

On his arrival in Singapore, Arch with seven others was posted to 36 and 100 Squadron, equipped with Vildebeeste aircraft.

Soon after the outbreak of hostilities, the Vildebeestes were to be replaced with Beaufort bombers being assembled at Fishermens Bend in Melbourne. Some of these new aircraft were ferried to Singapore. Not being fully equipped for action, all were returned to Australia and Arch flew back as one of the crew.

Later he became a member of 100 Squadron in Australia, but I have no information regarding his further career.

THOSE WHO DID NOT SURVIVE THE WAR

Lex Logan	— Observer
James Axon	— Wireless Air Gunner
Francis Gordon	— Wireless Air Gunner
Kenneth G. Holmes	— Observer
Gordon W. Clarke	— Wireless Air Gunner

LEX LOGAN — Observer — 60 Squadron.

Pilot Officer Lex was posted to 60 Squadron, as was Don Purdon. When hostilities broke out, the squadron had left Rangoon in Burma and proceeded to Kuantan on the east coast of Malaya on training exercises.

On the first day of hostilities, the 8th December, 1941, Lex was killed when seven Blenheims took off on an operational flight to search for enemy naval ships off Kota Bharu on the northern coast of Malaya. Two of the aircraft were shot down, with only one survivor, the pilot of the aircraft in which Lex was the navigator. The pilot was picked up by a Japanese naval ship, and taken as a prisoner of war to Japan.

JAMES AXON — W.A.G. — 100 Squadron

Flight Sergeant Jim Axon was a member of 100 Squadron and returned to Australia with the Beauforts in December, 1942.

He became a member of a crew in 100 Squadron flying Beauforts and lost his life on the 12th July, 1942, in an aircraft accident near Dromana on the south coast of Victoria.

FRANCIS GORDON — W.A.G. — 34 Squadron (Singapore) 22 Squadron (R.A.A.F.)

Flight Sergeant Francis (Flash) Gordon was a member of 34 Squadron based at Tengah, Singapore, equipped with Mk4 Long Nosed Blenheim aircraft.

Returning to Australia, he was posted to 22 Squadron, flying with Boston (A20) aircraft. He lost his life when his aircraft was posted missing on an operational flight off the coast of New Guinea on the 9th February, 1943.

KENNETH G. HOLMES — Observer — 100 Squadron — Singapore and with the R.A.A.F.

Flying Office Ken Holmes, then a sergeant, was a member of 100 Squadron in Singapore, flying Vildebeestes. In late December, 1941, he returned to Australia by QANTAS flying boat assigned to a crew ferrying Beauforts from Melbourne to Singapore.

He attained his commission in 1942. He was in 100 Squadron which became operational on Beauforts, stationed on one of the islands north of New Guinea. On the 21st May, 1943, Ken was a member of a crew on an operational flight at night off the coast of New Britain which did not return. The aircraft was posted missing with the loss of all the crew.

GORDON W. (CLICKER) CLARKE — W.A.G. — 62 & 27.
Squadron Malaya & Singapore No. 1. Operational Training
Unit West Sale.

Warrant Officer Gordon (Clicker) Clarke was a member of 62 and 27 Squadrons in Malaya, Singapore and Netherlands East Indies. On our arrival at Palembang in Sumatra, he became the wireless air gunner of our crew, with Jock Kennedy as pilot and myself navigator. He was an outstanding air gunner. He was with us when we crash landed at night on the 15th February, 1942 in Java, and when we evacuated from Tjilijap on the "Kota Gede" to Colombo.

In 1943, he was an instructor at the Air Gunnery School at West Sale. He lost his life in a flying accident on the 19th September, 1943, when an Airspeed Oxford crashed at night when landing on the Bairnsdale aerodrome.

THOSE WHO BECAME PRISONERS OF WAR

Ted Eckersley	— Observer
Peter Atherton	— Observer
Bert Cooper	— Observer
Jim Barnes	— Wireless Air Gunner
John Blunt	— Wireless Air Gunner

Pilot Officer TED ECKERSLEY - 100 Squadron

Ted completed his training at Mt. Gambier, and then came to Queensland for his embarkation leave, reporting to Sandgate E.D. He travelled with our group to Singapore on the S.S. "Marella" in September, 1941.

All the above five were members of 36 and 100 Squadron based at Seletar on Singapore Island, and equipped with Vildebeeste aircraft. These were bi-planes, carrying a crew of three in separate cockpits, with pilot in front and the W.A.G. at the rear. The top speed was approximately 130 m.p.h., but the cruising speed only about 90 m.p.h. They had two guns as armament, one forward and a Lewis gun at the rear. The plane's range was approximately 350 miles.

These planes were equipped to carry torpedoes. They were certainly easy prey for the Japanese fighters, and were mainly used as night bombers.

On the 26th January, 1942, the Japanese made a landing at Endau, about 120 miles north of Singapore on the eastern coast. It was a major landing with two large ships, supply ships, and escorted by a large naval force, previously sighted by our reconnaissance aircraft. A decision was made to send out the Vildebeestes in force to oppose the landing in daylight. At the briefing, the crews were told that Hurricane fighters would have cleared the skies of all Japanese fighters and that Brewster Buffaloes would also act as escorts.

Ted Eckersley was a member of a crew in the first wave of twelve Vildebeestes which reached their target and ran into the full force of Zero fighters. For some reason the Hurricanes and Brewster Buffaloes did not arrive, and five of the Vildebeestes were shot down by the Japanese fighters. Ted's crew was very fortunate to escape and completed the mission and returned to base.

In the second wave consisting of nine Vildebeestes and three Albacores, only four planes returned and most of the members of these crews were wounded in the action. Some members of the crews that were shot down miraculously made it back to base after harrowing experiences. The loss of thirteen planes out of twenty-four was very demoralising.

Ted evacuated with the Squadron to Java and operated from various aerodromes on the east of Java, the main one being Medeon. When the Japanese invaded Java on the 2nd March, Ted was a member of a crew bombing the invasion fleet and was shot down. He survived by swimming to the shore.

He was taken prisoner on the 6th March, 1944 and remained in Java until the end of hostilities in 1945.

Warrant Officer PETER ATHERTON
— Observer — 100 Squadron

Peter Atherton was the navigator in a crew with Bruce Appleby of the R.N.Z.A.F. as pilot and John Blunt as the W.A.G. This crew carried out several night bombing operations whilst they were stationed at Seletar, and were not called upon for the Endau mission as their aircraft had been slightly damaged in a Japanese air raid.

They evacuated from Singapore to Java and were stationed at a drome on the east coast inland towards Medeon. On the last day of resistance to the Japanese invasion they bombed the Kalidjati aerodrome, which was in the hands of the Japanese. They made three bombing runs and on the last run the plane seemed to get into trouble. The pilot called to Peter and John to bail out as he could not clear the hilly terrain. With John Blunt bailing out and Peter following, the aircraft crashed and the pilot was killed.

Peter and John landed in a tea estate with terraced ricefields. The time was about 2 a.m. and the two of them met up two hours later, making their way to a village. Next day they located the aircraft, with the pilot's body amongst the wreckage. It was the 6th March, 1942, and the Japanese were largely in command. This was recognised as being the last air flight in resistance to the Japanese invasion.

With Dutch forces capitulating over the whole island, Peter, John Blunt, Ted Eckersley and other survivors decided to make their way to the south coast of Java, and look for a boat in which to make their escape. None was to be found. They then considered forming their own group to continue the fight. Shortly after they met up with a party of Army officers who advised them against this, stating that if they ran into a Japanese patrol and were armed (as they were at that stage), the Japanese would not hesitate to take severe action. They were advised to dispose of their weapons and surrender.

Rather than let the guns fall intact into the hands of the enemy, they decided to dismantle them. In the process a revolver was discharged; the bullet entered the chest of Peter through his right hand side, just missing his heart and lodging just inside the skin on his left side. He was placed in a truck and driven about forty miles to the wife of a planter, who gave him first aid and cared for him. He was eventually taken to Bandoeng and placed in hospital, where the doctor in charge was Sir Edward "Weary" Dunlop. He was very fortunate to receive such expert treatment, and to survive.

Peter remained a P.O.W. throughout the war, initially in Java but for the final twelve months in Singapore. He returned to Australia late in 1945.

BERT COOPER — OBSERVER — 100 Squadron

Bert was not in a regular crew, being more or less in reserve. However, he was in a crew of the first wave of aircraft in the attack on Endau. Bert was also in one of the aircraft ferried through Palembang from Singapore to Batavia in Java.

He spent the whole of his time as a prisoner of war in Java.

JOHN BLUNT — W.A.G. — 100 Squadron.

John Blunt was in Bruce Appleby's crew in a Vildebeeste, with Peter Atherton as observer. His time in Singapore and Java has been covered in Peter Atherton's story.

John's last bombing strike when he bailed out of the aircraft with Peter Atherton was on Kalidjati aerodrome. On being taken prisoner, he thought it was most ironic that he should be sent to Kalidjati with others to clean up the debris and shrapnel. He was very careful not to let the Japanese know that he had played a part in causing the damage.

In December, 1942, John was sent in a draft under Sir Edward "Weary" Dunlop to Thailand, to work on the Burma railway. When it was completed, he was employed on maintenance at various camps in Thailand up to the Burma border.

Like so many other P.O.W.'s who worked on the Burma railway, John's health was severely affected. On return to Australia, it took quite a time for him to recover his original mental and physical strength.

In later years, I used to see John regularly when he came to Cairns on business matters. When I asked his opinion of the Japanese, his reply was — "I can forgive, but can never forget".

JIM BARNES — W.A.G. — 100 Squadron

Jim joined 100 Squadron stationed at Seletar flying Vildebeestes, and was amazed when he saw the aircraft — a 1929 vintage bi-plane with a top speed of 135 m.p.h., a cruising speed of 90 m.p.h. and an open cockpit for the air gunner and with a single Lewis gun for protection.

He was assigned to a crew with P/O Basil Gotto as pilot and Sgt. Brian Toohey (another Australian) as navigator. They carried out night bombing at Kuantan, Kuala Lumpur and Batu Pashat, and then came the daylight raid against the landing at Endau. He was horrified when they were attacked by a Navy O, and his Lewis gun jammed after firing only five rounds. His pilot took violent evasive action, and they got back to base.

At the end of January, 1942, they flew to Palembang in Sumatra and then on to Batavia in Java, eventually going to Medeon in central Java. They dive bombed a ship in the invasion at Rembang obtaining a direct hit, and then due to a mix up in navigation, crash landed in a padi field. Crash landing a Vildebeeste was rather difficult and dangerous because of its fixed undercarriage, and as usual it cartwheeled over on its back. They surrendered to the Japs on 8th March, 1942.

The next two years were spent in Java, doing most unpleasant jobs. On the 19th May, 1944, a draft of 775 P.O.W.'s — American, Australian, Dutch and British embarked for Singapore. After medical tests, they were loaded on a small ship in a convoy sailing for Japan. The first stop was Manila, then on to Formosa, where a violent storm damaged their ship. They were then transferred to a larger ship called the "Tamahoka Maru".

Shortly before midnight on June 21, 1944, the convoy was attacked by an American submarine which sank four ships. Jim's ship went down in about two minutes. After spending the rest of the night supported by wreckage, the survivors were picked up next morning by a Japanese whale chaser and taken to Nagasaki. Only 213 P.O.W.'s were left of the 772 on board. Of 267 Australians, only 72 survived. Sadly, his crew mate Brian Toohey was not one of them.

At the end of June, 1945, most of the P.O.W.'s were sent to work in the nearby coalmine at Omine, whilst the others worked in the foundry and steelworks of Mitsubishi.

On 1st August, 1945, there was a very heavy air raid by B29s on Nagasaki, and on the 9th August, Camp 14 was demolished by the atomic bomb which devastated the city. Jim was very fortunate, as he was working in the mine on that day.

Jim was returned to Australia, landing by Catalina on the Brisbane River, and discharged in late 1945.

INDEX

228